THE VITALITY OF OBJECTS

Exploring the Work of Christopher Bollas

Disseminations: Psychoanalysis in Contexts

Series Editor: Anthony Molino

THE VITALITY
OF OBJECTS

Exploring the Work of Christopher Bollas

Series Editor: Anthony Molino

Edited by

Joseph Scalia

continuum
LONDON • NEW YORK

CONTINUUM

The Tower Building, 11 York Road, London, SE1 7NX

370 Lexington Avenue, New York, NY 10017-6503

www.continuumbooks.com

First published 2002

British Library Cataloguing-in-Publication Data
A catalogue record for this book is available from the British Library.

ISBN **978-0-8264-5569-7**

Typeset by CentraServe Ltd, Saffron Walden, Essex

Dedicated to my parents,
Jessie and Joe,
who imbued me with both passion and devotion.

Contents

Acknowledgements

Arne Jemstedt's 'Idiom, intuition and unconscious intelligence: some thoughts on the work of Christopher Bollas' was first published in *Psychoanalytic Dialogues*, Vol. 7, No. 1, and is reproduced here, in much modified form, with the permission of the author and of The Analytic Press. It appeared there in 1997 as 'Idiom as an inherent intelligence of form: thoughts on Lawrence Jacobson's essay on the work of Christopher Bollas'. Adam Phillips's 'Futures' is an excerpt from the chapter of that name, which appeared in Phillips's *On Flirtation*, 1994; it is published here with the permission of its author and of its publisher, Faber and Faber. 'Transformational, conservative and terminal objects: the application of Bollas's concepts to practice' by Gabriela Mann, is reprinted here from the *British Journal of Psychotherapy* in 2000, Vol. 17, No. 1, with the permission of Gabriela Mann and of Artesian Books. 'Of knowledge and mothers: on the work of Christopher Bollas', which appeared in *Gender and Psychoanalysis*, Vo. 1, No. 4, is reprinted here with the permission of its author, Jacqueline Rose, and the journal's publisher, International Universities Press. Anthony Molino's interview of Christopher Bollas was first published in Molino's *Freely Associated: Encounters in Psychoanalysis with Christopher Bollas, Joyce McDougall, Michael Eigen, Adam Phillips and Nina Coltart* (Free Association Books, 1997) and in his *Elaborate Selves: Reflections and Reveries of Christopher Bollas, Michael Eigen, Polly Young-Eisendrath, Samuel and Evelyn Laeuchli, and Marie Coleman Nelson* (Haworth Press, 1997). It is reprinted here courtesy of The Haworth Press.

Notes on Contributors

Joel Beck received his PhD from the Committee on Social Thought at the University of Chicago. He is in the private practice of psychoanalysis and psychotherapy in New York, and teaches and supervises at the Training Institute for Mental Health Practitioners.

Malcolm Bowie is Marshal Foch Professor of French Literature in the University of Oxford, and a Fellow of All Souls College. He is the author of *Henri Michaux: A Study of His Literary Works* (1973), *Mallarmé and the Art of Being Difficult* (1978), *Freud, Proust and Lacan: Theory as Fiction* (1987), *Lacan* (1991), *Psychoanalysis and the Future of Theory* (1993), and *Proust Among the Stars* (1998).

Kate Browne is Artistic Director of Browne Barnes Productions, whose work has been presented in numerous theatres around the world. Two of her projects, *The Lost Tensions* (1998) and *Needles* (1999) were influenced by Christopher Bollas's (1985) *The Shadow of the Object* (1987). Ms Browne currently lives and works in New York City.

Joanne Feit Diehl is Professor of English at the University of California at Davis. She has published extensively in the fields of poetry by women, feminist critical theory, and psychoanalytic (particularly object relations) approaches to poetic texts. Her most recent book (1993) is *Marianne Moore and Elizabeth Bishop: The Psychodynamics of Literary Creativity*, published by Princeton University Press.

Greg Drasler is a painter living in New York. He began showing his work upon his arrival there in 1983. He has shown widely in the United States with exhibitions in New York, Chicago, San Francisco and Boston. He has taught painting and drawing at Williams College, Pratt Institute of Art, and is currently teaching advanced painting at Princeton.

James Grotstein, MD is a training and supervising analyst at several psychoanalytic institutes. He is the author, editor, and co-editor of several books and has published over 200 papers in scholarly journals. He is in private practice in Los Angeles. His most recent book is *Who is the Dreamer Who Dreams the Dream?*

Arne Jemstedt, MD is a Training and Supervising Analyst at the Swedish Psychoanalytical Association and is in private practice in Stockholm.

Gabriela Mann, PhD is Senior Clinical Psychologist and Supervisor, Member of the Tel-Aviv Institute of Contemporary Psychoanalysis, Director of the Program in Psychoanalytic Psychotherapy at Bar Ilan University, Ramat-Gan, Israel.

Anthony Molino is the *Disseminations* Series Editor. Co-editor (with Christine Ware) of the series launch title *Where Id Was: Challenging Normalization in Psychoanalysis*, he counts among his works *The Couch and the Tree: Dialogues in Psychoanalysis and Buddhism* (ed.) and *Freely Associated: Encounters in Psychoanalysis*. He lives in Italy, where he is a practising psychoanalyst.

Adam Phillips is a child psychotherapist in London, and General Editor for Penguin's new collection of the works of Sigmund Freud. His most recent works are *Promises, Promises: Essays on Psychoanalysis and Literature* and *Houdini's Box*.

Jacqueline Rose is Professor of English at Queen Mary University of London. Her books include *The Haunting of Sylvia Plath*; *States of Fantasy*; *Albertine: A Novel* and, most recently, *On Not Being Able to Sleep: Essays on Psychoanalysis in the Modern World*.

Joseph Scalia, MEd is a psychoanalyst in private practice in Bozeman, Montana, USA. He is the author of *Intimate Violence: Attacks Upon Psychic Interiority*.

Wesley Shumar, PhD, Assistant Professor of Anthropology at Drexel University (Philadelphia), is author of *College For Sale: A Critique of the Commodification of Higher Education* and co-author (with Anthony Molino) of the forthcoming *Culture, Subject, Psyche: Anthropology, Social Theory and Psychoanalysis*. He is the co-editor of the volume *Building Virtual Communities*.

Michael Szollosy is a PhD candidate in English Literature and the Centre for Psychotherapeutic Studies at the University of Sheffield. He is currently compiling an anthology of essays applying British object-relations theory to culture and literature.

Preface

Over the last fifteen years the work of Christopher Bollas has become an indispensable reference point, both inside the profession of psychoanalysis and outside it, in the wider arena of the Humanities. At a time when the Freudian legacy has been exposed to hostile critique from all sides, the behaviour of the main legatees – the psychoanalytic institutions themselves – has often been short-sighted and self-defeating. When recent criticism has been well-informed and cogently argued, it has seldom been welcomed as a stimulus to new thinking or treated as a basis for creative dialogue with other disciplines: the proponents of psychoanalysis have shrunk back into their specialized conceptual idiom and their isolationist professional practices. When such criticism has been of an ill-informed or scandal-mongering kind, few analysts have been prepared to defend their discipline publicly in clear and accessible terms. To make matters worse, psychoanalysis, instead of creating opportunities for dialogue between its own different traditions and tendencies, has suffered from extreme factional narrowness. Vast amounts of intellectual energy are still expended on what are essentially family squabbles.

Against this background, the theoretical contribution of Christopher Bollas has acquired its huge authority. As a writer, he is self-revealing, generous and inclusive. Psychoanalysis as he describes it is a matter both of possessing specialized concepts and of knowing when to let go of them in favour of a report on first-hand experience. Bollas's talk of 'objects' both external and internal, and of their inexhaustible interplay, has many virtues, as this volume makes plain, but perhaps the most compelling of these is that it allows him both to acknowledge the linguistic medium in which the entire psychoanalytic project unfolds and to spell out the fact – known to us all, lived by us all – that language, the whole hubbub of human exchange, can sometimes fall silent or go blank. Bollas rebels against what Perry Anderson, in a memorable phrase, called the 'megalomania of the signifier'. His encounter with Lacan is particularly fascinating in this regard, and already in *Forces of Destiny* (1989) had its characteristic 'yes, but . . .':

> In our true self we are essentially alone. Though we negotiate our ego with the other and though we people our internal world with selves

and others, and though we are spoken to and for by the Other that is speech (Lacan's theory of the Symbolic) the absolute core of one's being is a wordless, imageless solitude. We cannot reach this true self through insight or introspection. Only by living from this authorizing idiom do we know something of that person sample that we are.

Bollas reminds us, at moments like this, that the 'project' of psychoanalysis is creative, dangerous and all-absorbing. It is a way of being alive, of escaping from but always returning to our 'wordless, imageless solitude'. Language matters, but is not alone in mattering.

There is, of course, a 'Bollas doctrine', and others will expound it in later pages of this work. But there is also, as even the brief quotation above makes plain, a 'Bollas voice', and this in itself has a singular beauty. That voice is personal and ruminative, as Winnicott's was, and it speaks of many things. Bollas is someone who has heard both Giulini and Bernstein performances of Mahler and enjoys sharing such experiences of difference with his reader. But for all the charm and openness of his literary manner, there is always something strict and trenchant going on as well. The very phrase 'cracking up', in the book that bears it as a name, for example, is teased out, revisited, and made to yield new senses as the argument proceeds. Bollas is inventive and resourceful in the pressure that he places on ordinary language. And at the present moment his voice offers two complementary benefits: it encourages analysts to talk to each other across the barriers that exist inside the psychoanalytic profession, and – as this coherent and multifaceted volume demonstrates – it gives them ways of engaging with the many-voiced general culture that surrounds them.

Malcolm Bowie

Introduction

Joseph Scalia

An interdisciplinary anthology seems a fitting way to comment on and explore the work of Christopher Bollas, a practising psychoanalyst and author of seven influential books whose work has forged unexpected ties across the arts, social sciences and humanities. This comes as no surprise, as Bollas is as comfortable explaining or expanding a psychoanalytic concept in the context of, say, Melanie Klein's or Jacques Lacan's writings, as he is investigating or rethinking Willem de Kooning's paintings, Herman Melville's fiction, or Sylvia Plath's poetry. Indeed, attesting to both his influence and versatility as a thinker is the broad range of contributors to *The Vitality of Objects*, drawn from psychoanalysis, cultural anthropology, the visual and performing arts, feminist theory, and literary criticism.

Beginning in 1987 with his first book, *The Shadow of the Object: Psychoanalysis of the Unthought Known*, Bollas develops concepts that will remain present throughout the later writings, first and foremost among which is the centrality of what is innate in us, that defies symbolization, representation, or expression in cognitive terms. In a way, the work claims a space, in contemporary psychoanalytic thinking, for the ineffable dimension of human existence. Two years later, in *Forces of Destiny: Psychoanalysis and Human Idiom*, Bollas took up the distinction between *fate*, as that which is visited upon us, and *destiny*, understood as our idiom's or true self's call to unfold and actualize its potentialities. With the publication of *Being a Character: Psychoanalysis and Self Experience* (1992), it becomes clear that Bollas wants to explore just how we unfold through the elaboration of those potentialities. Invoking and ingeniously deconstructing the dynamics of Freud's dreamwork, Bollas envisions how those very dynamics inform the development of creative self-expression. (See, in this volume, the excerpt from Adam Phillips's essay 'Futures,' for a sense of the daring innovation of *Being a Character* in the literature of a discipline traditionally so oriented towards the past.)

Cracking Up: The Work of Unconscious Experience (1995) continues to map out the project of how a self evolves. Crucial to the work is the fertile concept of *dissemination*, what Bollas sees as the self's potentially infinite unfolding through its incessant tapping of the wellsprings of the unconscious. This is how any self grows, by establishing networks of thought that expand the mind and increase one's unconscious capability. Then came *The Mystery of Things*, a collection of essays written in the decade and a half leading up to the book's publication in 1999, portraying free association as Freud's revolutionary repositioning of the self's access to its own unconscious life, creating through this remarkable method a new form for human thought and individual creativity in that place we call psychoanalysis. In the same year that *Cracking Up* was released, Bollas co-authored *The New Informants: The Betrayal of Confidentiality in Psychoanalysis and Psychotherapy* with attorney David Sundelson. In this unique testament to the integrity of the psychoanalytic enterprise, psychoanalyst and appellate lawyer show how legally mandated therapist reports to insurance companies, child protective services (in child-abuse reporting laws), and law enforcement agencies (in the duty-to-warn law) violate patient confidentiality and erode the psychotherapeutic process at its foundations. And finally, in *Hysteria*, Bollas's most recent publication (2000), the central role of sexuality in this classic but persistent (and persistently misdiagnosed) malady is given vigorous and clear expression, while also adumbrating the role of sexuality in the lives of the other classical 'characters' of psychoanalysis. Needless to say, most of the central themes of these books are taken up in the essays here collected in *The Vitality of Objects*.

It is striking to note how these essays both avoid redundancy and yet consistently (and uncannily) resonate with one another. They converge remarkably around a need for delivery from a societal tendency to demystify 'the ineffable'. Inasmuch as concepts relevant to such liberation appear again and again throughout this collection, it may well be that Bollas's theorizing gives voice to inklings, intimations, and intuitions that thinkers across any number of disciplines are today struggling to articulate.

Perhaps one of Bollas's own richest contributions to psychoanalytic theory, also a thread throughout this book, has been his reconceptualization of the Freudian unconscious, long known as a *prisonhouse of repressed mental contents*. While insisting on the Freudian laws of the unconscious and of the dreamwork – those of condensation, displacement, and substitution – Bollas has writ large the idea of a *receptive unconscious*. The individual, for Bollas, in fact '*becomes the dream work of his own life*', 'simultaneously an actor inside a drama and an offstage absence directing the logic of events'. We not only repress unwanted mental contents into the unconscious, but the unconscious also contains our potential, waiting to receive experiences that will activate aspects of ourselves that have been latent within. In the pages that follow, philosopher and psychoanalyst Joel Beck's 'Lost in Thought: The Receptive Unconscious' explores the courage one needs in such moments of receptive opportunity, and discusses certain timeless philosophical and existential struggles in the light of Bollas's thinking.

Bollas's theoretically complex yet enlivened invoking of the self and its object worlds has a certain vitality about it which makes his writing readily accessible. Indeed, Adam Phillips refers to Bollas as 'the most evocative psychoanalytic writer we have', and it is perhaps Bollas's very capacity for evocation that so appeals to thinkers from disparate areas of the arts and sciences. For example, Bollas's articulation of objects into thought existence, for the self to use, is not only vibrant and compelling, but somehow quite simply *makes sense*, and can itself be used and applied, as the essays in this book attest. Of course, any number of terms and concepts basic to the Bollas canon appear throughout this collection. In privileging a few, let me cite: the *unconsciousness* of the unconscious; the ineffability of subjectivity; the multiple forms and functions of *the object*, that omnipresent psychoanalytic term which Bollas has broadly adopted and clarified to mean something more than 'the other', and more than the mere object of the subject's focus. Thus, *The Vitality of Objects*, where notable colleagues and students of Bollas's oeuvre all reveal something of his idiomatic way of naming and conceptualizing the world and, in the process, stamp his work with their own creative explorations.

Essentially, Bollas galvanizes our understanding of what the object *is* and of what happens when we encounter the objects, the endlessly variegated content, of internal and external experience. How each of us, given our own idiom, our own uniqueness, endows such objects – a streetcar, one's parent or spouse, a football, a mood, a swing, a single aspect of one's actual or phantasied analyst or analysand, for instance – with special meaning. Or how all objects have their own 'integrity', which upon use by any subject is realized through the 'processional' form of the object, as any object puts the user through that logic peculiar to its own shape. Bollas's descriptive classification of the object world – with its *transformational, aesthetic* and *aleatory* objects, to name just a few – enhances not only our understanding of both unconscious fantasy and the external world, but the dimensions of those inner and outer spaces as well.

As we journey through life, we are moved by 'objects'. Some we seek out, consciously or unconsciously, others we happen upon. Bollas has termed the latter *aleatory objects*, after the Latin *alea*, a dice game. It is with such a degree of chance that we stumble upon formative events and influences in our lives. James Grotstein develops this theme in his ' "Love is Where It Finds You": The Caprices of the "Aleatory Object" '. Here the reader will not only appreciate Grotstein's joyful reflections but will also encounter aspects of his *dual-track* theory, in which he argues for a necessary attention – often lost within as well as outside of psychoanalysis – to both the world's impact upon us and our own unique authorings of that same world.

Bollas prefers the term *idiom* to D. W. Winnicott's *true self*, specifying the uniqueness of personal character, which he understands as an irreducible intelligence in human form, or an *aesthetics of being*, unfolding into a person's character through its interaction with the environment. Anthony Molino and Wesley Shumar's 'Returns of the Repressed: Some New Applications of Psychoanalysis to Ethnography' finds idiom in some surprising places, and sees creative self expression where an earlier psychoanalysis might only have recognized defensive or self-protective manoeuvres. Investigating places as *other* and faraway as rural Appalachia or the mines of South Africa, and applying some of Bollas's intuitions to select classics in ethnographic writing, their study argues that a psychoanalysis inspired by thinkers like Bollas can make significant contributions to modern-day anthropological fieldwork. Of course, the question can always arise in such contexts: how does one know when one is encountering a person's idiom? Arne Jemstedt is convinced that we can indeed know, and exemplifies how in his 'Idiom, Intuition and Unconscious Intelligence'. Here, while exploring the conjunctions of conscious and unconscious experiences in a person's life and how these are, so to speak, 'registered', Jemstedt also examines a number of Bollas's theoretical contributions and suggests how it is that they have come to make such broad, multi-disciplinary impact.

And what about the role of the environment in the process of generating idiom? Bollas has coined the term *transformational object*, deploying a key aspect of W. R. Bion's usage of the concept of transformation in one's becoming what we know as human. The maternal environment is our first transformational object, but while foundational this object is also an ever-recurring *phenomenon* throughout our lifelong development, and appears in a variety of forms, including the aesthetic experience. Moreover, it is also wed with idiom to yield what Bollas calls the *unthought known*. Indeed, psychoanalysis has long devoted itself to what happens in the unfolding of the pre-verbal human person: that is, before we have language at our disposal, and before language itself becomes the *second human aesthetic*. Yet before articulation, there is knowledge that we have 'in our bones', that we enact through our very character without thinking it, and that is seen as being at the root of much of our reception of and acting upon the world around us. It is these dimensions of the *unthought known* that painter Greg Drasler explores, in his 'Painting into a Corner: Representation as Shelter', giving us a surprising look at how the visual arts reach to this core in both the audience and the artist.

Readers will have gathered that aesthetic experience is a principal focus of Bollas's work. With his notion of the *aesthetic object*, Bollas returns us to the inner space of our original and only *existentially* remembered transformational object, the mother. It is because of being derived from our fundamental experiences of how we were mothered that aesthetic experiences can have such haunting effects on us, allowing contact with our origins as well as opportunity for critical re-workings. Since the mother is seen, here and elsewhere in Bollas's work, as 'the prime mover', and given that Bollas comes out of the British Independent Group that many have seen as blaming mothers for psychopathology, Jacqueline Rose's 'Of Knowledge and Mothers' fruitfully challenges Bollas on this score and traces some of the developments in his thinking that pre-date the publication of his more recent *Hysteria*.

Objects also conserve. They conserve, that is, early states of being that we may not be able to remember cognitively but which we experience as moods. These *conservative objects* may be either generative of further growth or 'malignant': damaging, in fact, further personal unfolding while also serving as manipulative efforts to infect others with inner states a person wants to evacuate. Such objects, along with transformational and *terminal* ones – i.e., those we use in a way to terminate or foreclose the possibility of self elaboration as well as experiences of *integrity* – are here exemplified in Gabriela Mann's provocative and illustrative clinical essay.

Joanne Feit Diehl's 'The Poetics of Analysis: Klein, Bollas, and the Theory of the Text' takes up the use of language as a human aesthetic and examines three Elizabeth Bishop poems in the light of Bollas's and psychoanalyst Melanie Klein's contributions. The poetry of transformation and the transformative capacities of poetry are here brought to life by Diehl. On a parallel note, in his 'If My Mouth Could Marry a Hurt Like That', Michael Szollosy looks at Sylvia Plath and her efforts to 'author' herself through the use of the Word. It is Szollosy's thesis that while one might deem much of Plath's effort as classically 'defensive', there is also a case to be made for idiom's attempt to speak *through* her work, even though it failed to find her freedom.

Kate Browne's 'Cracking Up the Audience' discusses what constitutes good theatre and why it is so rare. Borrowing from the title of a book by Bollas, she argues that good theatre 'cracks up', that is, disseminates psychic intensities through its capacity for unconscious communication with the audience, and thus yields new insights that may not be immediately thinkable. Free association and its liberating potential are envisioned here and seen, literally, 'at play' in Browne's use of a theatre that seeks to creatively move us.

Bollas has often been asked if he is an essentialist or a postmodernist, a positivist or functionalist. Some have seen him as 'relational' or 'intersubjective', missing the mark. Is he Kantian, or Platonic? But as his work is not apprehendable by way of traditional categories, it is helpful to maintain a sense of his psychoanalytic pluralism, threaded through the eye of clinical work and his own receptiveness to the offerings and aleatory objects that inhabit our cultural and generational milieux. Some of this is made clearer in Anthony Molino's 1995 sparkling, in-depth interview with Bollas, which closes out the book and where Bollas can be seen already returning his attention – in a statement which long predates *Hysteria* – to the Freudian fields of the *psychosexual*. There, in fact, in our earliest sexual epiphanies, is the trauma that inaugurates both the end of any human innocence and, to use a Lacanian term dear to Bollas, the onset of our *jouissance*. It is my sincere hope that the vitality of that *jouissance*, through the diverse infusions of the contributors to this book, now pervades its pages, enriching the dialogue with one of the most prolific and ingenious psychoanalytic thinkers of our time.

In closing I would like to express my appreciation to a number of people for their help in compiling *The Vitality of Objects*. I owe a great debt of gratitude to Anthony Molino, the *Disseminations* Series Editor, for inviting me to edit this book in the first place, and then for his steadfast assistance and guidance. It was actually Lucinda Mitchell and I who together were originally invited to produce *The Vitality of Objects* but, owing to the uncontrollable hazards of life, Dr Mitchell was unable to carry through with the work. The book, however, is also imbued with her spirit. All of the book's contributors have been delightful to work with, in a variety of ways. Each has been an 'evocative object' for me and has helped me become more of myself. Katharine Turok once again helped me see a project through to completion, while adding her considerably engaging and personable self to our shared ventures. Finally, my wife and son supported me throughout the book's development, invaluably helping to create a space in which I could work.

Joseph Scalia
October 2001

PART I
Essays from Psychoanalysis

1

Lost in Thought:
The Receptive Unconscious

Joel Beck

ONE

The idea of an unconscious is coeval with the emergence of Western philosophy. In *Republic* IX, Socrates observes: 'Surely some terrible, savage, and lawless form of desire is in every man, even in some who seem to be measured. *And surely this becomes plain in dreams*' (*Rep.* 572B). It remained for Freud (1959) to develop the idea of the *repressed* unconscious into a concept and integrate it into a theory of mind by linking repression to dreams, symptoms, and misguided actions. According to Freud, repressed desire creates the unconscious. In the second topography, the notion of the id replaces the repressed unconscious. But the id bears an uncanny resemblance to Plato's (*Rep.* 329C-D) description of the experience of *eros* as the tyranny of many mad masters. It remains the site of lawless desires and death-bearing drives.

What if the unconscious, in addition to being the prison house of repressed desires, also functions as the condition of the possibility of creative thinking? What if it makes an essential contribution to the disclosure of personal meaning and the uncovering of truth for an individual? In *Being A Character* (1992) and *Cracking Up* (1995), Christopher Bollas argues that psychic meaning arises in an encounter between an evocative object and an unconscious that is fundamentally receptive, affected in multiple ways by its experience of a person, place, word, image or thing. Using the dream-work as his model, Bollas (1992) constructs a theory of unconscious thinking as an oscillation between condensation and dissemination.

Unconscious thinking, set in motion by the reception of an object, leads to the formation of what Bollas (1992) calls psychic genera. While indebted to Winnicott and, above all, Bion, Bollas's conception of genera involves nothing less than a rethinking of the nature both of the unconscious and of psychoanalysis as a curative process. The latter emerges as a process in which the repressed unconscious, created by trauma, is supplemented and complemented by the work of the receptive unconscious, inhabited by genera. Psychic change involves the development of new perspectives on self and other. It also means that the analyst assists the analysand in thinking about that which had been hitherto unthinkable thereby transforming structures based on trauma into genera.

The movement of my argument takes the following form. In the second section, I begin with a description of six fundamental characteristics of conscious thinking. In the third section, I develop the idea of unconscious thinking as an activity evoked by an encounter with an evocative object and oscillating between condensation and dissemination. In the fourth section, I argue that the notion of a receptive unconscious is implied by the notion of the evocative object.

I further argue that the receptive unconscious bears a strong resemblance to Kant's notion of the transcendental imagination as mediating between the activity of thinking and the passivity of sensibility (Kant, 1965). The unconscious thinks, in other words, by arranging and ordering elements into schemata. The latter furnish rules for organizing unconscious experience. Bollas calls these schemata 'internal objects'. One can distinguish between 'good' and 'bad' internal objects in terms of the purpose of the schematism. If its goal is the elaboration of idiom, the schema or organizing process functions as a good internal object. If its goal is the repression or evacuation of pain, the schema functions as a bad internal object. Finally, in the fifth section, I briefly discuss the relevance of the idea of genera for our understanding of psychic change.

TWO

My topic is Bollas's account of psychic genera. His hypothesis about generative psychic structures attempts to conceptualize the way in which the mind arrives at a new perspective. When this happens, we begin to think differently about the world and ourselves. But what does thinking mean? Brugger and Baker's *Philosophical Dictionary* (1972) defines thinking as 'the non-intuitive mode of knowing that is ordered to the existent and its essential relationships' (p. 417). This characterization of thinking defines it in the traditional manner as 'non-intuitive', i.e. as involving the formation of ideas or concepts about things.

To think is to synthesize, to unify substance and attribute or subject and predicate. When I say to myself, for example, 'this ball [both a substance and the subject of the assertion] is red', I think about the relation between the ball and one of its qualities, redness. This thought is true when it is 'ordered to the existent' or *corresponds to* what is actually the case. If the ball were green, the thought would be false.

Thinking, in other words, stands in a complicated relation to the conception of truth (Heidegger, 1962). Thinking can be, but does not have to be, true or false. When I think of my friend, for example, does it make sense to utilize the concept of truth? On the one hand, there seems to be a growing consensus among analysts that when I think of my friend, my thought is a construction. I unconsciously emphasize some of her qualities, neglect others and undoubtedly distort some rather basic features. On the other hand, no one would argue that one construction is as good as another. What, then, are the criteria for deciding between different, even conflicting constructs? While space does not permit an adequate treatment of this topic, we shall return to it briefly in the conclusion of this essay.

When Freud published *The Interpretation of Dreams*, he laid the foundation for an expanded conception of thinking and truth. Psychoanalysis holds that thinking is simultaneously a conscious and an unconscious activity. Following the example of Aristotle (1984), I shall begin my discussion of Bollas's conception of unconscious thinking with a brief statement about what 'is better known to us' or conscious thinking. Two thousand years of Western philosophy have shaped our understanding of the latter.

Conscious thinking has six characteristics that are relevant to Bollas's notion of the dialectic between the conscious and unconscious mind. First, conscious thinking begins when we withdraw from our practical and productive involvement with the world. During this withdrawal, we take the time to *stop and think*. Thinking as an activity, therefore, requires solitude. However, this solitude does not lead to loneliness. When we pause to think about something, we are 'together' with ourselves (see Arendt, 1978).

The second characteristic of conscious thinking is that it brings into being a two-in-one split in the mind. When we think, we engage in what Plato called 'a conversation that the mind carries on with itself about any subject it is considering' (*Theaetetus*, 198E). Conscious thinking happens as an interior dialogue.

Third, thinking involves a turning away from reality as directly perceived and experienced and a turning towards what Hannah Arendt (1978), for want of a better term, calls 'thought things'. The latter include memories, things imagined, opinions, hypotheses, concepts and ideas. While one can weigh and measure a sensible thing, one will never see, touch or smell a thought. Because our thoughts are invisible, we customarily describe them with metaphors drawn from the more accessible realm of the visible. For example, philosophers have traditionally compared thinking to a form of seeing. From this comes the metaphor of insight (literally a seeing into something) that has been so important for psychoanalysis.

Four, thinking can take a number of different forms. While conversing with ourselves, we can pay attention to whatever comes to mind in the form of wishes, hopes or fears. When we do this, we engage in subjective thinking. We can construct things that never were on land or sea, i.e. engage in imaginative thinking. Also, we can follow the connection between concepts and engage in purely logical thinking. Lastly, we can orient our thinking towards the way things are or engage in objective thinking (Brugger and Baker, 1972).

Fifth, no one thinks about anything in a vacuum. Our thinking is always in some way related to the thoughts and opinions of others, including parents, teachers, friends and society as a whole. Mostly, to think means to think the thoughts of others. This means that we can either think passively, following the paths trod by others, or think for ourselves, i.e. actively. The latter, authentic thinking, leads to the discovery of new insights. Authentic thinking creates psychic genera.

Finally, as noted above, the concept of thinking has always been closely related to the concept of truth. Just as there are different kinds of thinking, so there are different kinds of truth. Leibniz, for example, distinguished between truths of reason and truths of fact. Both types of truth share the characteristic of *compelling* the mind to assent to their existence. Logical thinking arrives at truths of reason. Two plus two equals four, for example, reveals itself as self-evident to 'everyone endowed with the same brain power' (Arendt 1978, p. 59). Truths of fact require witnesses to verify them. But to the eyewitness a truth of fact, such as the proposition that the allied armies invaded France on 6 June 1944, is just as compelling as the assertion that a triangle has three sides.

Bollas's conception of unconscious thinking takes these six perspectives into account. Bollas sees unconscious thinking as beginning with a withdrawal from our conscious involvement with whatever is at hand. This withdrawal of attention makes possible what Bollas (1992) calls the projective subjectification of reality. Second, he argues that unlike conscious thinking, which involves a complex self reflecting on its own experience [the two-in-one], unconscious thinking stems from the activity of a simple self that is lost in thought.

Third, unconscious thinking also requires an involvement with thought things. These thought things come into being in the unconscious during an encounter with an object. Bollas uses the term 'object' in a very broad sense to indicate anything that affects the psyche. Objects can take the form of self, the living of a life, other people, places, things, works of art and body parts (e.g. the breast as object). An object has the potentiality of evoking a particular self-experience. The self, then, represents its experience of the object visually, linguistically, sonically, gesturally and interpersonally. All of these modes of unconscious representation belong to the category of what Arendt (1978) calls 'thought things'.

Fourth, unlike conscious thinking that can be subjective, imaginative, logical or objective, unconscious thinking is more like dreaming. It takes the form of condensations and disseminations as the unconscious brings latent ideas into clusters and then breaks them up into chains of associations. Fifth, we saw that conscious thinking always begins with thoughts of others, which it either makes its own or follows passively. Unconscious thinking initially requires the facilitating presence of others who make available to us what would otherwise be unthinkable. Here the crucial distinction is between the traumatizing object that is either internalized and repressed or evacuated and the generative object that facilitates the development of what Bollas calls idiom.

Finally, Bollas as a psychoanalyst is concerned with the discovery of what I shall call individual truth or self-knowledge. The latter concept has generally lived on the margins of Western philosophy for two reasons.

First, Aristotle, the founder of Western science, held that science yields knowledge only of the particular, i.e. of the individual as subsumed under a concept, or, to put it a different way, of a substance in relationship to some attribute. An individual as individual (as opposed to instantiating an essence or related to an accident) is unknowable. I can know this ball as being red, round, and weighing six ounces. In each case, I am thinking about the predicates as examples of more general concepts such as redness, roundness, and heaviness.

To attempt to know the ball as an individual artefact with a particular history can lead one to two different contexts. First, it can move us in the direction of knowledge of the *whole* as the context within which the ball is embedded. In this instance, the ball appears as a toy used by a being with the capacity for play. Playing names a way of being. Human play can take elaborate forms because we have a unique relationship to reality. We understand that there are different forms of reality. The capacity for play rests on a determinate understanding of reality as expressed, for example, in the contrast between factual and imagined reality.

Playing engages reality imaginatively. When we play, we play with reality. This leads to a host of questions. What differentiates factual from imagined reality? Is the imagined less real that than the factual? If so, what does it mean for something to be real? To think about the ball as an individual can lead to the basic questions of metaphysics.

Second, we can ignore the context and confine ourselves to learning the history of this particular ball. Such knowledge inevitably lacks the universality and necessity required by philosophy or science because it offers nothing more than a sequence of contingent encounters which just as easily may not have occurred. At most, we would learn an interesting story about the relation of the ball to those who made or used it.

However, our problem does not concern an inanimate object but relates to human beings. One significant claim of psychoanalysis is that one can, through analysis, know an individual as an individual (as opposed to knowing her as a particular, i.e. as born in Russia, as Jewish, as a mother, etc.). What does it mean to know an individual person as an individual? How is the individual affected by such knowledge? What does it mean for an individual to know himself? Does he, in so doing, discover truths about himself that are neither truths of reason nor truths of fact? What kind of truth does self-knowledge uncover?

The whole topic of self-knowledge, which is at issue here, is extremely vexed in the history of philosophy precisely because the insights arrived at when we know ourselves generally lack the compelling character of truths of reason or truths of fact. This leads to the need for a concept of the truth of an individual, which I shall argue for in section five. In this context, although Bollas generally avoids the problematic of truth, I shall argue that the discovery of individual truth follows from the development of a new 'genera' of experience that expresses the idiom or inner truth of the self.

THREE

In section two I identified six characteristics of conscious thinking that are particularly useful for understanding Bollas's conception of unconscious thinking. In this section, I propose to look more closely at the notions of the moment of withdrawal, the role of the simple self, the functions of the evocative object and, finally, at Bollas's analogy between thinking and dreaming. I shall use the examples of Freud in Padua and looking at a text in art history to exemplify my points.

Being A Character (1992) begins with a description of a visit that Freud made to Padua. It describes how, returning to the city after an absence of twelve years, Freud had an insight. He identified certain figures that he had repeatedly encountered in dreams as being identical to some sandstone figures in the entrance to a restaurant. He remembered that that was the place where he learned that he would be unable to view some frescoes painted by Giotto. In the language of this essay, the story of Freud's recollection is the story of an insight or of a moment of truth.

We begin with the element of withdrawal. Presumably, Freud was making his second attempt at seeing the frescoes when he noticed the sandstone figures and paused. His moment of hesitation as withdrawal signifies his turning his attention from sightseeing to thoughts, particularly memories. Such a transition begins as a moment of what Bollas (1995) calls 'psychic intensity'. The latter reflects a 'slight degree of interest', arising in an instant, awakening 'memories, instinctual states and vivid emotions' (p. 52).

To see how these sandstone figures entered Freud's dream life we must take a closer look at the simple self. First, note that Freud recognized the figures as belonging to the day residue, i.e. 'to elements from the waking state of the day before which are found in the narrative of the dream and in the dreamer's free associations' (Laplanche and Pontalis, 1973, p. 96). In this case, Freud realized that the dream day occurred seven years ago.

Bollas (1992) argues that projective identification plays a crucial role in the formation of a day's residue. During the day, we select certain persons, places, objects and events as psychically significant. This happens when the subject projects an aspect of himself into the object, thus, in Bollas's language, psychically signifying it. To do this, he argues, the subject 'must "lose himself" in moments of experience when he projects meaning into objects' (Bollas, 1992, p. 22). At this moment, we exist as simple subjects, out of touch with ourselves. It is, then, the simple self that has the capacity to invest objects with meaning. While conscious thinking begins with a complex self, reflecting on its deeds and sufferings, unconscious thinking begins with a simple self, engaged in an act of projection.

The sandstone figures, in Bollas's interpretation, functioned for Freud as a mnemonic object. The latter conserves and holds an aspect of a self-state that one is not able to think about, usually because entering the self-state arouses too much anxiety. In this case, Freud's inability to complete his journey to see the frescoes may have unconsciously raised the spectre of his own incomplete self-analysis or it may have pointed to a painful contrast between Giotto's finished masterpiece and his unfinished work on dreams. In any case, the sandstone figures became the container for Freud's anxiety and reappeared as sinister shapes in a recurring dream.

In his account of the dialectic between conscious and unconscious thinking, which he compares to the contrast between waking and dreaming, Bollas is particularly interested in the role of the object as it is used and represented by the subject. Thinking begins when the object elicits a certain psychic intensity. In *Being A Character* (1992), Bollas enumerates six different ways that an object can evoke unconscious thought or be used to initiate a self-state. The subject can use the object sensationally, structurally, mnemonically, conceptually, symbolically and projectively. Each of these represents a way in which the object presents itself to the unconscious. That is, an object presents itself *as* sensible, *as* structured with a certain atomic specificity, *as* memorable, *as* related to certain concepts and signifiers, and *as* a transient container for projections.

To show how the same object can evoke or be used in many ways at the same time, I will make use of my own experience of coming across a reproduction of Paolo Veronese's *Marriage at Cana* while browsing through David Rosand's book, *Painting in Sixteenth Century Venice* (1997). In Bollas's language, I chose to use the book as an object of psychic interest because the bright colours and dramatic themes of Venetian painting resonate with certain aspects of my character. The reproduction was, however, an 'aleatory' object; i.e. I encountered it by chance, not expecting to find it in this book. I recognized it as a painting I had seen many times at the Louvre. Looking at the reproduction, I found myself in a state of reverie. Initially, the painting functioned as a mnemonic object evoking images of being at the Louvre and of summers in Paris with my first wife in the summers of 1978 and 1979.

In this sense, the painting had already been psychically signified because those visits to the *Marriage at Cana* at the Louvre were already associated with my own first marriage. They were also associated with my first sustained study of classical painting. In terms of the painting as a sensed object, I remembered it as a huge canvas, filled with bright blues and reds, located in a large room, packed with people taking photographs and murmuring to each other.

At the centre of the wedding feast sits Jesus, having just performed the miracle of turning water into wine. During my reverie, I thought of my own wedding when a violent thunderstorm left us without light and electricity. The painting's structure, its unique form stirred up associations connected with being married, then divorced. Was there something miraculous in the idea of marriage itself? The blue colours suggested the signifier 'blue' associated with feelings of sadness about time past and opportunities lost. Finally, the painting served as a container for a transient wish to escape the complexities of life in New York and to move to Paris, a city that I associate with pleasure and leisure. As I turned the page and continued browsing, I found myself feeling somewhat sad and depleted, as if part of myself had been left behind in the Louvre.

To exemplify how an object functions evocatively, I have put into words an encounter that took place in a few seconds. The print evoked a state of psychic intensity that gave rise to a brief reverie, punctuated by a feeling of regret. Such intensities, writes Bollas (1995), have the potentiality for developing into latent thoughts. In this instance, I have made some of the latent thoughts manifest but most latent thoughts remain unconscious. When the mind responds to a psychic intensity, when it acts on what it has received, meaning is created.

Up to now we have been considering the different ways in which the object acts on the subject during a self-experience. To get a deeper understanding of the vicissitudes of meaning, we shall turn to the self's experience. The latter begins with what Bollas (1992) calls 'the lifting' of the self. The experience of a psychic intensity lifts an aspect of the self out of its unconscious nuclearity and exposes it to the 'ego'. The term 'ego' does not here refer to the thinking ego associated with modern philosophy's conception of the subject. Instead, it refers to Bollas's own conception of the unconscious ego.

In *The Shadow of the Object* (1987) he writes:

> When I refer to the ego, I draw attention to that unconscious organizing process that reflects the presence of our mental structure . . . My intention here is to argue that the unconscious ego differs from the repressed unconscious in that the former refers to an unconscious form and the latter to unconscious contents. The unconscious form or idiom of the ego evolves from the inherited disposition, which is there before birth. (pp. 7–8)

I shall discuss the implications of distinguishing between an unconscious ego and a repressed unconscious in section four when I take up the topic of genera. In this context, suffice it to say that the unconscious ego functions as an organizing or forming agent.

At birth, we are endowed with a unique potentiality for giving shape to our experience. Bollas (1989) calls this unique potentiality *idiom*. We shall see that it is his way of approaching what I shall call the truth of the individual. In any case, we can idiomatically shape or represent experience visually, sonically, gesturally, linguistically or interpersonally. In its role as an organizing process, the ego finds itself spontaneously attracted by some modes of representing experience and indifferent to others.

Bollas and I share a predilection for linguistic representation, i.e. for putting things into words. From his writings, I gather that he is drawn towards the musical or sonic while I am drawn toward visual representations of experience in all forms [art, cinema, theatre]. That the ego finds itself moved to represent, i.e. finding meaning in its experience of objects in some ways rather than others, suggests to Bollas that the ego is moved by an *eros* of form, i.e. the desire to give a unique shape to what it experiences. The unconscious ego acts as 'thinking desire' or as 'desire thinking' (cf. Aristotle, 1984). Thinking entails an excitation of the mind that takes a particular form.

Thus far, I have focused on the moment of withdrawal; the role of the simple self, and the way the mind receives and represents the evocative object. When Bollas turns to the process of unconscious thinking, he makes use of an analogy to dreaming. In thinking's first stage, a psychic intensity develops into a cluster of images, memories, signifiers, and feelings *associated* with an object. The second stage of unconscious thinking involves *condensation*. Since Freud's *Interpretation of Dreams*, most analysts have considered condensation to be one of the essential modes of the functioning of the unconscious.

In condensation:

> a sole idea represents several associative chains at whose point of intersection it is located. What happens from the economic view is that this idea is cathected by the sum of energies which are concentrated upon it by virtue of the fact that they are attached to these different chains.   (Laplanche and Pontalis, 1973, p. 82)

The creation of unconscious meaning initially involves the conversion of psychic intensities into latent thoughts. The second stage of unconscious thinking involves the appearance of many unconscious *ideas* in the form of one idea or image.

When one encounters the term 'idea' in psychoanalytic theory, one should remember that it is a translation of a translation. We generally associate an 'idea' with a concept or universal, as in 'the idea of justice'. The German noun generally translated as 'idea' is *Vorstellung*. A more literal translation would be 'representation' which emphasizes something *placed before* the mind. The latter can take the form of a concept or an image. Thus, an image is also an idea. The German term *Vorstellung*, in turn, translates the Latin *repraesentatio*. The Latin word reflects the scholastic interpretation of the Greek *eidos* or 'form' which, first, presents itself as belonging to a thing, giving it its characteristic 'look' or 'shape' and is, then, 'represented' in the soul. Because as a psychic actuality, the 'form' is first present in the senses, then in the imagination and finally in the intellect, an idea undergoes a series of transformations (Aristotle, 1984).

Psychoanalysis, however, has revolutionized the meaning of idea, particularly in its conception of condensation as the production of images. In the psychoanalytic sense, the image, as one idea condensing many ideas, does not represent anything, at least not in the traditional sense of representation as re-producing something about a being. According to the theory of the dream, all dream thoughts are subject to conditions of representation. Latent thoughts must be translated into images if they are to appear in a dream. The initial latent thoughts 'undergo selection and transformation so as to make them capable of being represented by images, particularly visual images' (Laplanche and Pontalis, 1973, p. 389). The crucial step in the creation of unconscious psychical reality, therefore, is imagining. In this step, the many ideas evoked by the object are 'sublated', to use a term borrowed from Hegel. That is, condensation conserves, negates and gives new form to the original ideas. What is not preserved as condensed is no longer available to the unconscious.

Psychoanalysis has discovered that images can also refer to chains of linked ideas. Bollas's (1992) notion of the evocative object extends this discovery to everyday life. We live surrounded by objects we have dreamed. Objects have meanings to an individual that are private and deeply personal. We are unconsciously thinking about objects during much of our waking life. These thoughts are evoked by an encounter with an object but they do not have to refer to the object present to the conscious mind and most of the time they don't. Thus, in my example, Veronese's *Marriage at Cana* refers to very specific memories of being in Paris during the early days of my first marriage. The only way that one can know the unconscious referents of this object is to follow the mind's associations to it. The latter, however, represents many chains of associations, most of which are unconscious and resist being uncovered.

Because the point is so crucial, I wish to provide a second example, drawn from Bollas's *Cracking Up* (1995). There he describes starting out on a journey to the library. His conscious mind is focused on the project of writing a book about confidentiality in psychoanalysis. On the way to the library to research, he stops in a record store after he sees in its window an advertisement for Philip Glass's opera, *Akhnaten*. He enters the store, thinking about the first time he saw the opera, about his son who is studying Egypt at the time, about a friend whose brother-in-law plays for Philip Glass. He then thinks about silence, Nina Coltart and Susan Sontag. Bollas notes that these thoughts took a few seconds to think. He then shows how these thoughts and others, connected with a ride on the subway and a misplaced pair of spectacles, might be condensed into a single dream image of a glass.

Common sense teaches us to think about a glass as a utensil for drinking. We might even think of it as referring to a celebration or to a gift. But without some conception of the unconscious, we could and would never link the image of the glass to Egypt, silence, Nina Coltart or Susan Sontag. The referents in unconscious thinking, what unconscious thinking is about, are never given immediately. One must deconstruct unconscious thinking, argues Bollas (1995), by destroying the imagined object. This happens when the dreamer freely associates to the images in the dream or to an event in life that one can consider as having the structure of a dream. Association translates the images and narratives into chains of words or signifiers. Moreover, free association in the analytic session imitates what the unconscious mind does of its own accord when it 'cracks up' the dream into strings of signifiers emanating from the dream's core images.

Dissemination, Bollas's (1995) term for this 'deconstructive' cracking up of the dream, completes the dialectic of unconscious thinking. In the first phase, we encountered the simple self, lost in thought, immersed in the object world, engaged in unconsciously projecting parts of itself into objects or signifying them. In response to the encounter with an object, the subject 'splits into several ideational parts' (p. 61). I illustrated this by referring to my own encounter with the reproduction of *Marriage at Cana* and to Bollas's pause in the record store. To uncover an individual truth, in part, would be to establish the psychic link between a reproduction of a Venetian painting and the memory of summers in Paris. This memory dwells within the unconscious as an inner constellation of feelings, images, somatic registrations and body positions.

Note that what this waking dreaming of an evocative object elicits can also be called an internal object. Veronese's painting summons up associations connected with Paris as an internal object; the city occupies my mind like a ghost or spirit (Bollas, 1992). However, as soon as I try to think about this spirit, trains of thought carry me away, radiating outward from the felt presence of Paris in a variety of directions. I think of my daughter's artistic talents, of a restaurant where I dined, of Paris and Helen in the *Iliad*.

This movement away from the affectively charged idea suggests Freud's theory of displacement. However, Bollas (1995) distinguishes between displacement and dissemination. He points out that Freud insists on the connection between the new idea, say of my daughter's artistic talent, and of the original, noxious idea, in this case, painful thoughts about a failed marriage. Displacement conceals this relation. Bollas, on the other hand, insists on the liberating power of this movement of ideas. He argues that in addition to masking pain, it gives rise to new 'notions and interests', for example, a wish to learn more about Veronese's career. Bollas contends that the breaking up or deconstruction of an affectively charged idea is part of thinking itself.

Unconscious thinking includes the lifting of the self by an evocative object, the creation of latent thoughts, and the compression of these thoughts into an image and dissemination or the breaking up of the condensed idea into new latent thoughts. To illustrate this, Bollas (1995) uses a striking example. The wish to have a sexual relationship with a woman might appear in disguised form as the wish to see a particular actress in a film. An orthodox Freudian reading would consider the forbidden wish to be the truth of the symptom, which is the intense interest in the actress. For Bollas it is equally true to say that the wish for pleasure has taken a new form.

What brings the movement of thinking set in motion by the wish for the affair to a halt is an act, the decision to use an object. Bollas (1995) describes this as an act of aesthetic intelligence. The unconscious ego resolves on one form of satisfaction rather than another. The original contents of desire are deconstructed by the erotics of form.

Let us say that our hypothetical subject decided to see Jeanne Moreau in *Jules et Jim*. Seeing the film could sponsor associations about the passing of time, male friendship, relations between men and women and numerous other topics. This capacity to unconsciously deconstruct our desires and to release instinctual tensions by new and different forms of psychic desires constitutes a condition of mental freedom. 'Mental freedom,' writes Bollas, 'is a form of desire that supports but supplants the specific desires driven by instinctual life' (1995, p. 63).

Viewing the actress in the film 'supports' the desire by changing its object and its aim. At the same time, the ego represses the original desire for sex with the forbidden object. Dissemination supplants the original desire by finding an object that will evoke new associations and images.

This liberates us from imprisonment by the original 'noxious' drive representation. Without unconscious freedom, the aleatory object that evokes an intense instinctual response would forever imprison us.

So far I have focused my attention on what the unconscious does as opposed to inquiring into what Bollas thinks it is. One final element of the movement of thought needs mentioning. That is, the oscillation between association and representation, between dissemination and condensation is punctuated by what Bollas (1995) calls an essential nothingness. Gaps, omissions, forgettings, breaches, breaks and fissures interrupt thinking. An essential nothingness interrupts and thereby separates 'all ideas, visual images, auditory shapes, somatic registrations, evoked memories and libidinal propensities' (p. 58).

Three considerations, I suggest, motivate Bollas's introduction of this essential nothingness, an idea that bears the weight of two thousand years of philosophical speculation (Heidegger, 1962). First, thinking, both conscious and unconscious, does break down. 'In the course of ordinary self-experience', writes Bollas (1995), 'I lose grasp of my thoughts, am interrupted by forgettings, frustrated by my failure to find a word . . . stopped by the effort to think a thought that fails to come to cognition' (p. 59). These experiences point to moments when thinking encounters a limit and fails. Hence, the possibility of failing to achieve its goal haunts thinking as its shadow. The nothingness, says Bollas, is always there 'whether it momentarily mutes speech, swallows up memory, refuses to yield an idea struggling to come to thought' (ibid).

Second, an emphasis on the essential nothingness belongs to an economic interpretation of thinking. Unlike many North American analysts, Bollas (1995) affirms the existence of a death drive. The latter aims to preserve a constant state by ridding the individual of all excitement. Thinking, I pointed out above, is a form of excitation or desire. Objects that arrive by choice or chance excite the mind. The force of a psychic intensity disturbs the peace, unsettles things. As finite beings, we can only tolerate so much excitation, so much aliveness. The death drive, the wish for constancy, brings thinking to an end. At some point, the mind seeks to rid itself of the tension of thinking. In a famous passage of his *Nicomachean Ethics*, Aristotle argues that thinking is the highest and most divine of all human potencies and that we must 'make ourselves immortal, and strain every nerve to live in accordance with the best thing in us; for even if it be small in bulk, much does it in power and worth surpass everything' (*Nicomachean Ethics*, 1177b, 31–35). Psychoanalysis shows that the death instinct functions as a necessary limit to our efforts to 'make ourselves immortal' by thinking.

Third, if no one can always be thoughtful in living life, the crucial question becomes how much thinking, how much aliveness can we tolerate? The capacity to tolerate unconscious thinking is coeval with the capacity to create meaning. This includes the ability to lose oneself in objects, to immerse oneself in them. Those who suffer from character disorders and psychosis lack this ability. The person who suffers from a character disorder lacks the power to use some objects; the psychotic lacks the basic trust necessary to lose himself in any objects, and, if Bollas is right, lacks a functioning unconscious.

I shall return to this point in section four when I discuss Bollas's view of the nature of the unconscious. In section three, I have discussed at some length four characteristics of unconscious thinking. It begins with a moment of hesitation, when the subject pauses, withdraws and is lost in thought. In this moment of hesitation, the evocative object announces its presence. The self responds by projecting a part of itself into the object in order to psychically signify the object. At the same time, the self introjects or receives aspects of the object. In thinking the object, the self oscillates between association and representation, dissemination and condensation until either an act of unconscious choice or an essential nothingness brings the process to a halt.

FOUR

In this section I take up the last two characteristics of unconscious thinking. We saw that thinking never occurs in a vacuum. The thoughts, opinions and beliefs of others determine an individual's thinking. But an individual is never simply the sum of all those who have raised, taught and influenced her. To emphasize this, Bollas (1989) has introduced the term 'idiom' into psychoanalysis. Idiom refers 'to the unique nucleus of each individual, a figuration of being that can, under favorable circumstances, evolve and articulate' (p. 212). The structures formed when idiom evolves and articulates itself are genera. Each person, Bollas argues, has a 'defining essence' (ibid). Others however play an essential role in the development of this defining essence. They either traumatize or facilitate the development of genera.

The expression and acknowledegment of idiom is an aspect of what I call individual truth. The discovery of individual truth for Bollas presupposes the presence of generative structures. If one reads Bollas philosophically, one finds the basis for a response to Hannah Arendt's (1978) argument that one should distinguish sharply between truth and meaning. She points out that the uncovering of meaning, especially personal meaning, lacks the compelling character of truth. An encounter with meaning is evanescent. It does not generally survive the solitude of thinking or the moment of insight in analysis. Meaning can dissolve when the session is over or when one stops thinking. For Bollas (1995) this follows from the rhythm of thought itself. It is the destiny of thinking as desiring to deconstruct its own condensations. Second, although the expression of idiom is contingent on generative encounters with others, there is a defining essence of truth of the self. This enabled Winnicott to distinguish between a true and false self, a distinction that Bollas preserves although he finds a new word for truth of a self, i.e. idiom.

If meaning begins and ends with the unconscious, what is the unconscious if not the generator of meaning? However, in generating meaning, the unconscious is essentially receptive. Idiom finds its lexicon in the evocative object (Bollas, 1992). Trauma, on the other hand, obstructs the development of idiom. To say that the unconscious is a receptive agent is, in one sense, to remain faithful to the spirit of Freud who concerned himself with the conflicts between somatically based drives and the external world. Freud's psychology is one of conflict between the elements received. The unconscious is the dwelling place of rejected drives and ideas. Bollas (1992) seeks to expand our understanding of the unconscious to include the received and thereby reconceives it.

In this section I focus on the unconscious as a structure that generates meaning. But what exactly does 'meaning' mean? I shall begin by providing a very brief argument that meaning involves a relationship between an object [word, thing, person etc.] and a context. One 'understands' the meaning of something when one intellectually grasps something *as* something. The small word 'as' contains the enigma of meaning (Heidegger, 1962).

Take, for example, the meaning of computer I am using to write this essay. I grasp it as an instrument for writing. In doing so, I tacitly refer it to a context which includes paper, printer, light, books and the act of writing itself. I exhibit my grasp of the computer's meaning by using it. Its meaning is to be a utensil and, *pace* Arendt (1978), its meaning expresses what it truly is. I can also change the context and consider the computer as a thing with properties – having the shape of rectangle, black and weighing six pounds. Or, I can consider the computer as exemplifying the triumph of technology in modernity or, if you will, postmodernity. In each case, the object remains the same while the meaning varies. To think, then, is 'to interpret' in the sense of referring something to a context (Heidegger, 1962).

Consider Veronese's painting. I can think about the painting as exemplifying the Venetian style of the sixteenth century. I can interpret it as Veronese's particular way of thinking about the meaning of Jesus or about what it must be like to be present at a miracle. In section three we saw that the painting has a personal meaning for me – it belongs in contexts including summers in Paris, marriage and divorce, past and present. The discovery of the unconscious radically shifts our understanding of what it means for something 'to be'. It turns out that 'objects' can belong to hidden contexts, have concealed relations, and sometimes, for a terrifying moment, belong to no meaningful context at all.

To think an object unconsciously is to take it in, to be affected by it. The unconscious is basically a receptive organ. In his essay, 'Psychic genera' (Bollas, 1992), Christopher Bollas explicitly argues for the necessity of adding the idea of a receptive unconscious to our understanding of the repressed unconscious. In what follows, I shall argue that reception describes what the unconscious basically does.

Since Bollas's notion of a receptive unconscious is, to some degree, innovative, he begins with what his readers know better, a description of trauma. He observes that trauma have a unique temporal structure. This, we shall see, is less a point about time than a point about the generation of meaning. A child's initial response to being overwhelmed by anxiety may result in the evolution of a traumatic core that forms a structure within the unconscious. 'But it is only afterwards, in a second recurrence of the traumatic event, upon the reawakening of consciousness, that the trauma's disturbing nature is felt' (Bollas, 1992, p. 67). In the language of this essay, a traumatic core refers to an unconscious context that announces its presence 'afterwards' in the subject's life. The original trauma is the mind's failure to interpret what is happening to it.

The use of the adverb 'afterwards' refers to Freud's theory of deferred action or, in the original German, of *Nachträglichkeit*. Freud argues that not all experience undergoes transformation by deferred action but only 'specifically what . . . has been impossible to incorporate into a meaningful context' (Laplanche and Pontalis, 1973, p. 112). One cannot make sense, i.e. find meaning, in a traumatic event because one lacks a context for it. The traumatized internal object created by the event then becomes the archetype for all subsequent indigestible experience. It provides the repressed core of a new context. 'Deferred action,' argue Laplanche and Pontalis, 'is occasioned by events and situations or by experiences which allow the subject to gain access to a new level of meaning' (p. 112). The more recent events and situations allow the context to function as a context and meaning, albeit painful meaning is created.

Bollas (1992) provides an example of a deferred action's impact on the repressed representation of a traumatic event by presenting two hypothetical cases of child molestation. He compares the experiences of a five-year-old child with a thirteen-year-old. The latter may have a memory of the event that can be transformed into a narrative that offers a temporal context for experience. Something becomes meaningful by being assigned its place in time; it happened 'before this' but 'after that'. A thirteen-year-old has the cognitive skills to find a context for being abused by telling a story about the event. A five-year-old, lacking a developed sense of temporality, may be unable to do this.

Because the child cannot tell a story about his experience, cannot objectify this event in a narrative, Bollas (1992) asserts, the recollection of the trauma may not have a generative side to it. That is, no new meanings will become associated with it. However, when the child sexually matures, a later sexual experience may awaken memories of the abuse or 'generate a conscious experience of confusion' (p. 67). Inevitably, every child has painful experiences that she cannot make sense of and which consequently inflict trauma. But here Bollas concentrates on the exceptional case to illustrate a point.

The experience of confusion is the moment when deferred action announces itself. Henceforth, the subject may understand sexuality itself as confusing and therefore as dangerous. The adult, Bollas (1992) points out, may even be confused about whether the abuse really happened. The feeling of confusion about what is real recreates the initial isolation imposed by the trauma. Trauma, in one sense, resembles thinking. It separates us from the world around us. But while thinking flourishes in solitude, trauma imposes loneliness. When I think, I am together with myself. When I am traumatized, I feel abandoned by the world.

The reason for dwelling on the idea of trauma is that it initially provides a paradigm for understanding genera. The economic meaning of a traumatic event is that it overwhelms the ego. The unconscious ego, in effect, says 'no' to the traumatic object and represses it. The ego, on the other hand, says 'yes' to the generative object and provides for the psychic incubation of its libidinal cathexis. The traumatizing object impedes the development of idiom while the generative object facilitates it.

The small child's vulnerability, helplessness and cognitive and emotional immaturity leave him/her highly vulnerable to the impact of potentially traumatizing experiences. Therefore, the development of idiom requires the generative impact of parental care. For the sake of clarity, one can simplify and say parents have the possibility of being either generative or impinging in their responses to the ordinary vicissitudes of childhood (although the typical parent engages in a mixture of impinging and generative interactions).

The concept of genera offers a conceptual basis for thinking about the development of idiom as the defining essence of an individual. Primal genera constitute the fundamental elements of the infant's idiom that 'sponsor early aesthetic cohesion of the object world' (Bollas, 1992, p. 68). This means that the actualization of the elements of idiom imposes a kind of cohesion or unity on experience. Initially, we respond to the object world by experiencing it as pleasant or painful. The logic of good-enough maternal provision leads to the child spontaneously seeking objects that please. At the other extreme, the traumatizing parent leads the child to be more concerned with avoiding pain. The child does this by engaging in what Bollas (1992) calls 'binding'. The latter is a self-protective, conservative process by means of which the child attempts to control damage, to desensitize the self, to rid itself of painful affect.

To conceptualize this process of self-protection and to lay the basis for its contrary, the generative process of self-development, Bollas (1992) draws on the work of Freud, Fairbairn and Bion. From Fairbairn he takes over the concept of the bad object. At issue in Bollas's discussion of the bad object is the structuring of the unconscious. The internalization of the bad object creates an autonomous psychic structure. That is, the unconscious takes in the bad object to control pain and in so doing makes it part of itself. On the other hand, the good-enough parent, also internalized as a structure or schema, makes possible the independent search for novel experience. Put simply, the unconscious works by receiving objects, in wholes, parts and diverse combinations.

But the unconscious can also rid itself of what it takes in. From Bion, Bollas imports the idea of linking. Bion originally introduced this idea to describe the psychotic patient's attack on internal reality. The psychotic, he argued, severs emotional links to objects. Bion then expanded the notion of linking into his own theory of thinking, which I cannot explicate in any depth here. The most important aspect of his theory in this context is the description of the coupling of an empty thought with a sense impression. In order to engage in productive thinking, the unconscious mind must reach out beyond itself and fill its empty thoughts with content drawn from the experience of objects.

The second feature of linking that I wish to emphasize is its connection with projective identification. 'As a realistic activity, it [projective identification] shows itself as behavior reasonably calculated to arouse in the mother feeling which the infant wants to get rid of,' writes Hinshelwood (1989, p. 185). He adds:

> In this context the mother uses her feelings to understand what the child is feeling and initiates the K or knowing link. When the mother fails to understand the child's projective identification, the infant resorts to increasingly violent attempts to project into the mother and then develops the capacity of ridding the psyche of bad internal objects.

If the conscious can create meaning, it can also destroy it by evacuating bad objects. However, the mind can only evacuate what it has already received.

Bollas (1992) uses the idea of the K link (i.e. the link of knowing something emotionally) to distinguish between generative and traumatic parenting. A mother who has received the projective identification of the child and through her reverie managed to detoxify the projection will produce a child who seeks links between internal and external reality. Since emotional connections are at issue, this child will seek emotionally meaningful experience. The traumatized child, on the other hand, seeks to 'break links between contents referred to the unconscious and their preconscious derivatives' (p. 72).

The idea of links between internal and external and between unconscious and preconscious reality leads Bollas to introduce the topographic model which culminates in his revision of our understanding of what the unconscious is and how it functions. He develops a distinction between the repressed and the receptive unconscious. By supplementing Freud's theory or distinguishing a new aspect of the unconscious, reception, he has reconceived it.

My thesis is that unconscious processes mediate all thinking about the real. To mediate is to act as a go-between, to connect or to relate different things. Phenomenologically, our access to beings is mediated by our understanding of context. Our understanding of beings varies with the context to which we refer them. The unconscious names a basic placeholder for the contexts of our experience. There are thus three stages of the thinking or understanding of what it means for something to be a 'conscious' tacit referral to a context, a preconscious referral to the unconscious that is sparked by the experience of a psychic intensity and an unconscious reception of the referred. The referral to a context functions as the condition of the possibility of all understanding. Unconscious reception is the condition of the possibility of something mattering to us.

Bollas (1992) introduces the notion of reception by beginning with what is better known to his analytic readers, the theory of repression. He first reminds his reader that in repression 'an individual preconsciously represses unwanted feelings and ideas to the unconscious' (p. 72). Henceforth, the metaphor of place governs his discussion of the unconscious. In presenting the unconscious as a place, as a kind of internal space within the mind, Bollas returns to Freud's original topographic theory of the mind, i.e. the distinction between unconscious, preconscious and conscious processes. In 1914 Freud (1959) wrote, 'The theory of repression is the cornerstone on which the whole structure of psychoanalysis rests' (p. 168). Laplanche and Pontalis (1973) point out that 'it is clear from the formative notion of repression that it appeared from the beginning in correlation to the concept of the unconscious' (p. 392).

At this point the economics of repression becomes crucial to Bollas's (1992) argument. The unconscious ego strips or removes from consciousness an affectively laden idea. The unacceptable idea is banished to a different part of the mind. Because the unconscious idea retains a certain quantity of energy, it continues to press for discharge or action. Bollas emphasizes two points in his account of repression. First, he stresses the links between unconscious ideas. The latter form something like a colony of the oppressed that gains strength as more and more ideas are banished to the prison of the unconscious.

Second, he notes that it is an anticathexis that keeps the prisoners from breaking free. This does not come as a new story to analysts. But Bollas's argument is that this cannot be the whole story. If the unconscious as a mediating agency owed its existence only to conflict, as a receptacle it would contain only unacceptable, unwanted, and rejected ideas, feelings and wishes. Important as this is for understanding human behaviour, it does not do justice to the phenomenology of the creation of meaning.

At this point it may help the reader if I review the points I have made about the concept of meaning. I began by arguing that meaning is grasped in an act of understanding. One understands what a being is when one interprets it as being something. Psychoanalysis preserves the notion of context but distinguishes between conscious and unconscious contexts.

A context, a simple example of which is a narrative, confers meaning on experiences. A context provides a framework for ordering 'facts'. Bollas (1992) prefers to use the word 'perspective' to describe the same phenomenon.

However, his theory of genera intends to set forth an account of how the mind creates new contexts or changes its perspective. The theory of genera holds that the unconscious is the creative factor in the emergence of new perspectives. The new context may be as sophisticated and complex as Einstein's theory of relativity. Or it may appear as an insight in an analytic session during which the patient gains a new perspective on a parental figure. It may involve sensing a new quality in an old friend or having one's sense of reality changed by looking at a painting or reading a novel.

Bollas initially introduces the theory of unconscious reception as if it stood in a complementary relation to the theory of repression. He first argues that some ideas are received into the unconscious. He, then, revises the theory of anticathexes. The latter not only keep unwanted ideas out of consciousness, they protect germinating ideas. The agent governing reception is the unconscious ego as the organizer of experience. In the case of the received, it employs anticathexes in order to allow for the evolution of new emotional experience.

One might ask why the development of a new perspective requires the positing of an unconscious in which ideas germinate, grow and combine. One function of the unconscious ego is to reduce anxiety. The generation of a new perspective or the development of a generative structure always occasions the experience of anxiety. The experience of generative thinking therefore involves the experience of psychic pain, particularly in its initial stages. The ego acts to protect the mind from premature awareness of some of the pain.

In explicating the theory of genera, Bollas (1992) says that he will refer to topographical, object relational and ego psychological theory. In his reference to topographic theory, he indicates what is at issue in his argument, i.e. a new theory of the formation of the unconscious. The latter consists of the received as well as of the repressed. One can say there are two species of received ideas, the invited and the rejected, neither having access to consciousness.

Object relations theory enables Bollas to say more clearly what genera are. For the purpose of the clarity of exposition, he exemplifies the process of the formation of genera by referring to accounts of creative work given by poets and scientists. While one can see the process writ large in an Einstein or a Wordsworth, we all have had the experience of generative thinking. The formation of genera entails the creation of a new *internal object*. Bollas (1992) cites Hinshelwood's definition of an internal object as the 'presence of a structure that is mentally sensed' (p. 82). Genera are good internal objects.

Again one must bear in mind that I am sharpening the contrast between genera and trauma for the sake of clarity. Everyone's unconscious contains 'good' and 'bad' internal objects. Our lives oscillate between repetition and creation, between seeking new self-experiences and avoiding pain.

To explain the process of the formation of good internal objects, Bollas returns to Freud's account of the dream work. Acts of condensation result in the formation of genera. The elements condensed include: instincts, affects, memories and existential experiences. For Bollas the construction of genera is somewhat akin to dream work, as we unconsciously labour to receptively condense many phenomena into a psychic structure.

In section three, we saw that condensation involves the formation of an image that refers to several chains of associations. In this case, condensation leads to the formation of a structure. To understand how this works, I believe that at this point one must go beyond what Bollas says in his text. I am interested in two points. First, what kind of a structure does condensation yield? How can an image function as a structure?

This is precisely the problem Kant (1965) addresses in his discussion of the transcendental imagination. At issue in *The Critique of Pure Reason* is the unification of a concept or empty thought with something received by our senses. Since concepts (universals) and intuitions (things sensed) are heterogeneous, something must mediate their opposition if they are to combine to form knowledge. Kant argues that the imagination exercises the unifying function. A schema is an outline governed by a rule. More precisely, a schema structures by providing an ordering principle governing the construction of an image. Kant (1965) exemplifies by articulating the schema for dog. 'The concept "dog" signifies a rule according to which my imagination can delineate the figure of a four-footed animal in a general manner without limitation to any determinate figure such as experience or any possible image I can construct *in concreto* actually presents' (p. 182). The schema provides the rule for the construction of a prototype. The latter makes available an archetypal model that is then used as a standard for ordering experience. One does not have a conscious understanding of the rule. We discover that we are in possession of a new schema, or, in Bollas's language, a new internal object, when we have a new insight.

This new rule or principle for organizing a manifold finds its realization in an intuition. For the sake of clarity, Bollas (1992) cites Webster's definition of an intuition: 'Intuition is the direct knowing or learning of something without the conscious use of reasoning.' Intuition entails an apprehending, a direct taking in, and a receptive attitude towards what is. Intuition, the result of the incubation of genera, announces a new perspective on reality. The condition of the possibility of this new conscious response to reality is unconscious reception.

To describe this process of unconscious reception, Bollas (1992) uses the metaphor of a radio receiver. If intuition draws on the experience of seeing to metaphorize a mental process, the radio receiver draws on the experience of hearing. The unconscious ego knows how to listen to messages from the real so that these messages coalesce into new structures. What appears to be the immediate grasping of a new reality is the result of many 'unconscious and conscious thinkings'.

Bollas (1992) calls condensation the 'thoughtless movement of desire' (p. 83). By this he means that genera are formed when the unconscious ego spontaneously plays with ideas. It is free from the ordinary restrictions placed on thought by logic and habit. We saw in section three that one can characterize unconscious thinking as either thinking desire or desire thinking. Intuition represents the conscious appearance of thinking desire. 'Intuition is a form of desire associated with the ego's notion of what to look at, what to look for and how to do both beneficially' (p. 91).

The topic of this section has been the nature of the unconscious. Bollas's conception of psychic genera, while drawing on the thinking of Winnicott and Bion, involves revision of the traditional understanding of the formation of the unconscious. Bollas's unconscious is neither the repressed unconscious of the first topography nor the id of structural theory although it retains aspects of both. Like the repressed unconscious, Bollas's contains bad objects and colonies of repressed ideas. Like the id, the unconscious is the source of energy. But Bollas's unconscious functions as the fundamental organ for the reception of reality. It can say 'yes' or 'no' to the real. It can desire or avoid the real or do both at once. It moves towards objects that facilitate the development of primal genera. It avoids objects associated with trauma. Unconscious avoidance happens either as foreclosure (Lacan, 1993) or repression.

When the unconscious unconditionally rejects the arrival of the real, the result will be psychosis. In Bollas as in Bion, psychosis follows from the failure of the unconscious to assimilate the real. When the real is experienced as the cause of conflict, repression follows. When the real is experienced as inspiring the ego's *jouissance*, as facilitating the elaboration of idiom, reception takes place. I am distinguishing, in other words, between the unconscious as a receptive organ and reception in the narrower sense. The former refers to what is taken in and, then, repressed, received or evacuated. The latter results in the formation of a new perspective or the creation of meaning. We began by asking about thinking and its relation to meaning. In the next section, we will look back one more time on what we have learned. I will argue for a conception of psychic change as entailing the disclosure of individual truth.

FIVE

In his essay on 'Primal genera', Christopher Bollas (1992) returns to the first topography with the aim of developing a hypothetical account of how human beings arrive at new perspectives that is inconsistent with the idea of the unconscious. As an analyst, he is particularly interested in how patients change. New insight announces the arrival of psychic transformation. An analytic discovery, I am arguing, constitutes a new shape of individual truth. But although new insights may appear suddenly or in response to an interpretation, they reflect a great deal of unconscious work. This work reflects the incubation of psychic genera.

Just as the unconscious mediates our access to real as emotionally significant, the preconscious mediates between the conscious and the unconscious mind. Aiming at generating new structures, the preconscious responds to the experience of a psychic intensity by inviting a new idea into the unconscious and investing it with an anti-cathexis that protects the new idea from premature exposure to the critical judgements of consciousness. The preconscious responds to the experience of an emotional link between the new experience and an unconscious constellation of instincts, affects, memories and experiences.

This cluster, residing in the unconscious, is a form of thinking desire. As such, it constitutes a form of psychic gravity that attracts related ideas. Because genera begin as incubating psychic structures that exist in inchoate form, the ego must tolerate unconscious chaos while they are developing. As the process of condensation intensifies and unconscious desire becomes more forceful, the ego develops a sense that a few form of experience, what I have called a new unconscious context for meaning, is developing. 'Suddenly,' writes Bollas (1992) 'the person develops a fundamentally new perspective which is the manifestation of a new psychic structure' (p. 88). Bollas adds, 'This moment often *feels* revelatory' (ibid.).

To which I respond, nay, it *is* revelatory in Heidegger's (1962) sense of truth as an uncovering of the hidden. In this case, the hidden does not refer to the truth of Being but to the work of the receptive unconscious. This new truth that announces the arrival of new psychic structure may be as personal as my awareness that my interest in the painting, *Marriage at*

Cana, both reflected an unconscious conviction that marriage is linked to the miraculous and, in addition, functioned as a container for memories of past visits to Paris. It may be as cosmic as the theory of relativity or take the form of a complex poem such as Wallace Stevens's *Sunday Morning*.

Truth, in the form of new intuition about reality, a new 'seeing' of what is there, announces the appearance of a new psychic structure. In object relational language, the latter exists as an internal object. I have argued that internal objects are best thought of as schemata. They exist as unconsciously held rules for establishing or severing links between ideas, affects, memories and existential experiences. These rules function in a way that is analogous to Kant's description of the productive imaginative. Instead of rendering a concept sensible, they render the reception of an object psychically meaningful. Thus, there are schemata for sensing, structuring, remembering, conceptualizing, signifying and evacuating an object. To sense an object is to schematize it in a particular way. In addition, there are schemata for representing this experience. These include unconscious rules for processing experience visually, sonically, linguistically and/or interpersonally. Finally, the preconscious consists of schemata for the avoidance and pursuit of objects.

When the unconscious ego avoids an experience, we saw that it represses ideas and affects by assigning them to the unconscious. These unconscious, affectively charged ideas coalesce to form a bad object. The ego constructs genera in a manner that is precisely opposed to repression. By inviting ideas into the unconscious, it creates a space for the development of unconsciously held schemata for organizing experience.

Bollas, in conclusion, reconceives the unconscious to make room for the unconscious creation of meaning, particularly in the analytic process. The unconscious consists of affects, instincts, ideas, clusters, developing internal objects and fully formed internal objects. The latter are either bad or good objects. Object choice, however, is not simply contingent on whatever presents itself to the unconscious. The unconscious also contains primal genera, elements of idiom. Each one of us has a defining essence that we strive to actualize. However, this actualization of essence does not happen spontaneously. Because we are born relatively helpless and vulnerable, the expression of idiom is initially in need of generative parenting. Because some of us are restricted in our use of objects, we need analysis to facilitate more spontaneous reception of objects. This entails the emergence of a new schema.

Near the beginning of this essay, I enumerated six characteristics of thinking. We have seen that both conscious and unconscious thinking begin with a moment of withdrawal. Conscious thinking requires solitude to actualize the two-in-one while unconscious thinking requires being lost in thought so that one can projectively subjectify or psychically signify objects. Conscious thinking takes various forms: it can, for example, be subjective, imaginative, logical or objective. Unconscious thinking is always subjective in the precise sense that it obeys the logic of either idiom or trauma. Just as conscious thinking begins with the thoughts of others, unconscious thinking requires the facilitating presence of a good parent or the stimulating presence of an evocative object. Both unconscious and conscious thinking aim at truth. One way of formulating the difference is to say that consciously we seek to conform to what is; unconsciously we seek the truth of idiom.

I have deliberately left until last the third characteristic of thinking. It requires an involvement with thought things. We saw that these thought things do not appear to the senses. They are invisible and one can only describe them metaphorically. Therefore, one cannot, I would argue, evaluate Bollas's theory of thinking by empirically confirming it. Just as one will never see a thought, we will never see an internal object. The question is, does Bollas open a new perspective on the unconscious that enables us to think about what we are doing when we think as well as when we treat patients clinically. This essay has attempted to show how his theory of genera gives us a deeper understanding of the unconscious, something that we will never see on land or sea, but that is as close to us as the heart beating within and yet as distant as the most distant star.

REFERENCES

Arendt, H. (1978) *The Life of the Mind: Thinking.* Vol. 1. New York: Harcourt, Brace, Jovanovich.

Aristotle (1984) *The Complete Works.* Vol. 2. Princeton, NJ: Princeton University Press.

Bollas, C. (1992) *Being A Character.* New York: Hill and Wang.

Bollas, C. (1995) *Cracking Up.* New York: Hill and Wang.

Bollas, C. (1989) *Forces of Destiny.* London: Free Association Books.

Bollas, C. (1987) *The Shadow of the Object.* New York: Columbia University Press.

Brugger W. and Baker, K. (1972) *A Philosophical Dictionary.* Spokane, WA: Gonzaga University Press.

Freud, S. (1959) *Collected Papers.* Vol. 4. New York: Basic Books.

Heidegger, M. (1962) *Being and Time*. New York: Harper.

Hinshelwood, R. D. (1989) *A Dictionary of Kleinian Thought*. Northvale, NJ: Jason Aronson.

Kant, I. (1965) *The Critique of Pure Reason* (trans. N. Kemp Smith). New York: St Martin's Press.

Lacan, J. (1993) *The Seminar of Jacques Lacan; Book III, The Psychoses*. New York: W. W. Norton.

Laplanche, J. and Pontalis, J.-B. (1973) *The Language of Psychoanalysis*. New York: W. W. Norton

Plato (1961) *The Collected Dialogues*. Princeton, NJ: Princeton University Press.

Rosand, D. (1997) *Painting in Sixteenth Century Venice*. Cambridge: Cambridge University Press.

Idiom, Intuition and Unconscious Intelligence: Thoughts on Some Aspects of the Writings of Christopher Bollas

Arne Jemstedt

And now I think that she wordlessly expresses herself, through the space that surrounds her.

(from an art review in *Dagens Nyheter*, Stockholm, 1980)

When Eve enters my room for a session, is it possible to say that I sense the presence of her idiom? If I do, how is this conveyed to me? Is it through the way she moves, the way she closes the door? Is it something in her eyes, the way she looks or does not look at me? Is it in her quick laughter and in the way her pain and sadness silently come to the surface? Eve is intelligent and quite efficient in her work and studies, though below her capacity. Some years ago she had a breakdown leading to admittance to a psychiatric hospital. She feels unreal, 'there is no centre, only loose threads'. Her body feels disconnected, 'my feet don't reach down to the ground. I have never trusted the ground, floors even less'. She feels like a tree consisting of just light leaves, no stem, no branches. Time is without continuity, 'I have heard that goldfishes don't suffer from small aquariums, because they can remember only one second back in time. It is the same with me, though it is usually more than one second.'

For reasons that very slowly are becoming more clear and possible to formulate, she has great difficulties in communicating to me what is going on inside her, and there are often long silences. Yet the sessions seem meaningful, and there is a high degree of attention in both of us. There is a lot of pain in her – and the pain is what feels real to her, the rest feels like a robotlike shell – yet there is something both delicate and distinctive in her being. Again, how is this quality conveyed and received?

Jane associates in a seemingly meaningful way, moving between her relation to her father and to me, yet I feel that she speaks from a protective position: there is a kind of automatic scanning of how I might receive her communication, and pain is avoided, there is a flight from within. Her being does not inform her words, and there is no real use of me. With what sense do I perceive this?

After two years of analysis, Kate brings this dream: 'I am at a shore, standing in the water. I hold a stone in my hand at the surface of the water. A pattern in the water emanates from the stone. It is beautiful, it moves and changes. I think: "This is my pattern." I have a thought of trying to bring the pattern with me up from the water, but understand that it does not work. I walk up to the shore with the stone in my hand.'

Kate had come to analysis caught up in a network of self-accusations, aggressions, guilt feelings and compliance, and variations on these themes had coloured the sessions. This dream seemed to bring something new and we were both alerted by it. It carried a change of tone – there was a quality of beauty and clarity in the dream that had not been conveyed in Kate's communication before. There are several aspects to reflect upon in the dream – the stone, for example – but our attention converged on the pattern in the water: its beauty, its integrity and ever-changing variability, the impossibility to catch it, to get hold of it. Could the pattern be said to be an attempt at representational expression of Kate's *feel* of her idiom? Idiom itself cannot be symbolized; what can be symbolized is derivatives of it. You cannot grasp the wind, but you can sense its effects in the movements of the trees.

I will pick up the thread of 'idiom' soon, but first I will stay with the question that has accompanied these three vignettes: how does the analyst sense the sudden shift of emotional tone in a session, the presence or non-presence of the analysand in the room, the change of *specific gravity* in the patient's communication?

THE INTUITIVE SENSE AND THE COMMUNICATION OF PSYCHOANALYTIC EXPERIENCES

'The physician,' writes Bion (1977, p. 7), comparing psychoanalysis with the medical model, 'can see, touch and smell. The realizations with which a psycho-analyst deals cannot be seen or touched; anxiety has no shape or colour, smell or sound. For convenience I propose to use the term "intuit" as a parallel in the psycho-analyst's domain to the physician's use of "see", "touch", "smell" and "hear".' Bion (1992, p. 31) sees the analyst's 'intuitive capacity' as a fundamental capacity on which other capacities and functions, such as his interpretative function, are based, and it led him to formulate his celebrated recommendation that the analyst should eschew 'memory, desire and understanding' since the intrusion of these elements damages intuition.

What kind of sense is this? It is a special kind of attentiveness, paradoxically exercised in a wakeful, dream-like state. It is akin to the aesthetic sense, being sensitive to nuances, shifts, harmonies, tensions in that which is communicated.

The analyst's intuition, if it is used, is turned towards the 'music' of the patient's presence and communication, and towards the work of the unconscious as it unfolds in the patient's dreams and associations, and in the responses and shifting movements in the analyst's own inner space. With it goes an attempt to let go of what is already known, and to tolerate not knowing. It comprises an openness towards the logic of the primary process and towards the rhythm of displacement and condensation and a capability to wait for a new pattern to emerge without prematurely trying to find order in that which is not yet organized.

This dream-like quality of the session is the 'stuff of analysis' (Bion, 1977, p. 70). In a lecture in New York, Bion (1980, p. 31) suggested that someone instead of writing a book called 'The Interpretation of Dreams', should write one called 'The Interpretation of Facts', investigating the transformation of secondary process thinking into dream language.

Bion formulates his recommendation (of letting go of memory, desire and understanding) strikingly, but the content of it is, as we know, not new. It is there already in Freud's advice (1955 [1923], p. 18) to the analyst to 'surrender himself to his own unconscious mental activity, in a state of *evenly suspended attention*, to avoid so far as possible reflection and the construction of conscious expectations, not to try to fix anything he heard particularly in his memory, and by these means to catch the drift of the patient's unconscious with his own unconscious.'

When we tell a dream we have had to an analyst or a friend we encounter the impossibility of conveying the fullness of the dream experience, of seizing the elusive quality of the dream. Given the dream-like characteristics as the essence of the psychoanalytic session, the same is true of the analyst's efforts to communicate – outside of his consulting room – his psychoanalytic experiences. The major part of numerous changing associations, of vague bodily sensations, of meteorological variations of the atmosphere in the room, of shifts from obscurity to sudden clarity, is lost in the description of a session.

In his 'Commentary' to *Second Thoughts* Bion (1967, p. 142) states that 'the matters with which we [as psychoanalysts] deal are real beyond question, but have to be described in terms that from their nature introduce distortion.' And:

> The experience of the patient's communication and psycho-analyst's interpretation is ineffable and essential. . . . What has to be communicated [to the reader] is real enough; yet every psycho-analyst knows the frustration of trying to make clear, even to another psycho-analyst, an experience which sounds unconvincing as soon as it is formulated. We may have to reconcile ourselves to the idea that such communication is impossible at the present stage of psycho-analysis. Transformations of the psycho-analytical experience into formulations which effect communication between psycho-analyst and reader, remains an activity to be pursued.   (Bion, 1967, p. 122)

Among several other *vertices* (to use a Bionian term) these two – the intuitive sense and the communication of psychoanalytic experiences – are useful in discussing the writings of Christopher Bollas, and I will dwell on these for awhile, hoping that they will lead into the area of *idiom*.

'Much of what transpires in a psychoanalysis – as in life itself – is unconscious,' Bollas states in his Introduction to *Being a Character* (1992, p. 5), and one of the main threads in his work is the paradoxical endeavour to transform unconscious primary processes in the analysand, in the analyst and in the interplay between them into verbal secondary process language, without doing too much damage to the quality of the sheer *unconsciousness* of these processes. 'Psychoanalytic theory,' writes Adam Phillips (1994, p. 157), reviewing *Being a Character*, 'has always had a problem keeping the unconscious unconscious; it usually becomes a nastier, or more ingenious consciousness. . . . What is distinctive about Bollas's work is his commitment to the unconscious – the unconsciousness of everyday life – without becoming speechless or too mystical in the process.'

STYLE AND FORM

Not all psychoanalytic writers have a personal style. Those who have are those whose writings have the greatest impact on us, where the presence of the author's personality is felt in his texts. Winnicott had a kind of light, sensitive touch, and a special talent of using ordinary words to say extraordinary things. Bion's style is rigorously condensed, each sentence loaded with meaning. Bollas's style is also very much his own. It has a versatile *musicality*, conveying rhythm and resonance. His texts often disseminate in complex meanders of thoughtful associations to return to simple statements of high density. This form, this musical quality, in Bollas's writing is important. When he pictures unconscious processes, be they the transformational effect on the child of the mother's 'aesthetics of care' (Bollas, 1987, p. 35), or the formation of 'psychic genera' – of new generative psychic structures formed through gravitational processes towards receptive areas in the unconscious (Bollas, 1992, pp. 66–100) – the form and rhythm of his text interactively resonates his lines of thoughts.

This feature is essential in Bollas's efforts to convey the experience of the *aesthetic intelligence* of the unconscious and to capture phenomenologically the processes that unfold in a psychoanalysis. In Bollas's thinking form is as important as content, 'how' is as important as 'what'. When trying, for example, to formulate the elusive essence of idiom, he states that 'a person's idiom is . . . an implicit logic of form' (1992, p. 70) and when discussing analytic technique he maintains that 'inevitably we must turn to the aesthetics of form – the particular way something is conveyed – as an important feature of unconscious communication' (1995, p. 41). This quality, this appreciation of form, is paralleled in his way of writing.

In his first two books Bollas moves primarily in the domain of psychoanalytic theories and experiences. His theoretical meditations are creative and evocative – it is easy to suggest for consideration his by now well-known concepts of *the unthought known* and *the transformational object*, both of which carry with them a penumbra of deep associations. His clinical examples convey very much a sense of presence of both participants in the room. Whatever his theme is – and his themes are many – there is an appreciation of the uniqueness of each individual and an emphasis on the shifting conscious and unconscious interplay between the two human *subjects* that constitute the psychoanalytic couple.

From *Being a Character* and onwards Bollas increasingly turns towards the field of arts to investigate the movements of unconscious forming processes. When discussing the unfolding of processes between the analyst and analysand and inside each of them he moves between the psychoanalytic area and the area of artistic creativity and the artist's relation to his/her medium. 'Artists,' Bollas states, 'are gifted only in their exceptional use of otherwise ordinary human capacities, usually because they know more about the intelligence of form' (1992, p. 39).

In 'Creativity and psychoanalysis' in *The Mystery of Things* Bollas (1999, pp. 167–80) oscillates between Stravinsky's, Bacon's and other artists' accounts of their work, Freud's theory of dreams and free association, and the psychoanalytic practice and brings these facets together in a profoundly evocative interplay.

When Bollas uses the description different artists give of the evolution of unconscious creative processes to shed light on the work of the unconscious in the psychoanalytic situation, he often succeeds in communicating to the reader the detailed subtlety of these dreamlike processes. In this sense he approaches a realization of Bion's wish mentioned earlier, to find 'transformations of the psycho-analytical experience into formulations which effect communication between psycho-analyst and reader.'

INTUITION AGAIN

'It is,' writes Freud in *The Unconscious*, 'a very remarkable thing that the *Ucs.* of one human being can react upon that of another, without passing through the *Cs.* This deserves closer investigation, but, descriptively speaking, the fact is incontestable' (1955 [1915], p. 194).

One significant feature of Bollas's work is that he follows Freud's request for a 'closer investigation' of such communication and interaction. Bollas's focus on unconscious processes in general – in the first chapter of *Being a Character* he hopes 'to set the stage for an understanding of how the human subject *becomes the dream work of his life*' (1992, p. 13) – and in the psychoanalytic relation in particular, is inseparably connected with his attention towards the intuitive sensing of the flow of internal shifts in oneself and in the other. 'Perhaps', Bollas writes, 'the sense of intuition is our preconscious experience of the ego's intelligent work, leading us to consciously authorize certain forms of investigation in thought which are not consciously logical but which may be unconsciously productive.' He adds, of course, that 'the fact that intuition seems to be an immediate knowing should not obscure the fact that it is the outcome of sustained concentration of many types of unconscious and conscious thinking' (1992, pp. 90–1). These sentences reverberate a statement by Stravinsky on: 'the intuitive grasp of an unknown entity already possessed but not yet intelligible, an entity that will not take definite shape except by the action of a constantly vigilant technique' (Bollas, 1999, p. 171).

In *Cracking Up* Bollas elaborates his thoughts on intuition as a *separate sense* and I quote him at some length:

A psychoanalyst develops a separate sense for each patient, attuned to the analysand's precise intelligence of form, as the patient takes the analyst through a process that derives entirely from the patient's aesthetic in being. . . . The analyst comes to sense the basic assumptions peculiar to the analysand's being, out of which he develops a sense of his patient's idiom.   (Bollas, 1995, p. 37)

He continues:

As analyst and patient shape one another, the analyst's self works with an inner, intuitional ear, the analyst's perception may enable him to learn something at a deeply unconscious level about the nature of the other's forming intelligence, and just as the aesthetics of literature or music have much to do with timing, pausing, and punctuational breathing, it may well be that he, too, works technically – knowing when to make a comment, what diction texture to choose, when to remain silent, what image to pick up at what moment, when to use his feelings as the basis of an interpretation, or when to scrutinise a word presentation. These decisions are aesthetic choices, and should be in tune with the analysand's self – namely, his aesthetic presence and its articulation. Such 'technical decisions' involve work at the level of self to self, of the analyst's self sensing the patient's self. . . . There is a feeling there of one's being, of something there, but *not a something we can either touch or know; only sense and it is the most important sensed phenomenon in our life.*   (Bollas, 1995, pp. 171–2)

In these dense sentences – touching on intuition, idiom, unconscious communication and psychoanalytic technique – Bollas again makes an analogy between the analyst's perceptiveness and the artist's aesthetic capacity. In doing so, he is moving in an area into which many psychoanalytic writers do not enter, partly because their attention is turned towards the content of the patient's communication rather than its form, partly – and even more – because the elusiveness of these processes makes them inclined to avoid the attempt to capture them in words – they are implicitly acknowledged, but not objects of elaborate thinking.

    In the last sentence of the quotation, Bollas comes close to Bion's formulation of the intuitive sense, and when he emphasizes the significance of the analyst's *unknowing* of his patients (Bollas, 1989, pp. 62–4), he does so for the same reason that Bion recommends the eschewing of 'memory, desire and understanding': to increase the analyst's ability to sense the emergence of new patterns in the patient's communication.

TRUE SELF AND IDIOM

I return to the clinical vignettes from the beginning of this chapter. To Eve who feels she has no centre – or sometimes a centre like a small dot, that has to be kept still, that can only wait – who has a fine intellect and is afraid of words, since they easily begin to live a life of themselves, disconnected from inwards; to Jane who speaks from a withdrawn position, who has a good life in any ordinary understanding of the words 'good life', but who suffers from a lack of spontaneity and from a subtle, cautious compliance aimed at protecting her from a feeling of painful loneliness; to Kate whose dream might be said to represent her feel of a personal pattern.

These themes obviously embrace the issues of psycho-somatic connectedness or lack of connectedness, of the sense of a personal centre of gravity, of access to a spontaneous inner flow, communicated or not communicated – themes that are essential to Winnicott's notion of the true self.

In *Forces of Destiny* Bollas writes:

> When Winnicott introduced the term 'true self' to stand for an inherited potential that found its expression in spontaneous action, I think he conceptualized a feature of the analytical relationship (and of life) that had heretofore been untheorized. . . . Winnicott's theory of true self is, in my view, just such a concept through which we may describe something we know about analysis, but have until now been unable to think.   (Bollas, 1989, p. 8)

Winnicott himself wrote: 'I think you will agree that here is nothing new about the central idea. Poets, philosophers and seers have always concerned themselves with the idea of a true self, and the betrayal of the self has been a typical example of the unacceptable' (Winnicott, 1986, p. 65).

The notions of true self and personal idiom have a central position in Bollas's writings. He elaborates the concepts mainly in his first three books, working on them, finding formulations for them. After *Being a Character* they are as it were left to work for themselves, disseminated into his texts, informing them from underneath.

Why are these concepts important, and why are Bollas's elaborations of them valuable? Because they refer to a *quality* of a person's being and mode of relating which 'ordinary' psychoanalytic concepts do not capture. Terms such as internal good or bad objects, splitting, projective identification – though immensely useful – do not capture the experience of, for example, being or not being in one's body. True self/idiom also underline the uniqueness of each individual, which colours his/her appearance, thought processes, emotional life and ways of being ill, and they carry with them a respect for the *enigma* at the core of each person.

Winnicott's clinical descriptions of analyses where an individual's centre of gravity is shifted from a false self to a true self position, and Bollas's descriptions of 'ordinary regression to dependence' (1987, pp. 256–74) and of the analysand's use of the analyst in the arrival of instinctual and true self representations (ibid., pp. 77–92) – and the analyst's noninterpretative, receptive response to it – convey the patient's experiences of inner movements and transitions that are psychically very real though difficult to represent in writing. These experiences have qualities of depth, of psychosomatic rootedness, of a sense of interiority, of discovery, sometimes of wonder and beauty. They are in themselves fundamentally meaningful and valuable, much as a valuable poem retains its value whether it is discovered and read or not. A 'good life' in the ordinary, social sense of the term may or may not follow such experiences.

Several of Winnicott's well-known terms, such as 'the ruthlessness of the primary love impulse', 'the creative impulse', 'the spontaneous gesture' are ways of depicting aspects of the true self, as is, paradoxically, his description of its sensitivity and vulnerability towards impingements from outside. While Winnicott wrote extensively about the aetiology, the function, and the manifestations of the false self, he intentionally avoided an elaborated description of the true self:

The concept of a 'False Self' needs to be balanced by a formulation of that which could properly be called The True Self. At the earliest stage the True Self is the theoretical position from which come the spontaneous gesture and the personal idea. Only the True Self can be creative and only the True Self can feel real. . . . The True Self comes from the aliveness of the body tissues and the working of body-functions. . . . It is closely linked with the idea of the Primary Process, and is, at the beginning, essentially not reactive to external stimuli, but primary. . . . There is but little point in formulating a True Self idea except for the purpose of trying to understand the False Self, because it does no more than collect together the details of the experience of aliveness. . . . It is important to note that . . . *the concept of an individual inner reality of objects applies to a stage later than does the concept of what is being termed the True Self.*

(Winnicott 1979 [1960], pp. 148–9)

These qualities are present when Bollas elaborates and deepens his thoughts on 'true self' and 'idiom'. There is throughout his books a development and refinement in his way of thinking about these concepts. In *The Shadow of the Object* he stays close to Winnicott's formulation describing the true self as 'the historical kernel of the infant's instinctual and ego dispositions' (1987, p. 51), 'the core of the self' (p. 208) and – linking true self to primary repression – as 'that inherited disposition that constitutes the core of personality, which has been genetically transmitted, and exists as a potential in psychic space' (p. 278). He places the true self at 'the very core of the concept of the unthought known' (p. 278), though essential aspects of the unthought known are derived from the logic of parental care and from living in family moods. And, of course, the true self, being initially a potential, is for Bollas – as for Winnicott – fundamentally dependent on a facilitating environment for coming into being.

A substantial part of *Forces of Destiny* is permeated by Bollas's efforts to illuminate the notion of true self/idiom without vitiating the elusive quality of it. 'To some extent,' he writes, 'the inherited potential is objectified through self and object representation in the subject's internal world although this is always only a derivative of the true self, much as we know the unconscious through its derivatives' (1989, p. 9). And:

The true self cannot be fully described. It is less like the articulation of meaning through words which allow one to isolate a unit of meaning as in the location of a signifier, and more akin to the movement of symphonic music. . . . Each individual is unique, and the true self is an idiom of organization that seeks its personal world through the use of an object . . . the fashioning of life is something like an aesthetic: a form revealed through one's way of being.

(Bollas, 1989, pp. 109–10)

In *Being a Character* there is a shift from using 'true self' and 'idiom' as synonyms to explicitly substituting 'idiom' for 'true self', not only, I think, because 'our words . . . need displacing' since 'overusage of a term [true self] . . . [leads to loss of] meaningfulness through incantatory solicitation, devaluing any word's unthought potential' (Bollas, 1992, p. 64), but also because Bollas leaves Winnicott's concept more in the background as he moves along his own lines of thought. Bollas now develops his image of idiom as an 'intelligence of form' and his ideas of idiomatic object-usage. 'The idiom,' he writes, 'that gives form to any human character is not a latent content of meaning but an aesthetic in personality' (ibid., pp. 64–5). He views one's idiom as being articulated through one's choice and use of objects, both in the transitional sense (where inner and outer reality overlap, and where the question as to what comes from inside and from outside is kept suspended) and in the 'objective' sense, where one encounters the object's quality of being fundamentally itself, outside the sphere of projective mechanisms, what Bollas calls the *integrity* of the object.

> If idiom is, then, the it with which we are born, and if its pleasure is to elaborate itself through the choice of objects, one that is an intelligence of form rather than an expression of inner content, its work collides with the structure of the objects that transform it, through which it gains its precise inner contents. This collisional dialectic between the human's form and the object's structure is, in the best of times, a joy of living, as one is nourished by the encounter.
> (Bollas, 1992, pp. 59–60)

There is an echo here, of course, of Winnicott's seminal paper 'The use of an object', describing the child's joyful discovery of the object's authentic realness, outside the realm of the child's omnipotence, outside the web of projective/introjective processes, as a result of the object's survival of 'maximum destructiveness (object not protected)' (Winnicott, 1971, p. 91).

A central theme in *Being a Character* is the 'capacity to be the dream work of one's life' (Bollas, 1992, p. 53), where the individual's idiom is disseminated in the endless movements of the unconscious and informs them, and this capacity is at the basis of the creative forming of new 'psychic genera'. Later Bollas terms this 'freely moving work of the unconscious . . . "unconscious freedom"' (1995, p. 3), this freedom being equivalent to the individual's capacity to deploy his idiom. A somewhat different perspective is envisaged here of pathology in the true self–false self area from the one Winnicott gives, where the individual operates from a false self position out of touch with a hidden, not articulated true self. The image Bollas conveys is one where the essence of this kind of pathology is the obstruction – for whatever reason – of the idiomatic movements of unconscious freedom.

Each dream is a unique creation, and as the analysand free associates to it – breaking up the visual images into verbal ramifications that takes him far away from the manifest dream – and as the analyst – in an unintrusive, dreamlike, yet attentive state – receives the other's communication and responds to it, suddenly or slowly new links and meanings will emerge. This is the essence of the psychoanalytic method that Freud invented when he created a space for the two participants' unconscious communication. As the process deepens there is an increased capacity on part of the analysand – and the analyst – to sense the idiomatic work of his/her unconscious, to receive messages from within and to be sensitive to the nuances of the other's communication. This development of unconscious capabilities – of increased unconscious freedom – is in itself deeply meaningful.

THE UNKNOWABLE QUALITY OF IDIOM

Throughout Bollas's elaborations of the notion of true self/idiom is the idea – explicit or implicit – that 'each of us at birth is equipped with a unique idiom' (1992, p. 51), 'the it with which we are born' (p. 59). This position is obviously not unproblematic. It is questioned by the interviewer in a long interview with Bollas in *Psychoanalytic Dialogues* (Bollas, 1993, pp. 3, 405–9) and by Jacobson (1997, pp. 89–102). Though both find great values in Bollas's work, they come up against this position of Bollas, and oppose it. The interviewer states sceptically that '[t]his seems to suggest that there is some core feature of self-experience that is separable from the facilitating input of others,' and Jacobson – when discussing Bollas's considerations on 'the interplay between the inherited (true self) and the environmental', between the infant and its environment – states:

> If aspects of the maternal idiom were nonexploitive, then it is not clear how these aspects could be distinguished from true self, although they may have originated from outside . . . the problem is: after this shadow of the object, this unthought known, is in principle taken in account and articulated, what else is there? . . . [W]hen Bollas tries to say what [the] true self or idiom core is, things get obscure . . . Bollas wants us to conceive a genetic core of these true self manifestations. He wants to provide an objective reality-grounding to what we are relating to in the analysand.   (Jacobson, 1997, pp. 89–102)

It is inherent in Bollas's notion of 'true self/idiom' that we will never know what it is; we will never find an 'objective reality-grounding' to it.

We will never encounter the true self as such, we will never know the other's idiom (or our own), but will sense, 'intuit', its derivatives through the individual's form of being. In this is an appreciation of the unknowable, linked to Bollas's appreciation of the unconsciousness of the unconscious. 'Above all,' Bollas writes, 'our itness, or our idiom, is our mystery. We imagine, dream, abstract, select objects before we know why and even then knowing so little' (1992, p. 51).

There are parallels between this unknown and unknowable quality of 'idiom' and Bion's notion of 'O' and its inaccessibility. Bion uses the sign O to 'denote that which is ultimate reality, absolute truth, the godhead, the infinite, the thing-in-itself. O does not fall in the domain of knowledge or learning save incidentally; it can be "become", but it can not be "known"' (Bion, 1977, p. 26). Using Bion's terminology I believe it is possible to say that 'idiom' is the 'O' of each personality. 'It [O],' Bion continues, 'stands for the absolute truth in and of any object; it is assumed that this cannot be known by any human being; it can be known about, its presence can be recognized and felt, but it cannot be known. It is possible to be at one with it' (ibid., p. 30).

The efforts to understand the human being exclusively in relational terms echo the difficulties Guntrip had with Winnicott's statement of an 'incommunicado element' at 'the centre of each person' (Winnicott, 1979 [1963], p. 187). 'Here I am unable to follow him [Winnicott],' writes Guntrip. 'I do not see how a core of the self that is ... incommunicado can be a self at all. A self can only experience itself in the act of experiencing something else', and he is at great pains trying to catch Winnicott's thoughts on non-communicating in a web of relational terms (Guntrip, 1968, pp. 236–42)

In one of his replies in the interview, Bollas says: 'It is very, very easy to get things wrong here, to stress one factor (the innate) against the other (the environmental)' (1992, pp. 405–6). Throughout his writing Bollas emphasizes the interactional play between subject and object in the inter-mediate area or otherwise, be it between mother or child, analyst and analysand, or in general between the individual and world around him, exploring this mutual conscious and unconscious communicating and its influences. In the interview Bollas uses the analogy with an author's idiom in writing, taking Jane Austen as his example. After having taken into account the myriads of influences on all levels on Austen's writing, there would still be 'something there, an aesthetic organization of being ... that would be the Austen idiom' (ibid., p. 406). There is a quality here of idiom as something truly belonging to the individual: intrinsic, inherent – and

inherited. The idiomatic potential is there within us from the beginning as
we emerge from not being into being.

Michael Eigen, when discussing the depths of creative experiencing,
formulates the same idea in the following way:

> All three authors [Winnicott, Lacan, Bion] maintain the critical
> importance of not confusing creative experiencing with introjection
> (or internalization) of mother and father images or functions. The
> sources of creative experiencing run deeper than internalization and
> go beyond it. If one reads these authors carefully, one discovers that
> the *primary object of creative experiencing is not mother or father, but the
> unknowable ground of creativeness as such*. . . . Maternal or paternal
> object relations may subserve or thwart this experiencing but must
> not be simply identified with it.   (Eigen, 1981, p. 431)

And finally, to return to Bion and 'O':

> [The analyst's] freedom from being 'blinded' by the qualities (or his
> perception of them) that belong to the domain of senses should enable
> the analyst to 'see' those evolved aspects of O that are invariant in the
> analysand. The further the analysis progresses the more the psycho-
> analyst and the analysand achieve a state in which both contemplate
> the irreducible minimum that is the patient. (This irreducible mini-
> mum is incurable because what is seen is that without which the
> patient would not be the patient.)   (Bion, 1977, p. 59)

This 'irreducible minimum' could be called the subject's *integrity*, in the
sense Bollas uses the word integrity.

ESSENTIAL ALONENESS

A human being is more than the sum of his instincts and passions and
defences, and more than the sum of external influences. There is something
deep inside us that is not relational, that is fundamentally alone. 'I suggest,'
writes Winnicott, in deepening his thoughts on the true self, 'that in health
there is a core to the personality . . . that never communicates with the
world of perceived objects, and that the individual knows that it must never
be influenced by external reality' (1979 [1963], p. 187). 'There is,' he
continues, 'at the centre of each person an incommunicado element, and

this is sacred and most worthy of preservation . . .' It is forever immune from the reality principle, and for ever silent. Here communication is not non-verbal; it is, like the music of the spheres, absolutely personal. It belongs to being alive' (p. 192). This is the enigmatic core at the centre of each individual. Outside us, in outer space, there is an infinity that astronomers and physicists explore. A corresponding, deepening infinity exists internally. 'The blackness of the pupil,' writes Lars Gustafsson (1990, p. 156), 'is identical with the blackness between the galaxies.' There is a connection between the loneliness in our inner cosmos and the foetus suspended in the womb, in a loneliness that paradoxically comprises a maximal dependency, of which the foetus has no awareness (Jemstedt, 2000, p. 130)

The access to an inner, personal non-communicating place is at the basis of the capacity of healthy individuals to be alone. Not defensively with-drawn, but restfully alone, with an openness inwards. It is from here, from this aloneness, that the movement outwards, the idiomatic gesture towards others and the world around, arises.

REFERENCES

Bion, W. R. (1967) *Second Thoughts.* London: Maresfield Reprints.

Bion, W. R. (1977) *Attention and Interpretation. I: Seven Servants.* New York: Aronson.

Bion, W. R. (1980) *Bion in New York and São Paulo.* Perthshire: Clunie Press.

Bion, W. R. (1992) *Cogitations.* London: Karnac Books.

Bollas, C. (1987) *The Shadow of the Object.* London: Free Association Books.

Bollas, C. (1989) *Forces of Destiny.* London: Free Association Books.

Bollas, C. (1992) *Being a Character.* New York: Hill & Wang.

Bollas, C. (1993) An interview with Christopher Bollas. *Psychoanalytic Dialogues,* 3: 401–30.

Bollas, C. (1995) *Cracking Up.* New York: Hill & Wang.

Bollas, C. (1999) *The Mystery of Things.* New York & London: Routledge.

Eigen, M. (1981) The area of faith in Winnicott, Lacan and Bion. *International Journal of Psychoanalysis,* 62: 413–33

Freud, S. (1955 [1915]) The unconscious. *Standard Edition,* 14. London: Hogarth Press.

Freud, S. (1955 [1923]) Two encyclopaedia articles. *Standard Edition,* 18. London: Hogarth Press.

Guntrip, H. (1968) *Schizoid Phenomena, Object Relations and the Self.* London: Hogarth Press.

Gustafsson, L. (1990) *The Death of a Beekeeper.* London: Collins Harvill.

Jacobson, L. (1997) The soul of psychoanalyis in the modern world. Reflections on the work of Christopher Bollas. *Psychoanalytic Dialogues,* 7: 1.

Jemstedt, A. (2000) Potential space – the place of encounter between inner and outer reality. *International Forum of Psychoanalsis,* 9:1–2.

Phillips, A. (1994) *On Flirtation.* London and Boston: Faber & Faber.

Winnicott, D. W. (1971 [1969]) The use of an object and relating through identifications. In *Playing and Reality.* London: Tavistock.

Winnicott, D. W. (1979 [1960]) Ego distortion in terms of true and false self. In *The Maturational Process and the Facilitating Environment.* London: Hogarth Press.

Winnicott, D. W. (1979 [1963]) Communicating and not communicating leading to a study of certain opposites. In *The Maturational Process and the Facilitating Environment.* London: Hogarth Press.

Winnicott, D. W. (1986 [1964]) The concept of the false self. In *Home Is Where We Start From.* London: Penguin Books.

Futures

Adam Phillips

Though there is by now a recognizable psychoanalytic sensibility, for the most interesting (least slavish) theorists Freud simply punctuates traditions that predate him. He gives certain preoccupations a new kind of future. Psychoanalysis may begin with Freud but what it is about does not. . . . Christopher Bollas [has] been writing some of the most innovatory psychoanalytic theory of the last few years. . . . There is an unusual stylishness in [his] writing and an exhilarating ambition. Bollas's prose, immersed in the poetry of romanticism and the nineteenth-century American novel, allows him to be eloquently grandiloquent on occasions while being at the same time quite at ease with the tentativeness of his project. His prose often has the evocative resonance that his theory attempts to account for. And as his theory describes psychic life as a kind of haunting, we have to be alert to the echoes in his writing (and sometimes in his overwriting). When, for example, he describes the process of observing the self as an object – 'Emerging from self-experience proper, the subject considers where he has been' – it is integral to the process being described that we can hear the cadence of Coleridge's glosses on *The Ancient Mariner*. And echoes work both ways. . . .

For Bollas it is one of the difficult ironies of psychoanalysis that as a theory it seems to preempt the future it is attempting to elicit. Freud's 'account of human temporality', [as Malcolm] Bowie writes, 'serves . . . to place the future under suspicion, and to keep it there throughout a long theoretical career'. Like Bollas's definition of a trauma – 'the effect of trauma is to sponsor symbolic repetition, not symbolic elaboration' – it is as though, from a psychoanalytic point of view, the future can only be described as, at best, a sophisticated replication of the past; the past in long trousers. Theory itself becomes the symptom it is trying to explain. If in psychoanalytic theory the past, the undigested past, is that which always returns – both as symptom and interpretation – how can we return to the future, or get beyond the interminable shock of the old that theory and therapy too easily promote? Our theoretical habits, like our erotic habits, are the revenge of the past on the future.

In *Being a Character* Bollas suggests that the future – future selves and states of mind – arise through a process of evocation. Starting with the mother we unwittingly use the world and its objects to bring parts of ourselves to life. A combination of chance and unconscious intention, even our most concerted projects are forms of sleepwalking. 'Without giving it much thought at all,' Bollas writes, 'we consecrate the world with our own subjectivity, investing people, places, things and events with a kind of idiomatic significance ... the objects of our world are potential forms of transformation.' Our chosen objects of interest – and this can be anything from the books we read to the way we furnish our rooms or organize our days – are like a personal vocabulary (or even alphabet); we are continually, at our best, 'meeting idiom needs by securing evocatively nourishing objects'. It is as though we are always trying to live our own language, hoping to find 'keys to the releasing of our idiom' – what Bollas calls in one of many felicitous phrases, 'potential dream furniture' – as we go about setting the scene for the future. Objects – like different artistic media – have very different 'processional potential'; what Bollas calls the object's 'integrity' – whatever it happens to be, what it invites and what it makes impossible – sets limits to its use. The world in Bollas's view is a kind of aesthetic tool-kit; and unlike most psychoanalytic theorists he doesn't use a hammer to crack a nut.

It should be clear by now that Bollas has to draw on a repertoire of vocabularies to describe his new psychoanalytic landscape. Orthodox psychoanalysts are not in a hurry to use words like 'consecrate' or phrases like 'idiom needs' or, indeed, to take the outside world on its own terms. In Bollas's work the language of Winnicott and of American pragmatism – of 'use-value' – meets up with Wordsworthian romanticism; the world is sown with, and so made up by, bits of self, and yet retains its separatenesss, its sacrality, its resistance to absolute invention. In Bollas the Self is at once disseminated – all over the place – and intent, in relentless pursuit of what he calls 'props for the dreaming of lived experience'. The articulation of the self, as psychoanalysis has always insisted, is the transformation of the self; to speak is to become different. For Bollas the Self is like a rather meditative picaresque hero, the unwitting artist of his own life. Bollas is extraordinarily adept at describing the moment, or as he prefers to call it, the 'place where subject meets thing, to confer significance in the very moment that being is transformed by the object': and it is whatever baffles this moment that is pathology. The enigma of these meetings, these reciprocal appraisals – their sheer unconsciousness – is Bollas's overriding preoccupation in this book. And his paradigm for these processes is dreaming. Since 'a day is a space for the potential articulation of my idiom', then perhaps, he suggests, living a day is more like dreaming a dream than waking up from one.

In any day, Freud showed, quite unbeknown to our conscious selves we are picking things out to use as dream material in the night ahead. So in what Freud calls the 'dream-day' we are living out a kind of unconscious aesthetic; something or someone inside us is selecting what it needs for the night's work.

Things in the day have a significance for us, are meaningful, in ways we know nothing about until we work them back up in the quite different context of the dream. A perception, a thought, something overheard is noticed and then transformed by an exceptionally furtive artist. 'In a very particular sense,' Bollas writes, 'we live our life in our own private dreaming.' Bollas manages to convey, without simulating mysteries, an ordinary day as a dream landscape full of unexpectedly intense significance. In its account of living a day as a form of dreaming *Being A Character* becomes a truly startling book. It is as though without being spooky or vague, Bollas gets us close to the ordinary but absolutely elusive experience of making a dream; of how, quite unwittingly, in the most ordinary way, we are choosing objects to speak our secretive languages of self.

Psychoanalytic theory has always had a problem keeping the unconscious unconscious; it usually becomes a nastier, or more ingenious consciousness, a wished-for or a dreaded one. What is distinctive about Bollas's work is his commitment to the unconscious – the unconsciousness of everyday life – without becoming speechless or too mystical in the process (the best and the worst of psychoanalytic theory always verges on the mystical). But how much real unconsciousness can one allow into the picture and still go on practising and believing in psychoanalysis? If psychoanalysis is really a sleep-walking *à deux*, what is the analyst, and for that matter the patient supposed to be doing? Taking Freud seriously – which doesn't mean taking him all or taking him earnestly – involves acknowledging, as Bollas writes that, 'most of what transpires in psychoanalysis – as in life itself – is unconscious'. Since for Bollas dreaming is the model, patient and analyst use each other as part, though an intense part, of each other's dream day. The official emphasis is on the patient using the analyst as a transformational object, but in Bollas's model the reciprocity of the analytic process cannot be concealed. And the aim is not so much understanding – finding out which character you are – but a freeing of the potentially endless process of mutual invention and reinvention. For Bollas pathology is whatever it is in the environment and/or the self that sabotages or stifles both a person's inventiveness and their belief in this inventiveness as an

open-ended process. It is a psychoanalysis committed to the pleasures and
the freedoms of misunderstanding, and that Freud called dream-work;
distortion in the service of desire: not truth, except in its most provisional
sense, but possibility. The core catastrophe in many of Bollas's powerful
clinical vignettes is of being trapped in someone else's (usually the parents')
dream or view of the world; psychically paralysed for self-protection in a
place without the freedom of perspectives. Here what Bollas calls 'that
instinct to elaborate oneself' is thwarted: one is fixed in someone else's
preconception. Bollas's use of the word instinct here joins the language of
psychoanalysis with the languages of romanticism.

In four remarkable linked essays in the book – 'Cruising in the homosexual arena', 'Violent innocence', 'The Fascist state of mind' and 'Why
Oedipus?' – Bollas explores the causes and consequences of stifling a
person's internal repertoire of states of mind. For Bollas so-called mental
health (or rather, his version of a good life) entails the tolerance and
enjoyment of inner complexity; the ability to use and believe in what he
refers to as a kind of internal 'parliament', full of conflicting, dissenting and
coercive views. There is no final resolution here but rather a genuinely
political and psychic vigilance in the face of the insidious violence of over-
simplification. In what he calls the Fascist state of mind – a state of mind
readily available to all of us – 'whatever the anxiety or need that sponsors
the drive to certainty, which becomes the dynamic in the fascist construction, the outcome is to empty the mind of all opposition (on the actual stage
of world politics, to kill the opposition)'. This essay makes one wonder
which parts of the self need to be expelled to sustain any kind of political
allegiance; what happens to greed in left-wing sympathies or empathy in
certain versions of Toryism? Unusually activist for a psychoanalyst, Bollas
offers us in this book both ways of recognizing the seductions of apparent
political and psychic innocence – being on the side of Goodness, Truth and
Logic – and actual strategies for managing them. One of the bemusing
things about this remarkable book is that it is at once a genuinely radical
book, and also a curiously comforting one.

Bollas's lucid commitment to complexity – which never degenerates into
a stultifying relativism – has, as it were, its own complication built into it.
For Bollas the 'achievement' of the Oedipus complex is that the 'child
comes to understand something about the oddity of possessing one's own
mind'; and this means being a mind among others. The child inherits, or
wakes up to, the notion of point of view: I'm not only my mother's son and
possible lover, but also my father's, and my mother looks different from my
father's point of view, and my desire for my father looks different from my

mother's point of view, and so on. The super-ego – the internalized paternal prohibition – 'announces' Bollas writes, 'the presence of perspective . . . the child discovers the multiplicity of points of view'. And this ever-proliferating multiplicity, informed by desire, will become the 'it' he will call his mind. It is easy to see, as Bollas intimates, how this can begin to feel overwhelming and persecutory; too much music on at the same time. In one of the best speculative moments in the book Bollas suggests the possibility that many people cannot bear the complexity of their own minds and so take flight into the collusive solace of coupledom, or family life, or group allegiance. The 'madness' of being insistently with others is preferable to the 'madness' of one's mind. 'Given the ordinary unbearableness of this complexity,' Bollas writes, 'I think that the human individual partly regresses in order to survive, but this retreat has been so essential to human life that it has become an unanalysed convention, part of the religion of everyday life. We call this regression 'marriage' or 'partnership', in which the person becomes part of a mutually interdependent couple that evokes and sustains the bodies of the mother and the father, the warmth of the pre-Oedipal vision of life, before the solitary recognition of subjectivity grips the child.' In Bollas's terms this proposal itself might function as an 'object with evocative integrity'. What would it be like to live in a world in which people welcomed their own, and therefore other people's, complication; in which people did not allow their children to be simplified by conventional education, or coercive belief systems? Traditionally the numinous thing has been to simplify the moral life.

For Bollas trauma is that which oversimplifies the self; it is that which, because of the suffering entailed, leaves people with an aversion to their own complexity. Some people, Bollas writes, for good reasons of their own, 'insist that the invitational feature of the object be declined . . . they may narrow the choice of objects, eliminating the high evocative potential'. Curiosity is a threat to the self as idol; each new person we meet may call up in us something unfamiliar. So from Bollas's point of view psychoanalysis, as a form of therapy, has two implicit aims: to release – to analyse the obstacles to – a person's internal radar for finding the objects he needs for self-transformation; and to elicit, and enable a person to use, their essential complexity. It is part of the subtlety of this book to make these projects seem compatible.

Transformational, Conservative and Terminal Objects: The Application of Bollas's Concepts to Practice

Gabriela Mann

Christopher Bollas has been one of the most interesting contributors to the understanding of unconscious self-experience in contemporary psychoanalytic literature. During the last ten years he has written a number of significant books (1987, 1989, 1992, 1995, 1999) and essays (1996, 1997), dealing with subtle shifts and transformations in object relations. In a descriptive style uniquely his, Bollas portrays the way that self finds its echo in the particular object selected to portray and contain its subjective experience and 'private idiom'. From Bollas's perspective, objects are chosen as vehicles of transformation and can be used in multiple ways, and for this reason he has paid particular attention to delineating numerous kinds of objects: e.g. transformational objects, passionate and integral objects, conservative and terminal objects, transubstantial and interprojected objects. These various objects, or *usages*, are not simply a static or even dynamic representation; each 'object' represents a different link by which the subject employs the object, and simultaneously thereby defines and extends itself.

My purpose in this chapter is to focus on the concept of the transformational object, on the one hand, and conservative and terminal objects, on the other hand. I consider these concepts as best capturing Bollas's major contribution to understanding the vicissitudes of intersubjective experience. I chose these particular objects as signifiers for the kinds of transformation we hope for in psychotherapy. That is, as therapists, we can conceive of our work as helping our patients make a transition from conservative or terminal object usage to transformational object usage. I will present two clinical vignettes transformed by Bollas's thinking to illustrate how the therapist can facilitate the patient's use of the environment as an object that 'transforms' rather than 'conserves' or 'terminates' psychic evolution. I will further describe those qualities of the intersubjective interaction with an environment that facilitate the use of a transformational object, as opposed to other qualities of an environment that induce the use of conservative or terminal objects.

I hope my review will make clear the degree to which Bollas, who belongs to the Independent Group in psychoanalysis (Kohon, 1986; Rayner, 1991) and is an eminent believer in conscious and unconscious free association, draws from diverse theoretical sources in a free yet coherent manner. In this presentation, I will show how Bollas draws from and elaborates upon Freud's, Winnicott's, and Bion's ideas in a most creative way in order to account for the process of object usage. Bollas's unrestricted use of different theoretical frameworks, in fact, is consistent with his clinical technique favouring free movement between different modes of interpretation. I believe this flexibility of moving between modalities is, indeed, perhaps the chief distinguishing characteristic of Bollas's therapeutic style.

THE TRANSFORMATIONAL OBJECT

I will start by discussing Bollas's concept of *transformational object*, described first in his essay (Kohon, 1986) as well as in his book (Bollas, 1987), which I consider to be his most significant contribution. In this work Bollas discussed the critical role of the mother in early development and in parallel, the therapist's function during the therapeutic session. Applying and extending Winnicott's understanding of the 'environmental mother' (Winnicott, 1992 [1945, 1952]), Bollas describes the transformational *function* as 'the idiom of gesture, gaze, and intersubjective utterance' (p. 13), and defines the *transformational object* as:

> the mother's function as a processor of the infant. Known less as an actual other or as a formable internal object, the mother is an object known through her continuous action that alters the infant's psycho-somatic being.   (Bollas, 1989, p. 213)

These transformations of the self begin to occur through the mother who, in fact, changes the environment for the infant. The transformations continue as the infant develops his or her own capacities to become his/her own transformational agent (through movement, perception and, most of all, language). Later, further development occurs when the child creates a transitional object. From Bollas's perspective, then, the mother's importance lies not primarily in her being internalized into an abstract representation, but rather in being available to facilitate a recurrent experience of self. It is through this experience that the infant is enabled to move from states of unintegration to states of integration. To emphasize the early presymbolic nature of this important function, Bollas stipulates that he views the more familiar transitional phenomenon as the heir of the transformational phase.

Bollas goes on to state throughout life there remains a longing for the ability to submit to objects that will change the subject's self experience, some of which will no doubt be cast in the shadow of the earliest transformational objects. In adult life, this longing is expressed through religion or mystical processes, or, in formally non-religious individuals, through involvement in aesthetic aspirations such as music, painting, or hope (hope in a new job, immigration, a change). Underlying these never-ending quests are preverbal memories of the transformational object, even though this object has never been 'objectively' perceived (Bollas 1989).

The search for the transformational object or experience will be (or ought to be) reflected in therapy, when patients try to turn the therapist into a transformational object. Here it is important to reflect upon just how patients create and use the therapeutic object. In such cases, what is important is not simply the content of the therapist's interventions *per se* but also the capacity of the therapist to make available a transformative process via presence and empathy. This stage is often difficult for the therapist precisely because the process taking place is not a verbally negotiated aspect of therapy in the usual sense, but a process that evolves from the fact of the therapist's presence. Patients may react to interpretations that focus upon or presume this aspect of the work with indifference, grudge or downright anger. Alternatively, the formal or more generally recognized elements of 'therapy' may be experienced as an intrusive invasion into the patient's private being when transformational phases of the treatment are prominent. Verbalization and conversation, in this sense, are not really appropriate in the relationship with the environmental mother. Preverbal memory may not be formulated in words and may only be captured via holding and intuitive knowing. At such moments, when the patient can sense the therapist's ability to adjust to his or her needs, he or she may experience, perhaps for the first time in his or her life, transformational object relations.

Ironically it was Freud who, in spite of the fact that he never wrote much about mother–infant relations, or thoroughly analysed his relationship with his own mother, created the analytical space which would allow such processes to unfold (Anzieu, 1986). The therapeutic set-up is a reconstruction of the original rapport with the mother, which allows knowing that the therapist will find out how to perform the transformation.

Case illustration

D was a male student in his late 20s, the second of eight children. His next youngest sister was born when he was one year old. That is, D's mother had been pregnant during the first months of D's life. When D was four years old, his sister developed a severe skin disease which required daily treatments at home, and, at a certain stage, in various hospitals. The external signs of the disease were 'disgusting', in D's memory. The fact that he was going to the same school as his sister always made D feel, on the one hand, ashamed of his sister and, on the other hand, obligated to stand by her when other children would mock her.

By the time D turned 11, he already had in addition to his ill sister, five more siblings. The family was living in a small flat. D never had a place of his own, yet he managed to establish a favourite and private place inside one of the cardboard boxes underneath his father's desk. When he was slightly older, he developed the habit of stealing money from his mother's purse, buying himself a candy bar and walking for hours in the neighbourhood. During these long walks he would usually calm down, but this would normally be interrupted by his parents who had gone out to find him and angrily bring him back home.

When D initially came to therapy, he complained he was feeling stuck, that he 'did not belong to that same world as the others'. But he was constantly preoccupied with what 'others' thought of him. In spite of his objective success in the academic world, he saw himself as a person who failed. He experienced constant restlessness. Approximately seven months into the treatment, he reported the following dream:

> In the dream you were lying beside me. I am asleep and I want to wake up to tell you about my dreams, I don't need a pen and paper because you are there. I wake up and can't remember whether I told you the dream or not. People keep coming in and intruding, breaking my concentration. One of them was your adopted son. He was the kind of person who had 'safety' written all over him. You tell him to

wait outside. He did not bother me. This was a situation in which I just didn't have that belligerence I usually need in my life. That was okay by me.

I realized that D was telling me how much he needed me to allow him simply to be, without his aggressiveness, just with my presence. I heard his associations about the dream and told him that maybe he was telling me about two possible children he could have been to me: one who was self-confident and knew how to make things happen, and the other, a son who seeks a place where he could be without struggle, in the orbit of the therapist's quiet presence.

At the end of the second year of treatment D would come into the room, sink into the chair with a glassy-eyed look and within a few minutes he would fall asleep for anywhere between 10 to 40 minutes. I would sit facing him, feeling his loneliness being transferred into me, and try to imagine what he was communicating to me through his silence. Was this a sign of resistance? Depression? Or maybe he allowed himself to feel the privacy and restfulness he never had? Should I cover him with a blanket? Should I wake him up or would I be taking him out of his 'box'? Were we, together, realizing his first dream?

When it would be almost time to end the session I would wake him up. I shared with him some of the thoughts that crossed my mind when he had been asleep. I wondered how he wished me to be there for him. D said that the problem was that I did not say the right thing:

D: Sometimes what you say is just not it. It's logical. It's not in my language. Sometimes when I come here, the moment I come in, it's like I'm being sucked into a black hole. I feel dizzy. I can't say it in words. The moment I use words it is all spoiled; I have to surface.

Therapist: You're disappointed when I can't feel exactly how you need me to be for you.

D: Now you're saying it much better.

I felt how D was instructing me, telling me how to be for him during that period: no interpretations, no unnecessary questions. I thought of the 'aloneness' he created for himself in my presence and the space he took, in order to experience his own self for the first time. We spent long hours like that together, in his silence and his dream, almost without a word being said, but knowing that he was there and I was here, and that we were walking together at his pace.

This period lasted five or six months. One day, without any apparent reason, D came in and talked. In that period he had started, for the first time, to speak to his family and to share with them some of his inner conflict and pain. It seemed that he had allowed his true self to emerge.

This vignette is not intended to be a full case study, but rather as a demonstration of a particular way in which the patient can use the therapist as a transformational object during a certain period in psychotherapy, during which the patient needs his privacy and the legitimization to not communicate, both in the presence and in the non-presence of the therapist. In this context, Bollas wrote:

> To be sure, one of the features of such patients is their comparative unavailability for relating to the actual other – their obtuseness or excessive withdrawnness – but I think such characteristics . . . also point towards the patient's need to assert the region of illness as a plea for the arrival of the regressive object relation that is identified with basic ego repair.

> He [patient] appreciates the analyst's fundamental unintrusiveness (particularly the analyst not demanding compliance) not because it leads to freedom of association, but because it feels like the kind of relating that is needed to become well.   (Bollas, 1987, pp. 22, 23)

We see here a link between what Bollas defines as 'fundamental intrusiveness' and Winnicott's ideas concerning the notion of environmental mother (Winnicott, 1992 [1952]), the capacity to be alone in the other's presence (Winnicott, 1965 [1958]), and the way Winnicott describes the progress from object relating to the use of the object (Winnicott, 1971 [1969]). Finally, we recognize the high value Winnicott placed upon the legitimacy and value of not communicating (Winnicott, 1965 [1963]). Winnicott clearly prefers the therapist's silence and lack of knowledge, provided the therapist does not turn into a not-me object prematurely. We may observe here also an additional link to Bion (1967, 1970) who, in the same period, emphasized the importance of 'lack of memory and desire' in the therapist's listening stance as a key to the emergence of undistorted psychic reality. Bion, like Winnicott, warns against a forceful or missionary intention to 'cure' the patient, to bring him or her back to 'functioning' since this kind of intention tends to reduce and limit the scope of psychoanalysis. At the same time, neither Bion nor Winnicott relate these aspects of therapy to any particular kind of perception of the therapist's as an object of any particular kind.

CONSERVATIVE AND TERMINAL OBJECTS

Conservative and terminal objects differ from and are opposed to objects that are evocative and assist the self in deploying its idiom into the object world, towards transformation. The *conservative object* is 'a being state, preserved intact within a person's inner world. It is not intended to change, it is untransformable into symbolic order' (Bollas, 1987, pp. 110–11). It refers to a mental state in which the adult concretely re-experiences static being-states from his childhood *without mentalization*. Bollas submits that these mental states conserve something from the past that does not exist in the present any more, strictly speaking. This 'conserved' experience resides in the patient's inner world as a conservative object. It serves as an experiential container of a certain static self-state, a part of the true child self, and does not achieve symbolic representation.

Therapists cannot detect this kind of object use easily. When conservative objects prevail, the therapist tends to become increasingly attentive to a certain mood, or being-state, which on the face of things is unrelated to the actual events reported by the patient. This is so because the patient, even though wanting consciously to communicate, lacks the proper words to do so. The therapist has to use the mood he or she is induced into in the countertransference, and to attempt to give it translation. By virtue of doing so, the therapist begins to function as a transformational object. The therapist must perceive moods and give them an articulation that subtly changes their form from the realm of perception and intuition to the symbolic order.

An even more extreme version of resistance to transformation will be found in the employment of *terminal objects*: 'The terminal object is selected because it ends the self's disseminative movement. It ends the natural forward movement of those departing trains of thought that are the elaboration of any person's idiomatic experience of life' (Bollas, 1995, p. 75). The terminal object is an object to be avoided, with which one can certainly not lose oneself or develop unconscious creativity. The intersubjective experience with such an object has the quality of anti-relating. It is shallow and empty of contact with the complexity of real life.

The patient's use of terminal objects tends to influence the therapist's countertransference in compellingly unpleasant ways. Its echo in the countertransference is radically stronger than the echo of conservative objects. Bollas (1999) describes such self-experiences of the therapist as 'occasional madness'. The patient attacks the therapist's mind consciously or unconsciously and interjects into it a 'terminal' quality. The therapist experiences him or herself as unable to free associate, prevented from thinking and void of new ideas. It is the quality of this deadening blockage in the countertransference that gives the best indication that such object usage is prevailing.

Case illustration

When he came to psychotherapy, A was a 40-year-old single male. He was handsome and looked athletic. His reason for referral was: 'I'm particularly desperate about relationships. I've had relationships with many women, but in fact I've never had a relationship at all.' He felt that he did not advance in his work, either. He had been doing the same thing for more than 10 years and said that 'actually, I don't know where I've been all these years, everyone moved on and I'm the only one who remained in the same spot'.

He remembered nothing from his childhood initially. He came from 'a Jewish–Polish family where you don't speak, you don't feel and you don't get too close'. He knew that his father had been a Holocaust survivor and believed that his father was also stuck and at a standstill. A was not sure whether his father had been 'in Auschwitz, or maybe Bergen-Belsen or one of those alternative places'. A had actually made a video film documenting his father's life and yet he could not remember what his father had said in the film. His mother had been a child when the war broke out. A had heard from her cousin that she had been deported to Auschwitz, but his mother refused to speak about it. Approximately one month after the beginning of treatment, A presented the following dream:

> I was a 'homeless' in New York and I was with someone else. The other guy dragged me to a basement full of dead people and we were there. We lay on beds and pretended we were dead. Then someone came, like a policeman, to see if we were dead or alive or whether we just played dead. He [the policeman] tried to make me laugh. He put his face very close to mine and I couldn't breathe because I didn't want him to notice me breathing. I was on the verge of bursting into laughter.

In his associations A said that there was a lot of laughter in the dream, although in reality things were not so funny. I interpreted that he had something he needed to hide, maybe his vitality. I suggested – as this was the beginning of his treatment – that maybe he experienced me as a policeman trying to scrutinize him from a very close angle, while he felt that he should not disclose anything. In the dream, it seemed clear that if he let out the fact that he was alive, he would lose the only place he had to live in, which was a basement. I felt that, in his story, A wished to depict that he had successfully elicited my empathy and involvement.

A came to his sessions regularly, twice a week, but time and again spoke about how nothing changed. Moreover, most of the time he could not remember what it was he had spoken about in the previous session and described the experience in terms of dust which clouded his view. He said that he was living mechanically, did not think much or feel much. The only thing he knew well was how not to move. In fact, he had always been detached and unable to connect with the world. Apart from that he knew nothing and did not know where he should go. The clock was ticking and he was getting nowhere, he said. The truth was that I couldn't see any change either, apart from the knowledge that there was a relationship between us which I experienced as good, and that I felt genuine warmth towards him. However, very often I felt his deep despair catching up with me, freezing and paralysing me. It seemed that he was nipping in the bud any feeling of progression in our work. I often felt quite angry at him for stealing my vitality from me and for rendering me essentially as helpless as he was.

In the summer, approximately seven months after we started to work, I went on a vacation. When I returned, A said, as could have been expected, that nothing happened during the summer. He had had countless blind dates and none of them ever turned into anything. There were some small things but they were meaningless. At work he now had 'two and a half bits of something'. Apart from that he had started to play volleyball on the beach. What surprised him was that he was willing to do this without wearing a shirt 'in spite of these skinny muscles', he said. 'Who would have believed that someone so unathletic as myself would allow himself to do such a thing!' Suddenly he changed his tone and said: 'What is the meaning of all these talks? Nothing ever remains from our talks but dust. It leaves me just where I am, maybe even more hurt and depressed . . . I feel I need ventilation, a heart transplant,' and then:

> I don't know if I want to think. There are times I think that the
> mechanical solution is the most miraculous thing. I get up in the

morning, do my thing and then go back to sleep, try to disconnect but don't always succeed.

I replied that it was precisely in his inability and unconscious unwillingness to completely 'disconnect' that I saw hope. I realized that A was living in reality the life of the dead, and that in his dream he was living the life of the living. I realized that A was holding the death which was the fate of his parents' environment, while they, at least ostensibly, kept living. He identified with and conserved their dead part. At a certain point, maybe because I felt that nothing but a very blunt statement would make any difference, I said to him:

> Your sadness nourishes you more than anything else. You live for it. It is my impression that you own this sadness and that you are unwilling to allow anyone to take it away from you. It is wrapped around you and accompanies you wherever you go, as though it were your mother. Letting it go would be unbearable. I imagine you as a child who felt his parents' sadness and grief, while it was impossible to discuss it. Instead of talking about it, you made it your own.

I was suggesting that, having no other imaginable object, his chronic sadness had itself become a conservative object. I told him how his parents had managed to erase their factual histories but not their psychic realities, the mood that accompanied their life. This mood had become the object they rendered available to him, and he clung to it forcefully. I offered myself as someone who was there with him, who could feel the deadening part, which was overpowering him time and again. This itself made me seem dangerous yet, as the first dream suggested, capable nevertheless of being perceived as soothing.

In the year following that interpretation a surprising change occurred. A remained, for the time being, incapable of establishing long-term relationships, but his playing volleyball led him to start to try roller-blades, and after that he went on hikes to the mountains and took diving lessons. A's range of subjective experience had broadened considerably and allowed us, at times, to experience together moments of real pleasure, in view of his new experiences in nature, compared with the long periods of emptiness and hopelessness. Contrary to what I could have expected, change came from the sphere of the psychesoma, not by symbolization. I understood it as a spontaneous gesture of an adult person.

This vignette demonstrates a patient's choice of psychic deadness (Eigen,

1996) as conservative and terminal objects. The patient is attached to and conserves the deadening quality of his primary environment and turns it into an object to hold on to. He cannot take in anything that is not toxined by this deadness (Eigen, 1999). The therapist is perceived unconsciously as a 'cop' who tries to break through a protective shield (Kahn, 1963). In fact, the therapist herself is transformed (via projective identification) into a being that is like a carapace, or a person carrying an autistic armour, which is how the patient has lived all these years. It is only when the therapist makes an active interpretation that confronts this tendency in the patient, and disseminates its experience into the symbolic order, that the process can take a new track towards transformation.

UNCONSCIOUS INTERSUBJECTIVE IMPRISONMENT: THE INDUCTION OF AN ENVIRONMENT FOR CONSERVATIVE AND TERMINAL OBJECTS

Bollas (1992) maintains that an individual's ability to use objects for creative experiential transformation is related to the primary relationship between the infant and his environment. He then makes a significant distinction between two essentially different primary environments: an environment of genera and an environment of trauma. The first is a facilitating or generative environment, which enhances creative being, whether in psychoanalysis or otherwise. The second is the opposite traumatic environment, which inhibits and restricts psychic development. Children who experience their parents as facilitating the discovery of the uniqueness of their own private world develop an openness to possible contributions from and creative use of the world of objects. But children whose parents inhibit their unique expression accumulate traumatic experiences in an inner mental space, designed to restrict and prevent additional damage to the self. In their attempt to avoid pain they reduce as much as possible the scope of their subjective and intersubjective experiences. A child who experiences trauma will tend not to explore new avenues nor project symbolic expressions of his/her inner world, nor seek additional interactions with the world. The psyche that develops in trauma protects itself by attempting to desensitize any possible future events. Hence the link between a traumatic environment and the death instinct, which strives to preserve the present and evacuate the subject from stimulations which are connected to relations with external objects.

In our clinical practice we often meet people who lack the unconscious freedom for creative living. Their freedom is restricted and reduced to repetition of familiar situations, which allow for no new avenues of the self. This is most vividly seen in obsessive individuals who are incapable of unconscious freedom. The obsessive is preoccupied with a certain idea which fills his or her inner world with repetitive experiences. He selects an object which is devoid of transitional qualities and turns it into a terminal object. The terminal object is selected precisely because it cuts off the process of dissemination and allows no new unconscious or conscious elaboration to set off and transform into a new realm. Of note is, in this particular context, Bion's concept of 'attack on linking' (Bion, 1967).

UNCONSCIOUS INTERSUBJECTIVE FREEDOM: AN ENVIRONMENT FOR TRANSFORMATION

Based on numerous observations of mothers and their babies (Winnicott, 1941), Winnicott was impressed by the specific movements of each baby and named them 'spontaneous gestures'. These gestures, he said, are a reflection of the existence of a true self in the baby. If those gestures take place in the presence of the mother while she is in a state of maternal preoccupation (Winnicott, 1992 [1956]), the mother allows the baby the experience of obtaining in reality what it had hallucinated. Such encounters with a facilitating environment, when repeated over and over again, create the basis for the consolidation of a true self and creativity (Winnicott 1945, 1970). If the mother cannot maintain sufficient amounts of maternal preoccupation, the frustration engendered may become so prolonged that it destroys the infrastructure of the innate true self and creativity (Winnicott, 1971 [1967]), and leads to the development of a false self (Winnicott, 1965 [1960]) or the 'dead' mother (Green, 1986).

Bollas (1989, 1992) further developed the concepts of true and false self, and described their potential and their dialectic relation to the environment. He believes that each person has a personal form of self-expression, an idiom. When the individual is able to move freely within his environment and select objects through which he releases his potential, he will be able to live out his idiom, his true self. Bollas (1999) believes that it is mainly the unconscious sphere where the personal idiom is either experienced or muffled. This sphere operates in wakefulness as 'day space', as well as in dream space (Kahn, 1972).

In such states a process of deconstruction of conventional concepts takes place; they are transformed into something else, in accordance with the subject's private logic. If it is correct to say that, when dreaming, everything is possible within the maternal space (contradiction, timelessness, unintegration), then a similar experience of deconstruction may take place in other states as well: in love relations when the other's body becomes a means of transformation, or when one slips into a conversation and suddenly feels 'carried away'. Another example would be stimuli that evoke past memories: music that transfers us to a different period in the past, or scenery which reminds us of past experiences. In all these instances there is an act of finding an object, which enables us to allow the personal idiom to reach some sort of self-transformation. These objects unconsciously keep for us something we projected on to them; they act as an intermediate space designed for the private use of each and every subject. That is, the self's experience may take place when the subject chooses an object, and allows it to perform transformation in the transitional space of the experience.

It may be possible to see a theoretical basis for these ideas in Freud's 1915 essay, 'The unconscious':

> It is a very remarkable thing, that the Unconscious of the human being can react upon that of another, without passing through the Conscious. This deserves closer investigation ... but, descriptively speaking, the fact is incontestable.   (Freud, 1955, pp. 198–9)

Bollas imports Freud's contentions of immediate communications to the intrasubjective realm. He says that, if one's unconscious may affect another's unconscious, then, obviously, the latter may affect the former as well. He describes how this process evolves in the dialogue between the therapist's unconscious and the patient's unconscious. The therapist, possibly due to countertransference, projective identification, or other forms of so-called primitive communication of unconscious psychic material, suddenly remembers an association. This particular idea (*Einfall*) 'drops' into consciousness, as it were, which then enables the therapist to transform the patient's words in accordance with the laws of dreams. That is, he turns/ shifts the patient's narrative to a counter-narrative, sometimes condensing it with other things that the patient may have told him or with any other association evoked in him. The patient hears the new idea and, based on that new idea, he too creates a new thought.

Bollas (1995) defines the resultant process as 'dissemination': a long series of intrapsychic associations and counter-associations, where each association is broken into various other associations and then organized intrapsychically in a way that brings about new understandings or new concepts – only to then move on to the next dissemination. Thus the therapeutic dialogue can act as a trigger for the processes of dissemination, and in this sense intersubjectivity is related to but does not constitute the important process of dissemination. The therapeutic dialogue acts as a stimulant to the patient, who, like a painter, draws on his canvas, erases, and then draws again. The patient responds, sometimes to stimulants that derive from the intersubjective therapeutic space, and sometimes from other environmental factors. Seeing it this way, we are reminded again of Freud (1966, 1971), who conceived of the notion of displacement but failed to appreciate its creative potential. The process of dissemination is, in fact, an intrapsychic version of displacement.

Here we can also recognize once more Bion's significant influence on Bollas. Bion (1963, 1967) described 'beta'-elements as facts disarmed of meaning, raw and unprocessed perceptions, which precede the thinker and seek a 'mechanism' that thinks them out. Such elements are projected by the baby into the mother or, to be more precise, into the breast and, by the patient, into the therapist. If the mother identifies the baby's cues, she may, from her reverie, or her α-function, change the beta elements which are inherently unthinkable, into α-elements which are thinkable. That is, she contains them. The baby is appeased by the emotional experience of being 'understood' by the mother, that she can endow his/her distress with meaning.

What is emphasized here is not the end result but the process of transformation itself. Like the mother, the therapist may choose a way of relating to the patient out of intuition. Bion denotes this intuition by using the letter 'o' (as in original). This intuition constitutes knowing when to say what, which is not based on clearly defined rules, but on submitting to unconscious perception.

In such a therapeutic encounter, where one's unconscious meets the other's unconscious and may communicate with it in play – a new experience may ensue: two protagonists engage in dreaming (the patient's free associations) and counterdreaming (the therapist's associations). The therapist dreams of the patient in the session and brings him to another place, another time, changes him into other people, deconstructs the patient's words and creates something new. This all takes place if both the patient's and the therapist's work are based on unconscious freedom, that is, a free movement of the unconscious. Here one is reminded of Grotstein's (1981) essay 'Who is the dreamer who dreams the dream and who is the dreamer who understands it?' which delineates perceptively the subject–object relationship between the dreamer who dreams the dream and the dreamer who makes the dream understandable. I have suggested elsewhere that work on dreams contributes to the building of transitional space, where the formative environment of the patient has provided few opportunities for the development of transitional space, and subsequent traumatic experiences contributed to further limitation (Mann, 1998). One also thinks of Ogden's 'Reverie and interpretation' (1997), which seeks to account for the informative capacity of the analyst's reveries by viewing these as unconscious intersubjective constructions cogenerated by analyst and analysand.

Discussion of clinical material

In therapeutic work we attempt to help patients who grew up in traumatic environments to find or 'create' objects they can use to reconstruct their unconscious freedom. 'Working-on-the-trauma' means collecting elements of traumatic experiences and attempting to allow the patient to discover the transformational use of the therapist to expand inner psychic space, allowing unconscious being to become more flowing, more associative and, eventually, more creative. We try to help our patients to relinquish terminal objects and eventually the need to fill the inner psychic space with predetermined 'thoughts'. We try to help them to allow the freedom of new thoughts and ideas which would enable transformation. We try to give our patients, at least, a *generative* environment in which they can relocate the true self, the personal expression of which was left unvoiced for so many years.

At this point I wish to return briefly to the clinical examples presented above. Both cases illustrate the therapist's endeavour to help patients relinquish conservative and terminal objects that stifle their lives and instead use the environment in a more nourishing and creative way. We can see the emergence of transformational object usage in the course of psychotherapy.

D grew up in a family where he had to deal with the harsh reality of his sister's illness. He was doomed to be preoccupied with it himself. All of his childhood was accompanied by the lack of his mother's maternal preoccupation with him, as the mother was busy giving birth to and taking care of his other siblings. D's subjective experience was that his mother could not attend to his needs nor promote the existence of his own personal and unique expression. The mindlessness of his environment made it a traumatic one, in that he was not seen enough within his family, and certainly not given freedom to elaborate his idioms. D had therefore to restrict himself to his cardboard box or to long outings, which were the only ways in which he could allow himself the self-experience he so desperately needed.

In our therapeutic work we provided space for not-yet knowing both in the patient and in the therapist. Silence is often experienced as a period of not-communicating, which is significant and even crucial for the creation of a core of true-self in the patient. I believe that in this case the patient and I created together what Bollas calls an environment of genera, and what Ogden (1996) calls 'the analytic third', that is, a space or object dimension in which the patient and the analyst engage together in intersubjective construction of an experiential space for the patient's unconscious.

From this quotidian private place (six months dozing-off in dreamspace) D was able to generate substantial changes in his inner and external experiences. He learned to use objects in his environment for true-self transformations and became an object to himself. The principle according to which life is an object which needs to be used, not only lived, becomes a central feature in D's life.

A, my second patient, demonstrates a relatively more extreme case of an environment in which the significant figures were obsessively preoccupied with eradicating and erasing certain themes outside its experiential domain. In this respect, A's environment had been a traumatic one. A was left as the carrier of the erased part, the dead part of life. His keeping of a lifeless front was a way of protecting the hidden part of the vital true self, which did not dare to emerge. He had never thought about, much less verbalized, this situation. His experience was expressed for the first time in the private space between him and the therapist and, naturally, in the private space between him and his self. His psyche, which did not know itself, expressed its freedom for the first time not in the psychological but in the somatic world, that is, through his body. What had started as an obsession concerning his inability to relate to his environment transformed into a passion for hikes and excursions in nature. He shifted from conservative–terminal use of the environment to using the environment (nature) as a transformational object. This use of nature became a potential space where transformation was possible. His own unique and personal expression was allowed to come out, even if only partially, permitting him to live in an increasingly creative way.

A's case should remind us of many cases we see in clinical practice. In countries experiencing extreme violence, many of our patients are children of parents who have gone through a process of uprooting and were on the edge of non-existence. These people often preferred mute silence to the loss of their inner worlds, and survived by preoccupying their psychic space with obsession and preoccupation. In Bollas's terms, they created an environment populated by terminal objects as a means to survive. Such environments, saturated with trauma, tend to allow for the recreation of experienced violence; people living in such environments seek despair and surround themselves with objects that carry despair for them, and exhibit no tendency to be transformed.

Theory and technique correlated

Bollas's ideas support a 'no-split' approach in clinical practice. As we have seen, clinical work can be non-intrusive or active, depending on the circumstances. In 'Figures and their functions' (Bollas 1996, 1999) Bollas conveys his justification for this approach. He maintains that psychoanalysis is trapped in an oedipal struggle between Papa-Freud and Mama-Klein, between interpreting and holding, phallus and breast, patriarchy and matriarchy. He quite poetically describes the importance of the oedipal triangle as a basic developmental cell – while asserting the impossibility of arguing that either matriarchy or patriarchy is preferable. In his opinion, the endless debate between theories which advocate holding and those which prefer interpretation derives mainly from political considerations, as it is in fact impossible for one to exist without the other.

Bollas believes that different psychoanalytic groups cling to certain parental body parts, the breast, the penis or the womb; others declare that 'they know everything about envy and destruction', while others emphasize empathy and 'potential space'. Every such approach, in fact, proclaims the 'preferred' child – that is, the maternal or paternal child. Adherents of the maternal-type theories (which generally relate to holding or the environment and holding) listen to the pre-oedipal elements as signifiers of the 'deeper' truth. Adherents of the paternal order (symbolization, the use of language, interpretation) listen to Oedipal elements as signifiers of deeper truth.

Bollas states that keeping the two approaches separate will transform psychoanalysis into a science which reduces itself. He suggests that such a distinction is impossible in practice:

We may wonder, for example, why a typical analytic session or, perhaps better yet, a series of sessions could not naturally be a mixture of these two positions, with the analyst sometimes quiet for long spells of time, implicitly supporting the generative development of internal association (in the patient and in himself) and other times talkative, bringing both himself and the patient into a more 'objective place'. The associative place would be operating within the maternal order, the interpretive within the paternal order, and the patient's participation in both worlds, indeed, the patient's need for both positions would constitute a structural usr of the paternal couple.

(Bollas, 1996, p. 11)

For psychoanalysis to be creative in practice it will have to acknowledge both theoretical perspectives that belong to the oedipal constellation used in various ways. This requires, first and foremost, the therapist's freedom of thought and flexibility in technique; that is, the ability to move, at any given moment, between silent holding (as in the case of D) and active interpretation (as in the case of A). Otherwise, the theory and practice of psychoanalysis will evolve into what might be referred to as a 'single parent family'.

REFERENCES

Anzieu, D. (1986) *Freud's Self Analysis*. London: The Hogarth Press and the Institute of Psychoanalysis

Bion, W. R. (1963) *The Elements of Psychoanalysis*. London: Heinemann Medical Books; reprinted Karnac Books (1984).

Bion, W. R. (1967) *Second Thoughts*. New York: Jason Aronson

Bion, W. R. (1970) *Attention and Interpretation*. Tavistock; reprinted Karnac Books (1984).

Bollas, C. (1987) *The Shadow of the Object: Psychoanalysis of the Unthought Known*. New York: Columbia University Press

Bollas, C. (1989) *Forces of Destiny: Psychoanalysis and Human Idiom*. London, Free Association Books.

Bollas, C. (1992) *Being a Character: Psychoanalysis and Self Experience*. London, Routledge.

Bollas, C. (1995) *Cracking-up: The Work of Unconscious Experience*. New York, Hill and Wang.

Bollas, C. (1996) Figures and their functions. *Psychoanalytic Quarterly*, LXV: 1–20.

Bollas, C. (1997) Wording and telling sexuality. *International Journal of Psychoanalysis*, 78: 363–7.

Bollas, C. (1999) *The Mystery of Things*. London: Routledge.

Eigen, M. (1996) *Psychic Deadness*. New York: Jason Aronson.

Eigen, M. (1999) *Toxic Nourishment*. London: Karnac Books.

Freud, S. (1955 [1915]) The unconscious. *Standard Edition*, 14. London: Hogarth Press.

Freud, S., (1966 [1916]) Introductory lectures on psycho-analysis. *Standard Edition*, 15. London: Hogarth Press.

Freud, S. (1971 [1916]) Introductory lectures on psycho-analysis. *Standard Edition*, 16. London: Hogarth Press.

Green, A. (1986) *On Private Madness*. London: Hogarth Press and the Institute of Psychoanalysis.

Grotstein, J. S. (1981) Who is the dreamer who dreams the dream and who is the dreamer who understands it? In *Do I Dare Discuss the Universe? A Memorial to W. R. Bion*. London: Maresfield Library, 358–416.

Kahn, M. M. R. (1974 [1963]) The concept of cumulative trauma. In *The Privacy of the Self*. London: Hogarth Press, 42–58.

Kahn, M. M. R. (1996 [1972]) The use and abuse of dream in psychic experience. In *The Privacy of the Self*. London: Karnac Books, 306–15.

Kohon, G. (1986) *The British School of Psychoanalysis: The Independent Tradition*. London: Free Association Books.

Mann, G. (1998) From disintegration to unintegration: the creation of potential space through work with dreams. *The Journal of the American Academy of Psychoanalysis*, 26(3): 389–416.

Ogden, T. H. (1996) Reconsidering three aspects of psychoanalytic technique. *International Journal of Psychoanalysis*, 77(5): 883–99.

Ogden, T. H. (1997) Reverie and interpretation. *Psychoanalytic Quarterly*, LXVI: 567–95.

Rayner, E. (1991) *The Independent Mind in British Psychoanalysis*. London: Free Association Books.

Winnicott, D. W. (1965 [1958]) The capacity to be alone. In *The Maturational Processes and the Facilitating Environment*. London: Hogarth Press, 29–36.

Winnicott, D. W. (1965 [1960]) Ego distortion in terms of true and false self. In *The Maturational Processes and the Facilitating Environment*, London: Hogarth Press, 140–52.

Winnicott, D. W. (1965, [1963]) Communicating and not communicating leading to a study of certain opposites. In *The Maturational Processes and the Facilitating Environment*. London: Hogarth Press, 79–192.

Winnicott, D. W. (1971 [1967]) The location of cultural experience. In *Playing and Reality*. London and New York: Routledge, 95–103.

Winnicott, D. W. (1971 [1969]) The use of an object and relating through identifications. In *Playing and Reality*. London and New York: Routledge, 86–94.

Winnicott, D. W. (1986 [1970]) Living creatively. In *Home is Where We Start From*. Harmondsworth: Penguin Books, 35–54.

Winnicott, D. W. (1992 [1941]) The observation of infants in a set situation. In *Through Paediatrics to Psycho-Analysis*. New York: Brunner/Mazel, 52–69.

Winnicott, D. W. (1992 [1945]) Primitive emotional development. In *Through Paediatrics to Psychoanalysis*. London, Karnac Books, 145–56.

Winnicott, D. W. (1992 [1952]) Anxiety associated with insecurity. In *Through Paediatrics to Psychoanalysis*. London: Karnac Books, 97–100.

Winnicott, D. W. (1992 [1956]) Primary maternal preoccupation. In *Through Paediatrics to Psychoanalysis*. London: Karnac Books, 300–5.

'Love Is Where It Finds You': The Caprices of the 'Aleatory Object'

James S. Grotstein

'He never loved at all who loved not at first sight.'[1]

Thomas Marlowe

INTRODUCTION

In *Being a Character*, following as it does so many previous uniquely creative works, Christopher Bollas (1992) gives birth to yet another creative concept, one that complements the theme of his *Forces of Destiny* (1989), and one that is almost whimsical in nature until one begins to consider the mystery, enigma, and ineffability of its unpredictable occurrence. I refer to his idea of the *aleatory object*, by which he means the object we meet by *chance*, not by the anticipation of *desire* (or destiny). Having read over this work many times, it only slowly dawned on me that Bollas was both filling a gap in Winnicott's (1969, 1971a) concept of the subjective object *and* establishing a unique, ontologically-tinged format for understanding inter-subjectivity from a new perspective. Conflating Freud's (1905) concept of libidinal drive theory, Lacan's (1977) concept of desire, and Winnicott's notion of the subjective object,[2] Bollas boldly shifts perspective (Bion, 1962) and reveals the missing complementary agency of the Other and its ineffable impact upon us, particularly the unique capacity of the unexpected object to surprise us, not only in regard to its own mystery, but also in regard to its mysterious ability to evoke from within our own unknown depths surprises to us about ourselves and what (and whom) we have been unwittingly harbouring. Obviously, the psychoanalytic experience comes to mind, yet so do friendship, love, theatre, reading, and the whole gamut of near and remote experiences with objects. Moreover, I believe that the aleatory factor interdigitates with Bollas's (1979, 1987) notion of the *transformational object* insofar as the latter is imbued with the capacity to bring out of us abilities of which we had been hitherto unaware.

THE INFANT'S RENDEZVOUS WITH 'FAMILIAR OBJECTS'

The aleatory object must be distinguished from the rightly anticipated familiar object. We have two separate psychoanalytic theories (if not more) about the infant's rendezvous with its objects. Originally, it was thought that the infant directly internalized (via incorporation and/or introjection) the (image of the)[3] object as it really was. It was only with Klein's (1952, 1955) discovery of the alteration of the image of the object imparted by projective identification that allowed us to understand the profundity and extent of the object's transformation upon becoming internalized (Heimann, 1949). Put succinctly, Klein's belief was that the object first became known through our projective identifications into it (our image of it); thus, our initial picture of the object is a subjective one. It is only in the depressive position, after the infant withdraws its projections from the object, that the reality of the object become recognized in its own right. Winnicott's (1969, 1971a) concept of the subjective object designates the former. Fairbairn (1952 [1940], 1952 [1944]), on the other hand, believed that the infant recognized the reality of the object from the start, selectively internalized the intolerable aspects of the object, identified with them internally, and then idealized the remaining portion of the object. Thus, with Fairbairn, the reality of the object was primary; its distortion, secondary – the opposite point of view from Klein.

Bion (1962, 1963) tells us that, because of our Platonic and Kantian repertoire of inherent preconceptions as Ideal Forms, noumena, things-in-themselves, and primary categories, we as foetuses are able to anticipate the arrival of the breast-mother, the realization of which experience promotes her, as it were, to a *conception*, and then, after many iterations of confirming experiences, to a *concept*, an even higher order internal road-map whereby to think about objects. Mother, father, siblings, relatives, and peers constitute familiar objects.

In recent contributions I united Klein's, Winnicott's, Bion's, and Fairbairn's conceptions of our initial encounter with objects and our creation of their internal counterparts within us with two concepts, that of *autochthony* and of the *dual-track* (Grotstein, 1997, 2000). In the former I hypothesized that all perception is really apperception, by which I mean, following Winnicott (1969, 1971a, 1971b, 1971c, 1971d), that the infant phantasizes that he 'creates' the object simultaneously with or prior to 'discovering' the object. In other words, creation must accompany, if not precede, discovery. Thus, the newly discovered object becomes a stimulus for us to create it, by which is meant that we first subjectify or personalize it with the hues of our own personalness before we can engage with its separate objective actuality. I also postulated that trauma consisted in the sudden intrusion of the object before we have the opportunity to have 'created' it. The dual-track, on the other hand, acknowledges Fairbairn's idea that we know the reality of the object from the beginning and make allowances for it so that we can survive. Thus, myth (phantasy) and reality can be thought to occupy a dual-track of binary opposition from the very beginning.

I also postulated that, following our autochthonous 'creation' of the object and then our discovery of the idiosyncratic uniqueness of its Otherness, we then then re-autochthonize our image of the object in terms of *self-organization* (Schwalbe, 1991), by which I mean that we 'digest' our experience of the impact upon us of the object so that the legacy of that impact fits within the parameters of our basic nature. In other words, it becomes 'personalized' to our nature. The concept of social *co-creationism* (Hoffman, 1992, 1994) also deals with the dual aspects of internalization but does not explicate the final personalizing process that self-organization exacts from the impact of the other to render it 'self'. By self-organization I am referring to the ultimate recombinatory processes whereby the strange becomes familiarized by virtue of the 'enzymes of self', as it were, that the subject casts upon the object and its products so as ultimately to make it self. One can visualize this process in infant observation when the infant salivates an object so as to territorialize it.

THE INFANT'S RENDEZVOUS WITH UNFAMILIAR OBJECTS

There are two major references to unfamiliar objects in psychoanalytic theory. One is that of the stranger, and the other is implicit in Freud's (1957 [1910]) formulation of the oedipus complex. Spitz (1950) discovered that at around nine months of age the infant develops 'stranger anxiety', that is, that it becomes markedly fearful when confronted by individuals with whom it is not familiar. Bowlby (1969, 1973, 1980; personal communication) posited a link between stranger anxiety and 'prey–predator anxiety', which he believed inhered in all mammals, including humans. This stranger anxiety can even be applied to familiar objects who have been absent past a critical period of time from the infant's presence. It seems probable that the infant may adaptively need the idea of the stranger to represent the container for its split-off persecutory feelings so as to preserve the illusion of its parents' goodness.

The other idea of the stranger is buried in Freud's concept of the oedipus complex. One recalls that in the original oedipal legend, Oedipus was abandoned and exposed by his parents in Thebes and was raised by strangers in Corinth. One reading of this is that the oedipal child must forfeit his/her claim to possess the parent and delay the pursuit of their sexual desire until they are old enough to leave home and find a stranger as a mate. That mate is waiting off-stage in the metaphoric wings of the theatre of our future life – as the aleatory object, the one that not only finds *us* when we do not realize that we are looking for him or her, but whom *we* believe we find as if by destiny – as if we have finally located our lost second self. This unexpected – and highly romantic – object also locates within us those aspects of us to whom (s)he has always corresponded – as if by *déjà vu*. The same idea is conveyed in Plato's concept of the androgyne, originally a combined entity which suffered a division into its male and female components, each forever searching for its lost counterpart to become complete once more.

BOLLAS'S CONCEPT OF THE ALEATORY OBJECT

Bollas's ideas about the nature of this object are so rich that I should first like to cite some of them before further discussing them. Bollas states:

> In a sense we are intermediates, engaged in an interplay between our idiom and its subjective objects. Some self experience arises out of the thing's play on the subject as much as from the subject's use of the object, because as we move through space and time many things pop up by chance (as aleatory objects) and sponsor a unit of experience in us that has, as it were, been contained in the real.
>
> (Bollas, 1992, p. 21)

Then:

Because a day is a potential space which we characterize by choosing certain objects and releasing varied self states, it is not necessarily an act of unconscious willfulness, as much of the time we are responding to the arrival of events sponsored by other subjects or the aleatory movements of objects. Nonetheless, each of our days begins to achieve its symbolic status as the dialectic between our unconscious wishes, needs, defenses, anxieties, and elaboratory self-states engages with chance as the environment telephones us, writes to us, offers us new books, displays wonderful-looking people, and so on.   (ibid., p. 26)

Bollas goes on to describe 'the ironic position':

[T]his duality of object arrival – by desire or by chance – mirrors the ambiguity of being that constitutes the human, who experiences himself both as the arranger of his life and as the arranged. The double experiencing of objects as vehicles of wish and spontaneous eliciters of inner experience echoes the nature of self experiencing when we are the initiators of our existence as well as the initiated . . . [T]o be with the other is to be played by them (through the other's projective identifications) as much as it is to evoke parts of themselves by virtue of the actions of our own character. It is a remarkable part of our life that this interplay takes place at such a deep level of both unconscious ego-to-ego negotiation and dynamically unconscious plays of mental content that the subject is indeed very much a simple self, inside this field, this intermediate space, where two very complex creatures are at play: idiom-to-idiom.   (ibid., p. 28)

Shortly later he states:

[F]our stages can be identified in what we might consider the dialectics of self experiencing:
1. *I use the object.* . . .
2. *I am played by the object.* . . .
3. *I am lost in self experiencing.* The distinction between the subject who uses the object to fulfill his desire and the subject who is played upon by the action of the object is no longer possible. The subject is in the third area of experiencing. . . .
4. *I observe the self as an object.* . . . This is the place of the complex self.   (ibid., pp. 30–1)

He goes on to say:

> Objects . . . often arrive by chance, and these aleatory objects evoke
> psychic textures which do not reflect the valorization of desire. We
> have not selected . . . the aleatory object to express an idiom of self.
> Instead, we are played upon by the inspiring arrival of the unselected,
> which often yields a very special type of pleasure – that of surprise. It
> opens up, liberating an area like a key fitting a lock. In such moments
> we can say that objects use us, in respect to that inevitable two-way
> interplay between self and object world and between desire and
> surprise.   (ibid., p. 37)

If I understand Bollas, he is making a significant distinction between
objects we not only desire but also unconsciously create, on one hand, and
objects which come into our lives by unpredictable chance, the latter of
which 'object-use' us. Another implication of the effect of the aleatory
object is that it seems to unearth or cause to epiphanize the 'unthought
known' within us (Bollas, 1989).

RESISTANCES TO ENCOUNTERING THE
ALEATORY OBJECT

Bollas's poetic elaboration of the surprise trajectory of the aleatory object
into our unsuspecting lives traverses the narratives of psychoanalysis,
romance, and the vagaries of everyday life. In fact, if I read him correctly,
we may have resistances to being available for encounters with the aleatory
object because of its propensity to precipitate 'catastrophic changes' (Bion,
1970) within us. The human being loves and fears surprises. He loves
surprises in order to offset the claustrophobic boredom and numbness that
his routinized life fashions for him, yet he clings to his 'escape from
freedom' (Fromm, 1941) so as to defend against the boundarylessness of
chaos, which Bion (1965, 1970) terms 'O'. Put simply, we must inescapably
adjust to the newly arrived object after we feel stimulated and opened up
by its presence. We must then evaluate our capacity to bear the impact –
and the internal cost of that impact, i.e., the internal rearrangements of our
values and limitations – before we proceed to engage with it. In other
words, the healthier we are, the more we become open to the arrival of the
aleatory object.

SURPRISE AND *DÉJÀ VU*: THE ALEATORY OBJECT
AND THE LOST SECOND SELF

The point that I am getting at is that the aleatory object represents a paradox in which both surprise and strange familiarity often counterpose one another. If the aleatory object awakens aspects within us that we had hitherto unsuspected, as Bollas states, then it would mean that it would represent a shibboleth, a separated-off part of a whole entity that, when matched up with its other torn half, reconstitutes the whole entity. Whereas Freud (1955 [1919]) believed that the ultimate origin of the *déjà vu* phenomenon resided in the subject's desire to return to the womb, one can also utilize Bion's idea of inherent (as well as secondary) preconceptions, the unborn 'thoughts without a thinker' awaiting a thinker to think them. This thinker-who-thinks-them is often the psychoanalyst who awakens these preconceptions and meets them half-way with interpretations. Can there be objects which are absolutely aleatory, that is, absolutely extraterritorial to our unconscious anticipation? This is a difficult question to answer. If we think of Plato's Ideal Forms and Kant's noumena and things-in-themselves, we would have to say no. Yet the romantic in us suggests yes.

CASE EXAMPLES

I[4]

A young, single, English-born physician entered psychoanalysis with me complaining of his inability to get along with women. In the course of revealing his background he mentioned that he had been born during the Second World War in a small English West-Country village. He had never met his father, who died fighting with the British Eighth Army in the western desert of Africa. Soon after his father's death, his 'mum' met a Yank soldier who was stationed at a nearby Army base. The Yank came from a wealthy American family and wanted to marry his mother and adopt him. After the marriage they all came to this country where he was subsequently raised.

Not long after he had graduated medical school, he made one of his return trips to his home town in England in order to visit his grandparents. During this particular visit he and his grandfather went to the local pub for a pint. While there, he began to look at an older man standing at the other end of the pub bar. He was fascinated by him and couldn't explain why. The other man occasionally caught his glance and desultorily waved his pint towards him and would then look away. Strange feelings began to develop in the patient. He thereupon enquired of his grandfather if he knew this man. His grandfather pretended at first not to hear his question and then, when pressed by the patient, answered him: 'He is your father!' The patient obviously was quite surprised – and yet not surprised at the same time. His father revealed to him that he had been a 'poor bloke without any expectations' and therefore arranged with his wife, the patient's mother, to play dead so that the wealthy Yank could rear him in the way he wanted his son to be raised. These revelations, however, turned out to be anti-climax in a way. What really most impressed the patient was the experience of the uncanny in regard to this strange man's presence before the revelation.

Comment

This case demonstrates the unsuspected surfacing of an object which corresponds to the uncanny *déjà vu* phenomenon. The landscape of the tale is almost mythic insofar as the uncanny stranger secretly bore information about the patient that had been hitherto unknown to him. The recovery of his lost father was of less importance to the patient that the recovery of the earlier boy, the 'unthought known', who was lost without his father.

II[5]

A 60-year-old single film-industry executive, now in re-analysis after an initial twenty-year analysis with another analyst, revealed the following episode from his past. During the Second World War he was attending a crowded party in New York just before being shipped overseas for duty in the European Theatre of Operations. At that party he chanced to look across a crowded room and met the eyes of a beautiful woman staring at him. This was a celebrity party; therefore there were many beautiful women there, but this one stood out. When their eyes met, he began to cry in longing. He also could see that she seemed to be attached to a man. Later that evening they actually met and introduced themselves. She informed my patient that she was engaged to the man he had seen earlier and that they were scheduled to marry in a few weeks. They continued to talk. As they talked, the patient felt haunted by this woman. He knew that he had never met her before. He said, 'There was something uncanny about her. It's as if I've known her all my life, and I've just met her – and too late. She brought up all kinds of strange feelings within me. I was going overseas and didn't want to think about my future. While talking with her, I began to think about having a career in show business after the war. I felt energized and hopeful.' The evening was coming to an end. He took the great risk of asking her for her telephone number, which, miraculously, she gave him. He wrote it down on the back of a match book.

The next morning he realized that he had slept deeply and happily and had happy dreams. When he looked for the match book with her number, he couldn't find it. He had apparently lost it. He became inconsolable. Years then decades passed after the event, 40 years, actually. He had actually become a film studio executive in the meanwhile. One day he was reminiscing about the event and decided to investigate where she now was. He hired a private detective to investigate the matter. All he had to go on was the name of the man who had hosted the party and the fact that she had been born and raised in Santa Barbara, California. The investigation surprisingly after all the intervening years, bore results. To his incredulous surprise, it turned out that she was alive and was living down the block from him on the same street in Beverly Hills! He summoned up his courage and went down to meet her. He knocked on her door, and a beautiful young woman answered. For all the world it was as if time had stood still. This *was* the woman he had met and fallen in love with 40 years earlier, he instantly felt. He addressed her by her first name. The woman answered, 'No, that's my mother's name. She died last week.'

It took him quite a while and a lot of analysis to absorb the double loss. A year or so later he was in his studio office when a young actress who had an appointment with him, was ushered in. He took one look at her eyes. She, who was 35 years younger, took a return glance at him. They each cried. He stated to her, 'It's as if I've always been waiting for you, and you take different forms, but you're always you.' She stated, 'You're the man I want to marry and you're the father I never had.' They subsequently married and 'lived happily ever after'. I see him from time to time for follow-up.

Comment

When the patient cried to his wife, 'It's as if I've always been waiting for you, and you take different forms, but you're always you,' he was acknowledging her as occupying an archetypal role that transcended her personhood but without ignoring her own uniqueness. This incident illuminates the 'pheromonal'[6] aspects of love insofar as the love object constitutes an archetype (an inherent and then an acquired preconception) based upon early object experiences combined with innate aspects of our self constituting our 'alter ego' (Grotstein, 1999). But it was not love that was the epiphanal aspect of this tale; it was the recovery of his 'able-to-love' self, his 'unthought known'.

III

W.B. is a 70-year-old married physicist of Hungarian birth who has found his way into the higher echelons of venture capital investments. His marriage has been one of convenience, his wife being more of a business partner than an intimate one. They have no children. By temperament he is severe, hard and ruthless but honourable in business, and is a loner. His only pleasure is playing tennis, and this he does daily and aggressively. Over the years and decades of his life he has dated many beautiful and talented women, some of them famous beauties, but he had never experienced love or closeness to any of them. They were merely 'trophies for the moment'.

One day while visiting the gymnasium adjacent to the tennis courts, he suddenly encountered a tall, extremely thin young woman, who was almost repulsively ugly to him. He noted that her cheeks showed the 'chipmunk' effect; therefore he concluded that she suffered from bulimia. He fell instantly in love with her and felt foolish at the same moment. She was nineteen years old. The May-to-December nature of the encounter reminded him of Vladimir Nabokov's adventures with *Lolita*. He felt overwhelmed by veritable oceans of love and longing. He perfunctorily introduced himself to her and asked her if she would like to hit some tennis balls. He had no idea then that she had been internationally ranked. They proceeded to play tennis. The patient realized then that he was in the throes of love for the first time in his life – with a deformed and ugly teenager. 'Love,' he commented, 'was a lethal weapon.'

They quickly developed a 'fantasy relationship' in which she would frequently toy with him by asking him to adopt her, even though her parents turned out to be his nearby neighbours. The relationship never became sexual. It was 'pure, ethereal love', he protested. He felt that at long last he had found a soul mate, a friend.

Enquiry into his past history turned up significant material. His mother died of thyrotoxicosis when he was five years old. This illness is often characterized by extreme loss of weight and high energy, as was the case with his 'friend'. He had a younger brother with whom he had little or no relationship up to the present time. His father remarried, but the little five-year-old had already sealed off, secretly 'divorced' his family, and left home forever when he became old enough.

An analysis he had undertaken many years ago dealt with his mother's death but apparently incompletely. I raised the possibility that his friend may represent not only the reincarnation of the ghost of his lost mother whose loss was and still is unfathomable to his little boy self, but was also the surfacing of his own gaunt, starving, distorted feminine self that went into hiding a long time ago and was mysteriously brought to life by the encounter with this girl. This interpretation seemed to produce a galvanizing effect. He instantly recognized that she had reactivated his long lost other self.

Subsequently, the 'affair of the heart' continued (non-sexually), and his earlier ardour seemed to have become greatly diminished in intensity and become sublimated into a father–daughter relationship. He had never had children and didn't want them – until he had met this girl. And then something happened! As their relationship deepened, she became aware of her power over him – and used it! She began playing coy tricks – of not being available, of delaying answering her phone and e-mail messages from him, asking for more favours, not showing up on time for their daily tennis engagements, and other similar sorts of behaviour. The patient finally came to the realization that he was being 'played' (object-*mis*used). Now he had a triple mourning on his hands: the reactivated mourning for his mother, his own lost child self, and now for the young girl 'friend' whom he thought she was and was now no longer.

Comment

This young girl seemed instantly to present the attributes of exactly the right type of object that mysteriously unlocked the key to his redoubtable heart. The concept of lock and key is an important component of the aleatory object phenomenon, as Bollas suggests. She was emaciated and ill like his mother and young and innocent like his own erstwhile buried self. The rest was mystery. Again, the key point here is that the young girl represented an aleatory object who 'object-used' the patient so as to revive his own lost, needy, loving self, his 'unthought known'.

The dénouement, his belief that she had been disingenuous to him all along, nevertheless did not erase the aleatory benefits he had derived from the relationship – the uncovering of his ability to love, to mourn, and to care. Thus, this case example is the exception which proves the rule: falling in love is in itself not an aleatory phenomenon; what the experience with the other brings out in us *is*.

DISCUSSION

I return to a central thesis in Bollas's definition of the aleatory object which I cited earlier:

> Objects . . . often arrive by chance, and these aleatory objects evoke psychic textures which do not reflect the valorization of desire. We have not selected . . . the aleatory object to express an idiom of self. Instead, we are played upon by the inspiring arrival of the unselected, which often yields a very special type of pleasure – that of surprise. It opens up, liberating an area like a key fitting a lock. In such moments we can say that objects use us, in respect to that inevitable two-way interplay between self and object world and between desire and surprise.   (Bollas, 1992, p. 37)

I have re-cited a portion of Bollas's definition to italicize the uniqueness of the aleatory object. In short, it object-uses *us* and is extraterritorial to our desire for it – at first. It discovers *us* and what is within us that we may not have discovered otherwise, i.e., our 'unthought known'. In the cases I discussed above, *the discovery of love was incidental to the epiphany of an aspect of the self that could love.* This is the essence of the other half of true intersubjectivity, an essence that has hitherto been neglected in the literature. In other words, object usage, the instrument of idiom and desire is but one half of a binary-oppositional structure, the other half of which is the aleatory phenomenon, which accounts for chance-surprise encounters that challenge our idiom–desire pretensions. The aleatory object lies outside the safety perimeter of our ability to predict or anticipate its occurrence. We can only nakedly react when it confronts us. It is the other side – and better half – of trauma.

At the beginning of this contribution I cited a portion of a poem by Thomas Marlowe to the effect, 'He never loved at all who loved not at first sight.' With apologies to Marlowe, I should like to amend the line thus: '*He was never loved at all who was loved not at first sight.*'

NOTES

1. Please note my unauthorized alteration of this line at the end of this contribution.
2. It must be remembered that Winnicott's notion of the subjective object is his own idiosyncratic rendition of Klein's (1952, 1955) conception of projective identification, to which he adds that the locale of the projection is not within the object per se but in the 'potential' or 'intermediate space' between them.
3. Curiously, the image has become the missing third in virtually every psychoanalytic theory of interaction, yet it is central to our understanding of object relations and/or intersubjectivity. For instance, we cannot project into an object; we can only project into our *image* of an object (Grotstein, 1995, 1999, 2000).
4. I have also discussed this case material in another contribution (Grotstein, 2000).
5. I have also discussed this case as well in another contribution (Grotstein, 2000).
6. By 'pheromonal' I am referring to the 'chemistry' of love.

REFERENCES

Bion, W. R. (1962) *Learning From Experience.* London: Heinemann.

Bion, W. R. (1963) *Elements of Psycho-analysis.* London: Heinemann.

Bion, W. R. (1965) *Transformations.* London: Heinemann.

Bion, W. R. (1970) *Attention and Interpretation.* London: Tavistock Publications.

Bollas, C. (1979) The transformational object. *International Journal of Psychoanalysis,* 60: 97–107.

Bollas, C. (1987) *The Shadow of the Object: Psychoanalysis of the Unthought Known.* New York: International Universities Press.

Bollas, C. (1989) *Forces of Destiny: Psychoanalysis and Human Idiom.* London: Free Association Books.

Bollas, C. (1992) *Being a Character: Psychoanalysis and Self Experience.* London and New York: Routledge.

Bowlby, J. (1969) *Attachment and Loss. Vol. I: Attachment.* New York: Basic Books.

Bowlby, J. (1973) *Attachment and Loss. Vol. II: Separation Anxiety and Anger.* New York: Basic Books.

Bowlby, J. (1980) *Attachment and Loss. Vol. III: Loss: Sadness and Depression.* New York: Basic Books.

Fairbairn, W. R. D. (1952 [1940]) Schizoid factors in the personality. In *Psychoanalytic Studies of the Personality.* London: Tavistock, 3–27.

Fairbairn, W. R. D. (1952 [1944]) Endopsychic structure considered in terms of object-relationships. In *Psychoanalytic Studies of the Personality*. London: Tavistock, 82–136.

Freud, S. (1905) Three essays on the theory of sexuality. *Standard Edition*, 7: 125–245. London: Hogarth Press.

Freud, S. (1955 [1919]) The 'uncanny'. *Standard Edition*, 17: 217–52. London: Hogarth Press.

Freud, S. (1957 [1910]) The psychoanalytic view of psychogenic disturbance of vision. *Standard Edition*, 11: 209–18. London: Hogarth Press.

Fromm, E. (1941) *Escape from Freedom*. New York: Rinehart.

Grotstein, J. (1995) Projective identification reappraised: Projective identification, introjective identification, the transference/countertransference neurosis/psychosis, and their consummate expression in the crucifixion, the Pieta, and 'therapeutic exorcism'. Part II. The countertransference complex. *Contemporary Psychoanalysis*, 31(3): 479–511.

Grotstein, J. (1997) Integrating one-person and two-person psychologies: Autochthony and alterity in counterpoint. *Psychoanalytic Quarterly*, LXVI: 403–30.

Grotstein, J. (1999) The alter ego and *déjà vu* phenomena: Notes and reflections. In *The Plural Self: Multiplicity in Everyday Life*. (Eds) John Rowan and Mick Cooper. London, Thousand Oaks, and New Delhi: Sage Publications, 28–50.

Grotstein, J. (2000) *Who is the Dreamer Who Dreams the Dream? A Study of Psychic Presences*. Hillsdale, NJ: Analytic Press.

Heimann, P. (1949) Some notes on the psycho-analytic concept of introjected objects. *British Journal of Medical Psychology*, 22: 8–15.

Hoffman, I. (1992) Some practical implications of a social constructivist view of the psychoanalytic situation. *Psychoanalytic Dialogues*, 2: 287–304.

Hoffman, I. (1994) Dialectical thinking and therapeutic action in the psychoanalytic process. *Psychoanalytic Quarterly*, 63: 187–213.

Klein, M. (1952) Notes on some schizoid mechanisms. In *Developments of Psycho-Analysis*. (Eds) M. Klein, P. Heimann, S. Isaacs and J. Riviere. London: Hogarth Press, 292–320.

Klein, M. (1955) On identification. In *New Directions in Psycho-Analysis*. (Eds) M. Klein, P. Heimann, S. Isaacs and J. Riviere. London: Hogarth Press, 309–45.

Lacan, J. (1977) *The Four Fundamental Concepts of Psycho-Analysis*. London: Hogarth Press.

Schwalbe, M. L. (1991) The autogenesis of the self. *Journal for the Theory of Social Behaviour*, 21(3): 269–95.

Spitz, R. (1950) Anxiety in infancy: A study of its manifestations in the first year of life. *International Journal of Psychoanalysis*, 31: 138–43.

Winnicott, D. W. (1969) The use of an object. *International Journal of Psychoanalysis*, 50: 711–16.

Winnicott, D. W. (1971a) The use of an object and relating through identifications. In *Playing and Reality*. New York: Basic Books, 86–94.

Winnicott, D. W. (1971b) Playing: A theoretical statement. In *Playing and Reality*. New York: Basic Books, 38–52.

Winnicott, D. W. (1971c) Playing: Creative activity and the search for the self. In *Playing and Reality*. New York: Basic Books, 53–64.

Winnicott, D. W. (1971d) Creativity and its origins. In *Playing and Reality*. New York: Basic Books, 1971, 65–85.

PART II

Essays from Other Disciplines

6

Returns of the Repressed: Some New Applications of Psychoanalysis to Ethnography

Anthony Molino and Wesley Shumar

> Consciousness nourishes itself by recentering itself around its Other: cosmos, bios, or psyche. It finds itself by losing itself. It finds itself instructed and clarified after losing itself and its narcissism. . . . This is why we must admit that the meaning of psychoanalysis as an event within modern culture remains in suspense and its place undetermined.
>
> (P. Ricoeur)

In an article entitled 'Psychoanalysis and the movement of contemporary culture', Paul Ricoeur (1974) makes the point that the human sciences remain far from achieving an integrated hermeneutical model – or what he calls a 'philosophical anthropology' – that can account for the discoveries and insights of Marx, Nietzsche and Freud. But while Marxist and Marxian applications have always found fertile ground in anthropology, the deconstructionist spirit of Freud remains for the most part on the margins of mainstream ethnographic practice. In fact, to say that the place of psychoanalysis as a model for anthropological research is undetermined is more than an understatement. To risk claiming as much, in some quarters, is tantamount to heresy. There is, we believe, with regards to psychoanalysis, a form of narcissism that shapes and informs certain strands of modern-day ethnography. It is a form of 'narcissism', if you will, that derives in part from anthropology's 'othering' of psychoanalysis and its repudiated object of study, the unconscious. It is a narcissism highlighted by Katherine Ewing when she suggests that a primary reason for anthropology's 'almost visceral rejection' (Ewing, 1992, p. 251) of psychoanalysis has been its inability to move beyond Freud's early drive model and the metaphor of depth on which it relied. As that which is recondite and removed from the surface of observable cultural data cannot, a priori, constitute or be framed within the anthropologist's object of study, the psychological dimension of human experience came to be equated with the private sphere, and thus excluded from ethnographic consideration. Banished, according to Ewing, were issues related to symbolization processes, personal motivation, and the generative dynamics of the ethnographer's field encounters and relationships. (While the first two, fortunately, have been rescued for anthropology in works like Gananath Obeyesekere's *Medusa's Hair* (1981), the importance of the interpersonal dimension of ethnographic work has had to wait for a new generation of self-reflexive anthropologists before gaining in currency and credibility.) Culture became abstracted, as communications between people became, in Ewing's words, 'only cultural [acts] revealing nothing of psychological or idiosyncratic processes. [Clifford] Geertz relied on this image of the [deep and private] psyche to construct a firm barrier dividing anthropology from psychology, the study of culture from the study of the individual and the mind' (Ewing, 1992, p. 254).

To limit one's understanding of psychoanalysis to but a single one of Freud's own multiple models (or to simply limit an update of the tradition to Lacan's school) is the equivalent, roughly, of restricting one's study of physics to the day an apocryphal apple chanced upon Newton's head. For anthropology to have remained focused on the early drive model has meant the neglect of Freud's entire lifework which, however flawed as an expression of the dominant ideological discourses of his time (of nineteenth-century enlightenment 'science' and the vestiges of an ancestral Judaeo-Christian patriarchy), was nevertheless to spawn the rich and often competing traditions of the Kleinian school, ego psychology, object relations and the British Independents, Lacan's 'return', self-psychology, neo-Freudians and French feminists – not to mention the similarly rich and rebel traditions of Jung and Adler. And yet many, if not all, of these influences have remained largely extraneous to mainstream anthropology, which has ignored the multiple visions and theoretical sophistication of the new generation of today's psychoanalysts.[1]

In these 'postmodern' times, when the fieldworker's subjectivity is known to infiltrate every stage of the creative process, right up to and through publication of the ethnographic text, ethnography cannot help but be challenged and engaged by today's psychoanalysis in a way that subverts the tendency that has traditionally characterized interdisciplinary work between the two disciplines. Whereas much of the literature bringing together psychoanalysis and the social sciences has used, to date, a reductionist psychoanalysis to analyse aspects of culture (or to identify 'syndromes' found in other cultures but foreign to the West), rarely has a more sophisticated effort been engaged to assess the parallel development of models in psychoanalysis and the social sciences, and the impact of these models for social theory.

Not unlike anthropology, psychoanalysis is itself in the concurrent throes of a 'self-reflexive' moment of its own; and, not unlike anthropology, psychoanalysis too is burdened by its past, as it suffers and problematizes the sins of its Father, in the hope of delivering on the promise of what Adam Phillips (1995) calls a 'post-Freudian Freud'. The critique produced from within psychoanalysis points, in fact, to a model of investigation into human life and relationships that is increasingly less invested in the preservation of psychoanalysis as a master discourse than in problematizing its own tools and traditional strategies. It is, in fact, through the deployment of new strategies concerned with reflexivity, representation, narrativity, and literary and feminist discourses, that psychoanalysis now situates its basic insights about the nature of consciousness and the construction of the self within a world that is increasingly 'multiple' and fragmented.

In this light, psychoanalysis can itself be seen in the throes of a fertile crisis of 'identity' and redefinition that parallels the reconceptualization of the ethnographic project and context. In psychoanalysis, for example, not only is the authority of the analyst's interpretations increasingly questioned, but the very therapeutic efficacy of any interpretation is generally assumed to be but one factor in a more complex relational 'cure'. Similarly, no longer viewed as a catalogue of the exotic serving to authoritatively categorize a collection of 'objective' data, ethnography nowadays concerns itself increasingly with *texts* and innovative modes of representation (personal, poetic and dialogic). In point of fact, the 'postmodern turn' in ethnography moves towards a reconfiguration of the ethnographic Other (the object) within an intersubjective matrix that invariably involves a questioning of the status of the Author (the subject). Ethnographer and social theorist Kathleen Stewart's idea of 'contamination' (see below) points most clearly in this direction, in a way that converges strikingly with developments in psychoanalytic thought. In both contexts, the supposed neutrality of the subject/analyst is exploded, as the messy indeterminacy of subject and object transposes the struggle over power and meaning into a relational encounter in which *two* actors are potentially transformed.

This *turn* in anthropology is also evidenced by the marked concern with issues of reflexivity, as is attested by the shifts in ethnographic writing towards personal and 'confessional' styles. Hence, it is concerned with the dispersion of the self into texts where truth (including one's own) is not pre-given but interrogated in the process of a *literary* construction. In an essay entitled 'Ethnicity and the post-modern arts of memory' (1986), Michael Fischer illustrates a singular aspect of this turn, while also pointing to new ways in which the contemporary ethnographic project can draw on psychoanalysis. Starting out from the premise of a 'pluralist, multidimensional, or multi-faceted concept of self', Fischer sees the relationship between identity and ethnicity as one being fruitfully explored, in a series of ethnic autobiographies, through 'processes analogous to the dreaming and transference of psychoanalytic encounters' (Fischer, 1986, p. 196). In his review of the genre (in which he includes Michael Arlen's *Passage to Ararat* and Charles Mingus's *Beneath the Underdog*), Fischer identifies what he calls 'transference-like techniques of repetition, indirection, and reworking' that are also deployed as textual strategies in works more generally regarded as ethnographic. Citing Gananath Obeyesekere's *Medusa's Hair* (1981) and Vincent Crapanzano's *Tuhami* (1980) among his cross-referencing examples, Fischer suggests

> reading ethnographies as the juxtaposition of two or more cultural traditions, and paying attention both in reading and in constructing ethnographies to the ways in which the juxtaposition of cultural traditions works on both the conscious and the unconscious level.
>
> (Fischer, 1986, pp. 199–200)

In his essay, Fischer thus returns us to the problem that is the unconscious for anthropology. Over the years, the discipline's unfortunate reliance on a metaphor of 'depth' for its critique of psychoanalysis has had as one of its corollaries what might be called a positivist/functionalist understanding of the unconscious. The unconscious, in fact, has posed a problem for anthropology to the extent that it not only lay 'beneath' the surface of the privileged, observable 'data' of culture, but precisely because of its supposed 'location', it could not be unequivocally situated or 'identified'. An assumed material quality, a quality of 'thing-ness', seemed to colour prevailing understandings of the unconscious which, combined with its encased and sedimented interiority, made it not only mysterious but impermeable to the research methods of a positivist science. Thus, it was easier – and understandable – for the unconscious to be disavowed, especially since anthropology had for the most part already disavowed the study of subjectivity.

Nowadays, however, it is interesting to note how the very depth/surface metaphor that informed yesterday's critical positions has yielded to a more pervasive concern with the so-called 'inner/outer' boundary. At one level, this transposition – from a vertical to a horizontal metaphor – readily denotes the assumption, on the part of anthropology, of a discourse of subjectivity. The boundary in question, in fact, is to some extent (if not altogether) clearly inspired by an evocation, or prefiguration, of the body of the human person: that is to say, of the human 'subject' in his/her materiality, as a (semi-)permeable membrane of sorts (and not only as an abstract discursive production) presumed to exist in an intersubjective context. It is through this light that we can begin to see how the residue of an outdated understanding of the unconscious can still mark the discipline's present-day foreclosures to psychoanalysis. Granted, alternative ideas of an unconscious do involve, if you will, an attitude of 'faith': in this sense, the unconscious does demand of the investigator an attitude similar to the one expected, for instance, of any intelligent reader of *The Divine Comedy*, when confronted by the 'reality' of Dante's odyssey through the afterlife. For there is no available 'proof' of the 'existence' of the unconscious; there is no incontrovertible 'scientific' demonstration of its 'presence' and influence. But neither do the privileged postmodern paradigms of 'ideology', 'discourse' or 'power', insist on such proofs to legitimate their status as tools of research. If anything, like the unconscious, these tools are also 'evidenced' by an analysis of their *effects* – which are, in turn and invariably, themselves subject to 'framing' and interpretation. In this sense, then, the unconscious *is* 'occult' – to borrow Stephen Tyler's term (Tyler, 1986). But: think of the radical change in conceptualizations of the unconscious from the time, say, of culture-and-personality studies in anthropology. Think of how anthropology might orient itself differently towards psychoanalysis today if understandings of the unconscious, and of the self, like those put forth by Christopher Bollas, were more widespread throughout the anthropological community.

For Bollas, the self is a process of becoming that involves the selection and use of objects and others in our world, and the ways those objects and others work upon us. The selection process itself is a product of our idiom: an inherited disposition, or orientation, towards life and the world that is shaped and first articulated through contact with the mother, and enhanced as we grow and become transformed by this meaning-invested world of objects. Like Lacan's, Bollas's model of the unconscious avoids the essentializing and ontologizing of the unconscious that for so many years met with anthropology's criticism. Again, the unconscious is not a thing; it is not simply a locus of symbolization or container of repressed memories, but an evocative, generative structure which informs and articulates the self. Bollas (1992) uses the notion of the waking life as a dream, in which each moment leading us to the next is determined by the past but also reshapes and reinterprets that past. Such 'dis/located' visions of the unconscious dovetail with and lend themselves to many of the contemporary representational devices deployed by a postmodern ethnography, roughly summarized by Fischer as 'transference, dream-translation, talk-story, multiple voices and perspectives, the highlighting of humorous inversions and dialectical juxtaposition of identities/traditions, cultures, and the critique of hegemonic discourses' (Fischer, 1986, p. 202). In this context, however, it is especially important to recognize that when experimental ethnographers turn their attention to the implications for social research and cross-cultural understanding of an unproblematized inner/outer boundary, what they are also performing is a critique of the traditional, disciplinary boundaries of anthropological knowledge. It seems to us near-sighted, in fact, to look to challenge traditional, objectifying understandings of the ethnographic Other, as well as the established rhetorics of anthropological representation, while insisting to exclude psychoanalysis as a viable methodological instrument. It would be regrettable, in fact, if the so-called 'crisis' in anthropology, concomitant with the general breakdown of boundaries across the territory of the human sciences, for some reason necessitated that a line of demarcation and exclusion, an inner/outer boundary of sorts, be drawn at the 'site' of psychoanalysis.

*   *   *

In 1980 anthropologist Michael Taussig's *The Devil and Commodity Fetishism in South America* significantly advanced anthropological thinking about the self and subjectivity. An exploration of magical practices that have grown around colonialist exploitation and the consequent grafting of capitalist economic structures onto subsistence communities, *The Devil and Commodity Fetishism in South America* moves beyond functionalist thought on the role of belief systems in human society. Through his study of small villages in Colombia and Bolivia where peasants worked on plantations and in tin mines, Taussig developed an alternative explanation to the devil worship cults that emerged in these contexts. Traditional anthropological explanations follow the functionalist notion that magic reduces anxiety; the reason one worships the devil in a tin mine is that an offering to the devil gives the illusion of control over a situation in which one is powerless. Taussig suggests however, that such practices are not just attempts at gaining control over circumstances; they are also ways to make sense of the world.

Using Marx's notion of commodity fetish, Taussig suggests that the world the mine owners bring – a world of private property, wage-labour, money, interest, etc. – represents a reified set of ideological categories that we in the West take for granted. For example, we understand the metaphorical meaning of 'your money works harder at such-and-such bank'. But for people not socialized into what Taussig calls the 'commoditized apprehension of reality', the expression is gobbledygook. Everyday business-as-usual practices turn the world upside down for people reared in a pre-industrial subsistence culture: no longer are social goods distributed fairly, and those who work hard get poorer while those who own the means of production get richer. The devil, in this context, is a reasonable explanation for what is going on.

While Taussig has at his disposal a language to talk about the *social* aspects of the above interpretation, he does not have available a language of subjective process. Such a language could contribute useful insights into the ways symbols are motivated and mobilized in particular cultural contexts. For example, when Taussig points out that many of the images of the devil are traditional and indigenous (i.e., as when miners report a reverie or an image of the devil walking around the mine), these are often unknowingly described as one of the European owners. Aware of this paradoxical imagery, Taussig wonders if there are unconscious processes operating in the production of the Bolivians' way of understanding their experience as exploited workers. It is our contention that it is precisely in such situations that a model like Bollas's can be fruitfully appropriated by anthropology, with tremendous implications for research that attempts to link the object world and the subjective states of individuals.

Bollas talks about how objects get infused with personal meaning, and how an idiom grows out of infantile experiences, forming a way of relating to self and world. Attributing to objects an inherent vitality that makes of them elements of transformation, Bollas theorizes the conception of multiple relationships capable of being generated by any object (be this a person, a piece of music, a toy or a pitchfork), and the dialectical interplay between the object and the way it is used and reinterpreted by an individual. The individual, in turn, is herself 'used' by the object – that is to say, her existence is aesthetically shaped and emotionally impacted by the object's material, evocative quality. While Bollas's theory is quite complex and cannot be done justice here, there are some implications that can be drawn from his work and have potential impact for efforts like Taussig's. For instance, devil worship, essentially a repetitive magical practice, could be compared to the psychoanalyst's discussion of trauma, in that it involves symbolic repetition rather than symbolic elaboration. (Bollas, 1992, pp. 69–70). Thus, while magic – as a creative response to a situation of oppression – gives meaning to a heretofore meaningless capitalist world, like trauma it has limited or no liberatory potential. (This is significantly different from the application of a reductionist psychoanalysis that sees magic and ritual as expressions or features of obsessional neurosis in the culture.)

In an article entitled 'The madman and the migrant', Jean and John Comaroff (1992) have developed ideas similar to those of Taussig. In their work on the Tshidi of South Africa, the authors observe that official local history, written by those in positions of power and constructed in linear narrative, is more likely to be the story of the oppressor than of the oppressed. In order to understand the peoples and cultures of Southern Africa, it is necessary to combine political and economic analysis with what might be called the poetics of everyday life. The Comaroffs' madman is one who expresses such a poetic, as his clothing and accessory symbols merge the world of wage-labour in the mines with the social life of Tshidi villages. This poetic merging is an articulation of the horror of oppression and death at the hands of Western colonial powers. To the white doctors in the hospital, the madman's behaviour was psychotic nonsense. To black African patients, he was a healer.

Through the story of this unlikely prophet, the Comaroffs illustrate how the Tshidi have symbolized the contact of their world with colonialism by constructing different categories. The world of work in the village is contrasted by the Tshidi with the world of labour in the mines; the first is seen as life-affirming, while the second is associated with death, both literal and symbolic. The Comaroffs' major point is that human actors strive together in specific cultural and historical contexts to represent themselves and their worlds. Further, the poetic expression of one's existence is no less compelling or important than a 'realistic' account of the local history; on the contrary, it might capture lived experience in a way impossible to achieve otherwise.

This concern with everyday poetics and how the mind articulates experience calls for the strengths of psychoanalysts like Bollas, who shares with another exponent of the British school, Adam Phillips, an attitude towards psychoanalysis that is at an infinite remove from the understandings most anthropologists have about psychoanalysis. When Phillips (1994, p. xi) writes, for example, in his preface to *On Flirtation*:

> For me, psychoanalysis has always been of a piece with the various languages of literature – a kind of practical poetry – taking its life, as theory and practice, from the larger world of words

he is expressing an altogether new psychoanalytic sensibility, with implications and possible applications for researchers like the Comaroffs, whose own poetics neglect conscious/unconscious process in the context of how subjects come to interpret their world. Like Taussig, the Comarroffs do make a political point about the poetics of everyday life and how this is a viable lens through which to view the world. They point out that while we have a tendency to see official history as the truth, the truth of people's lives is often missed or deleted by official history. In their poetic truth, the Tshidi find in the madman a voice that brings some comfort and helps make sense of their lives. The madman's own redeeming effort to find a voice, moreover, occurs in a world where the Tshidi have not only lost culture, life and family, but the very ability to represent themselves to themselves. It is against this background that an applied psychoanalytic sensibility, like that of Bollas or Phillips, can only enrich the perceptual tools of the ethnographer. Imagine, for example, a 'reading' of the madman's self-representation inspired by the following reflections of Bollas:

> I think that 'character' is an aesthetic. If our way of being refers to our very precise means of forming our world, both internal and intersubjective, then each of us is a kind of artist with his or her own creative sensibility. We know that the distinctiveness of that creation is the particular form we have brought to it. . . .
>
> It is a pleasure to express and articulate the self: there's an erotic dimension to that kind of representation. . . . My own view is that in the formation of character we similarly have a pure arc of the pleasure of representation: except I would say that, instead of there being (as in Freud's instinctual arc) a pure line from source through aim and object, there are many lines that fragment and break, in something like a vast symphonic movement which is, in and of itself, a pleasure . . . the pleasure is in the entire movement: which nonetheless remains something far too complicated and condensed, too thick, to be reduced to a single meaning, or even to two or three meanings.
>
> (Bollas, in Molino, 1997, p. 9)

Clearly the madman and the patients in the mental hospital are not experiencing any ordinary sense of pleasure. And yet, there is an unequivocal 'erotic' quality to the madman's idiosyncracies. He is a healer and a prophet for his ability to bring together the contradictory symbols of oppressor and oppressed, and there is an odd sensuality in his presentation of self. In the words of the Comaroffs:

> Famous for an ingenious costume he would never remove, the man was, literally, a prophet in polythene robes. His crazy clothes spoke the language of his obsession. His boots, standard issue for mineworkers, were topped by intricately knitted leggings, the painstaking product of many unravelled orange sacks. He wore a cloak and a bishop's mitre, fashioned from black plastic garbage bags. Across his chest stretched a brilliantly striped sash, on which were stitched three letters: SAR.[2]   (Comaroff and Comaroff, 1992, p. 155)

While the language of the Comaroffs betrays the madman's sensuality, it cannot help but fall short in any attempt to fathom or convey how the particular objects that inform and constellate the madman's 'idiom' work to foster both subjective and shared meanings. For in the intersubjective context of the Tshidi, the madman does help patients to experience a healing pleasure – a therapeutic outcome which also reflects, if you will, an unconscious 'grammar' of relationship. Clearly, while the local miners resonate with the madman's objects and idiomatic expressions, the doctor's estrangement from and devaluation of those same expressions is what leads to a very different apprehension of (and response to) the madman's and his patients' reality.

Finally we would like to briefly mention a critical article by Kathleen Stewart, 'On the politics of cultural theory: a case for "contaminated" cultural critique' (1991). In this article Stewart also draws upon a poetics of everyday life, 'picturing' articulations of self through processes of narrative and dialogue. One image she offers is of an Appalachian man expressing the loss of culture and habitat in his critique of the strip mining practices in the area. The man's discourse is a fertile poetic reverie, in which self and community are imaginatively constructed in the space left barren by the mining companies; it is also, however, a denunciation completely misunderstood by the city slicker/social worker to whom the story is told. As in this instance, such benevolent outsiders, with no sense of the way 'place' and 'talk' work together to construct what Kirkpatrick Sale (1991) calls *dwellers* (people who are part of the landscape and *belong* to a place), often presumptuously fill in the spaces and gaps in the local discourse with their own self-righteous sense of what needs to be done about the loss. By interpreting the local rhetorical style as one of helplessness, the outsider attempts to fill in the meaning he sees 'missing' in the discourse by redefining the local in cosmopolitan terms.

The resulting image of the redefined local is one Stewart uses to express her concern for an anthropology that constructs a barrier between ethnographer and informant, and then makes a virtue of the barrier. Stewart, drawing upon the work of Mikhail Bakhtin, suggests that a contaminated critique is preferable; an attitude that recognizes that interpretation is not a neat scientific process but one where ethnographer and informant struggle together to define and understand each other in a polysemic and dialogic process. This process will yield no seamless results but will rather be one in-filled with uncertainties, gaps and mis-recognitions.

The struggle that Stewart describes is about power and who has power over meaning; but it is also one where important questions about truth and knowledge are recognized in all their ambiguity. This is very similar to the interpretive struggle engaging many post-Freudian analysts. For instance, Stewart's use of the word *contaminated* reflects the relatively recent turn in psychoanalysis that places increasing emphasis on the dynamics of the so-called 'countertransference'. In a move away from Freud's ideal of the analyst's 'neutrality' and 'blank screen' function (akin to the fiction of the ethnographer's 'decontaminated' distance from his/her object of analysis), focus on the countertransference can well be understood in terms of 'making the analyst more vulnerable to something that someone like Bakhtin would call trans-subjective relations' (Stewart, personal communication). It is in this sense that the transference/countertransference dynamic, as it unfolds in a mutually constitutive space (thus lessening the patient's 'responsibility' for the quality of the emotional engagement and experience) also forms a relational, trans-subjective field.

*   *   *

In 'Grief and a headhunter's rage', anthropologist Renato Rosaldo (1989) discusses his perplexity over trying to understand the Ilongot of the Philippines and their ritual expression of grief through murderous rage and the desire to take the head of an enemy. Rosaldo points out that all of his efforts to intellectually understand the Ilongot system fail until he meets with a personal tragedy of his own. The grief Rosaldo experiences, at the loss of his wife in a fieldwork accident, leads him to deep feelings of rage; finally, it is only through empathy that Rosaldo gets a sense of how the Ilongot feel. For Rosaldo, this personal story is emblematic of the ethnographer's dilemma and the existential gulf between self and other. While this gulf can be reduced by efforts to understand other ways of life, there is a level at which cultural experience is just that: experience, of the kind that remains inaccessible from the outside. But Rosaldo's story is also a story about a common humanity: a common humanity that opens another door for understanding, empathy, and the space to share the experiences and emotions that make us who we are.

The psychoanalytic perspectives that we have been discussing here have, like the newer vistas in anthropology, moved away from a naïve position where the analyst assumes s/he can know the other through the power of scientific models, to a position of greater ambiguity but potential wisdom. In admitting that we cannot know the other we open up possibilities for ways of knowing and understanding ourselves and others. The researches of psychoanalysts like Bollas, Phillips and a host of others working and writing today have value for the social sciences in ways which extend far beyond their original clinical applications. In fact, in a dizzying global economy that operates through vast and dense semiotic systems (in ways that acritically promote and develop our desires in every possible direction), the insights of psychoanalysis can only contribute to prevailing models for understanding contemporary articulations of the self, desire, multiplicity and our relationship to the objects in our worlds.

NOTES

1. Since our conception of this paper in the mid-1990s, this trend has begun to be reversed. To cite just two of the more notable works refocusing the work of anthropologists in the direction of contemporary psychoanalytic thinking, see Katherine Ewing's *Arguing Sainthood* (Duke, 1997) and Nancy Chodorow's *The Power of Feelings* (Yale, 2001).

2. The initials 'SAR' stand for South African Railway, an object that for the Tshidi mediates between the world of their villages (that the people symbolically associate with life) and the world of the mines (which evokes death). The Comaroffs themselves make this point, in a way that is consistent with Object Relations theory.

REFERENCES

Bollas, C. (1992) *Being a Character: Psychoanalysis and Self Experience.* New York: Hill and Wang.

Comaroff, J. and Comaroff, J. (1992) The madman and the migrant. In J.

Comaroff and J. Comaroff, *Ethnography and the Historical Imagination.* Boulder: Westview Press.

Crapanzano, V. (1980) *Tuhami: Portrait of a Moroccan.* Chicago: University of Chicago Press.

Ewing, K. P. (1992) Is psychoanalysis relevant for anthropology? In *New Directions in Psychological Anthropology.* (Eds) T. Schwarz *et al.* Cambridge: Cambridge University Press.

Fischer, M. (1986) Ethnicity and the post-modern arts of memory. In *Writing Culture: The Poetics and Politics of Ethnography.* (Eds) J. Clifford and G. Marcus. Berkeley: University of California Press.

Molino, A. (ed.) (1997) *Freely Associated: Encounters in Psychoanalysis with Christopher Bollas, Joyce McDougall, Michael Eigen, Adam Phillips and Nina Coltart.* London: Free Association Books.

Obeyesekere, G. (1981) *Medusa's Hair: An Essay on Personal Symbols and Religious Experience.* Chicago: University of Chicago Press.

Phillips, A. (1994) *On Flirtation: Psychoanalytic Essays on the Uncommitted Life.* Cambridge: Harvard University Press.

Phillips, A. (1995) *Terrors and Experts.* London: Faber and Faber.

Ricoeur, P. (1974) Psychoanalysis and the movement of contemporary culture. In P. Ricoeur, *The Conflict of Interpretations.* Evanston: Northwestern University Press.

Rosaldo, R. (1989) 'Grief and a headhunter's rage.' In P. Rosaldo, *Culture and Truth: The Remaking of Social Analysis.* Boston: Beacon Press.

Sale, K. (1991) *Dwellers in the Land: The Bioregional Vision.* Philadelphia: New Society Publishers.

Stewart, K. (1991) On the politics of cultural theory: a case for 'contaminated' cultural critique. *Social Research*, 58:2, 395–412.

Taussig, M. T. (1980) *The Devil and Commodity Fetishism in South America.* Chapel Hill: University of North Carolina Press.

Tyler, S. (1986) Post-modern ethnography: from document of the occult to occult document. In *Writing Culture: The Poetics and Politics of Ethnography.* (Eds) J. Clifford and G. Marcus. Berkeley: University of California Press.

7

Of Knowledge and Mothers:
On the Work of Christopher Bollas

Jacqueline Rose

About ten years ago a student who had been taking a course on Freud and feminism with me at the University of Sussex came to me in a state of some anxiety. It seemed to her, from her reading of the late papers on femininity, that psychically speaking there were only mothers in the world. If the boy desires the mother, and if the girl's main psychological task is to detach herself from a maternal presence whose traces are never fully dispersed, then all love objects are in a sense mothers. (In first marriages, Freud argues, it is the relationship to the mother that surfaces and most often as not wrecks the home.) Or to put it more crudely, there is no getting away from mothers. They are there where you least expect them, most troublingly when you thought you had left them behind.

I must admit that I did not have a way of alleviating this student's anxiety, since it seemed to me she had touched on something important. No amount of trying to stress the infinite plasticity of the unconscious, the fluidity, transferability, mobility of its objects quite worked – which should suggest the opposite, that there is no stopping point, that whoever you think you are dealing with, it is always also somebody else. It was as if everything we had discussed, with equal emphasis, about unconscious process was in a sense powerless in the face of this mother, her capacity to draw back everything to herself. Freud famously ignored the mother, but as many commentators have pointed out, her figure haunts the work.[1] The somewhat triumphant, absolute, nature of her arrival on the scene of those late papers bears all the marks, one might say, of the return of the repressed.

I start with this anecdote because what the student experienced is, I think, not wholly dissimilar to the feeling I find myself experiencing whenever I read the work of Christopher Bollas. There is, I think, no psychoanalytic writer in English – and this becomes more and more the case in the most recent writing – who conveys such a strong sense of the ungraspable unconsciousness of the unconscious, and the endless, unstoppable, play of its work. But equally, there is no psychoanalytic writer who gives me such a strong, and at moments sinking, sense of the utter unmoveability of the mother. This paper will address what I see as the dynamic tension between these two components of the writing: between on the one hand the unconscious as a limit to knowledge, as a break on what it is possible for any subject of the unconscious to know of either the other or herself; and on the other, the mother as a figure there to be uncovered, the one you always somehow knew would be there.

Freud himself provides a precedent for the relationship between mothers and the question of knowledge in his 1925 paper on 'Negation' (Freud, 1961). At the start of the essay, in what might appear as an exemplary moment of self-analysis, he uses the example of denial of the mother to usher in the discussion of the origins of thought: 'You ask who this person in the dream can be. It's *not* my mother.' We amend this to: 'So it *is* his mother' (Freud, 1961, p. 235). In Freud's paper, the mother stands twice over in the place of knowledge. First in this example, for analytic certainty, the moment when the analyst can be most unswervingly sure. But as the paper unfolds, she appears again, this time as the founding condition of judgement since it is in relation to her body that the function of acceptance and rejection of what constitutes a world comes to be. 'To affirm or negate the content of thoughts is the task of the function of intellectual judgment [. . .] Expressed in the language of the oldest – the oral–instinctual impulses, the judgment is "I should like to eat this," or "I should like to spit this out."' (Freud, 1961, pp. 236–7). In this famously dense paper, Freud manages, not for the first time, to set the mother up as blindness and insight. No one is so inept, so embarrassingly giveaway as the mother-denying patient, but without a capacity for denial, grounded in that primordial connection to her body, there would be no such thing as thought.

It is customary to read the development of object-relations theory in Britain, with its focus on the mother, as remedying a glaring deficiency in Freud. My question, however, is not whether we should be talking about mothers – I assume that on the whole to be a very good thing – but what happens to our relationship to knowledge when mothers are around. When the traces of the mother are uncovered in analysis, is it the end of the line? Can we think about mothers and keep an open mind? Can we think ironically about mothers? (This is not the same as Winnicott's question as to whether a mother can relate playfully, ironically, tongue-in-cheek or, in Christopher Bollas's most recent work, comically with her child.) What does thinking about mothers do to thinking? If you make the mother *the* unconscious object, what hermeneutic arrest have you stumbled into, what

violence have you committed to the unconscious as process, or to use one
of Bollas's most famous formulas, to the category of the 'unthought'?

In fact that's only half his formula, only half the story, since his concept
is more exactly the 'unthought known'. To put the question in terms closer
to the language or spirit of his work: Is the 'unthought known' the place
where knowledge unravels from its own self-possession, from its pretension
as knowledge; or is it the place where the mother, the imprint of her care
on the being of the subject, is once and for all to be found? Are we dealing,
to use his own words from an essay in *Being A Character*, with 'a force of
dissemination that moves us to places beyond thinking' (Bollas, 1992a,
p. 17); or, by analogy with the mother in one of her most famous
incarnations or stereotypes, with a type of first and last resting place? And
if the second, does the mother acquire the status of only truth or rather the
only place – given that psychoanalysis could be said to have made the idea
of one truth its first casualty – where truth is still allowed to be? It is
probably already clear what I would like the answer to that question to be,
but of course nothing is ever that simple.

It has often been pointed out that the mother has a lot to answer for in
the writings of the Independent School. These quotes are almost all taken
from *The Shadow of the Object*, Bollas's first collection of essays; 'his
mother's absence' (1987e, p. 127); 'his disappearing and dismissive mother'
(1987g, p. 189); 'the refusing mother' (1987g, p. 195); 'the contagious
confusion of the mad mother' (1987g, p. 199); 'strange and absent mother'
(1987h, p. 212); 'cumulatively dis-incarnated by maternal failure' (1989b,
p. 136); and perhaps most devastating of all, 'she hired a nanny' (1987h,
p. 39). It is, one could fairly say, and especially in the early work, something
of a refrain. But it seems to me to be a trap, too easy – although that is
exactly what I have just done – to just list these instances, to see them only
as marking a blindspot in the writing, where one feminism, the feminism
that sees psychoanalysis as a pure emanation of patriarchy, would read the
ideological prejudice of a whole tradition, and one form of psychoanalysis
(the Lacanian) would see a failure to acknowledge the absence at the heart
of being, a way of laying at the door of the mother what is irredeemably
incommensurable about human desire.

One of the problems of those kinds of objection, even though they may
each have a crucial point, is that they blind themselves to the institutional
histories out of which theories are made and unmade. It therefore seems
important to recognize the argument to which this appeal to the mother
belongs. What worse fates is this dreadfully failing mother being called on
to save us from? Paradoxically, it seems as if this hopeless mother, in

relation to whom no doubts are entertained, is intended to ward off another form of certainty, knowledge, omniscience. In a strange twist, which I see as central to Bollas's project, the dulling sameness of her invocation is designed to protect the patient from the potential tyranny of psychoanalysis itself. Better her neglect than its coercion. Better to have been overlooked in the beginning than to find yourself bound, in the analytic setting, to an interpretive presence that won't let go. More explicitly, this emphasis on the mother's powers, in the reality of a patient's past, to move and stall a life – a power I would not wish to dispute – has two targets. On the one hand it is aimed at Kleinian hermeneutic confidence about deep phantasy, on the other at the version of object–relations interpretation which reads everything in the analytic setting in terms of that setting alone, as having as its sole referent, with a no less oppressive sameness, the analytic here-and-now. As Bollas puts it, not without a trace of irony, in the final paper of *Forces of Destiny*, his second collection of essays: 'the British analysts of the 1940s freed the boring patient from the analyst's narcoleptic countertrans-ference [. . .] by understanding the patient's narrative as a metaphor of the patient's ego experience of the analytic object, the clinician was suddenly alive in a field of meaningful plenty' (1989c, p. 194).

Bollas's constant reference to the mother is, if I have understood correctly, part of an appeal to history. Hence his repeated stress on her actuality. Again, despite my own caveat, I found myself listing the number of times, also in the early work, that the insistence on a concrete retrievable reality appeared, a reality almost invariably given the status of single determinant or cause: 'This is *objective fact*' (1987h, p. 33); 'a belief that was a fact in his infantile life' (1987g, p. 187); not meaning, as it might appear, that his phantasy was a psychic reality to the child, but that his belief accurately reflected his world: 'It was a *fact* that neither parent, for different reasons, could identify with their child's needs' (1987g, p. 187) (this is both parents, but it is the mother's disappearance early in the child's life that precipitates the problem); 'an *actual family setting* with which [the ego] cannot cope' (1987a, p. 77). 'It is a source of puzzlement,' writes Bollas in disagreement with Bion who, as he sees it, attributes the source of the child's attacks on alpha functioning to the child alone:

why madness within the mother or the father, or between the parents, or in that atmosphere that is created by all participants in the child–parent interaction, should be eliminated as one of the potential sources of disturbance in the child's development of alpha function.

(Bollas, 1987f, p. 142)

If we place the work in this tradition, it seems clear that, after Winnicott, Bollas wants to reassert early environment against phantasy, what is done to the infant against what the infant or patient projects onto her world. But in Bollas's case, the argument about reality avoids the obvious critique – that this move is a positivist reduction, that psychoanalysis must be about phantasy before anything else – because of the way it is constantly run into the question of knowledge (How much can we ever know? How sure can or should the analyst ever be?). It is almost as if the irreducible nature of phantasy, partially or momentarily lost to the objective facts of the case, resurfaces in the form of a radical uncertainty which gives back to the unconscious its greatest unsettling force. And insofar as it was in relation to the mother that Bollas seemed originally so sure, it is appropriately her figure who stands to lose (or rather gain) most from any such loss of conviction. By linking the Winnicottian stress on environment to the question of knowledge, Bollas therefore opens up a rift in his own work which allows us fruitfully to track the implications of this centring of the mother for the category of the unconscious. For the rest of this discussion, I want to trace the ways in which his writing incrementally unravels that early hermeneutic certainty about the mother and in the process provides some dramatic, and at moments disturbing, insights into what a mother can carry, for theory, for analysis, for being a subject in the world.

There is a moment in H. D.'s *Tribute to Freud* (1956), the poet's account of her analysis with Freud in Vienna, when she describes the symptom – writing on the wall – which of all her symptoms, he confessed to finding most disturbing: 'of a series of strange experiences, the Professor picked out only one as being dangerous, or hinting of a danger or a dangerous tendency or symptom' (H. D., 1974, p. 41). Freud analyses this hallucinated writing as desire for union with the mother, but later he comments: 'I must tell you (you were frank with me and I will be frank with you), I do *not* like to be the mother in the transference – it always surprises and shocks me a little. I feel so very masculine' (H. D., 1974, pp. 146–7). On the wall, or off the wall ('Off the wall' [1989d] is the title of one of Bollas's papers from his second book), what flashes up as a moment of danger in H. D.'s symptom, and the moment of analytic frankness it precipitates, is the point where the boundaries of consciousness are transgressed, where the limits between inside and outside, between a subject and the world of objects that surround her, breaks down. As with the 'oceanic feeling', which in his famous exchange with Romain Rolland he declared himself immune to, Freud

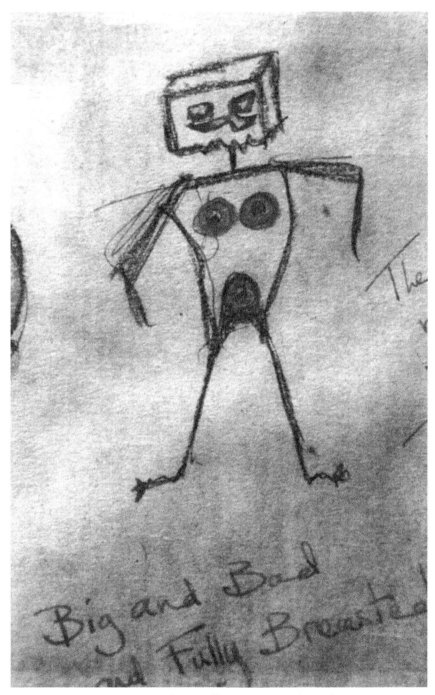

Plate 1: *Needles*, drawing by Kate Browne. Photograph © Eric Etheridge

Plate 2: *Needles*, written and directed by Kate Browne. Left to right: Sarah Moore as Evil 1 and Molly Powell as Evil 2. Photograph ©Amy Freeth

Plate 4: *Sling,*
1993, by Greg Drasler.
Oil on canvas (80˝ x 70˝)

Plate 3: *Umbrella,*
1992, by Greg Drasler.
Oil on canvas (80˝ x 70˝)

Plate 6: *Load,*
1995, by Greg Drasler.
Oil on canvas (58" x 52")

Plate 5: *Cows in the Corn,*
1996, by Greg Drasler.
Oil on canvas (70" x 50")

(1959) responds by an intimate confession which in fact involves a rigid redemarcation of lines.

If object-relations theory, in its Winnicottian form, has taken upon itself to enter the space where Freud did not dare to tread, this particular form of danger – that there might be a world without boundaries where all founding distinctions are lost – seems, for the most part, to have been ignored (rerepressed one might say). Indeed you could argue that the emphasis on the adequacy and inadequacy of the mother – what she can and should do – has served to make safe or occlude this space: not the space of a necessary lack-in-being in Lacanian terms, but the opposite, a space too full, a space that will become our dream of the mother, but which is in fact a space with no single origin, and for which no one is accountable, where the divisions inside my own mind, and between me and the other, are unclear. One of Bollas's strongest early points – and a great deal follows from here – is that if Freud refused the mother as referent, he more than embraced her into the setting of analysis (Freud's blindness as the insight of analytic work). It would then be possible to read Bollas's writing as going back over this ground, unearthing its latent implications, shadowing forth its hidden shape.

More and more in the essays, analysis is a dream setting, 'a kind of countertransference dreaming', a meeting of one unconscious with another, the analyst as 'medium', processing in his body the unintegrated instincts and affects of a hysteric with nowhere else to go (1995a, p. 12).[2] If at first this feels like an extraordinary maternal idealization of the analytic encounter, in which feminism would see simply the inverse image of the mother who fails, it is only for a moment. And that is because the very movement which makes of this analyst all-receiver, reparative mnemic trace for what failed before, also dissolves all identity, wrests from us any certainty of being, turns us into shadows, spirits, ghosts.

'I seem to be saying,' writes Bollas in 'Off the wall', 'that analysts are mediums for the psycho-somatic processing of the patient's psyche-soma' (1989d, p. 59); or again, from *Cracking Up*, the analyst bears 'the analysand's psychic state in his own body' (1995a, p. 12). This quote from the title article of *Being a Character* could, I think, be taken as a type of manifesto of the later work, certainly for the last two books:

Being a character means that one is a spirit, that one conveys something in one's being which is barely identifiable as it moves through objects to create personal effects, but which is more deeply

> graspable when one's spirit moves through the mental life of the
> other, to leave its trace.   (1992b, p. 63)

The opening essay of *Cracking Up*, 'Communications of the unconscious'
draws out even further the extent to which, if you go down this path, what
you begin to lose is the possibility of any conviction that there are,
conventionally speaking, two separate consciousnesses in a room. 'Unconscious communication' takes off from this remark from Freud's paper on
'The unconscious' (1957): 'it is a very remarkable thing that the Ucs. of one
human being can react upon that of another, without passing through the
Cs' (Freud, (1957) [1915], p. 194). We are close here to telepathy which, as
other recent commentators have pointed out, is, no less than femininity, an
undercurrent to Freud's work (not in either case its wild fringe, but
something whose links with the discoveries of psychoanalysis are unavoidable but difficult because in each case they push it over its own theoretical
edge) (see especially, Derrida, 1988, pp. 3–41). First dismissed by Freud,
telepathy then returns in the 1932 essay 'Dreams and occultism', rather like
mothers we might say (everything clearly returns in the 1930s). 'The
phenomenon of thought-transference,' Freud writes, 'which is so close to
telepathy and can indeed without much violence be regarded as the same
thing' (Freud, 1932, p. 39); 'by inserting the unconscious between what is
physical and what was previously called "psychical" [psychoanalysis], has
paved the way for the assumption of such processes as telepathy' (Freud,
1932, p. 55).

It seems to me therefore that there are two very different mothers, or
fantasies of the mother, at work in Christopher Bollas's writing. Mother as
fact, the one safe haven of interpretation; but then mother, or her space, as
the vanishing point of all identities, where no form of knowing could ever
reach. For if it is the case that in this second space subjects pass through
each other like spirits in the night, more intimate, closer than any other
form of contact could hope to be, the one thing that Bollas insists on is that
this insight spells the end of the fantasy that subjects could ever know each
other, or be known. '[I]t is interesting', he continues in 'Communications
of the unconscious', 'that psychoanalysis, which would have us look truth
in the eye, also makes use of the most powerful illusion we generate: that
we convey ourselves to other people' (1995a, p. 19).

Compare that comment with this one from 'The analyst's multiple
function': 'Is not one pleasure of loving and being loved the realisation that
one is truly known? . . . In other words, to love and to be loved is an act of
deep appreciative knowing' (1989a, pp. 112–13).

And here is the mother: 'Maternal care, then, is a knowing that is an act of love, and whether we have our right to a destiny or whether we are to have a fate will, in my view, depend on whether a mother can love her infant in a knowing way' (1989d, p. 113). Which I would simply wish to qualify; to save the child from such maternal omniscience, with this remark by Bollas from 'Off the wall': 'Each analyst who comes to know his patient [. . .] must unknow him' (1989d, p. 63).

Paradoxically, then, it is by invoking the maternal space as powerfully as he does, pushing the metaphor as one might say to its furthest limits, that Bollas himself 'unknows' the mother, undoes her as referent, placing the whole scenario – what it is to be an analyst, a patient, a human subject – beyond knowing's reach. Hence my sense that the most immediate feminist response to this tradition, crucial as it is, is too limiting. For if you simply demand that the Winnicottian image of the mother be modified – saved from her total accountability, recognized even more fully than it did in its radical ambivalence – or more simply demand that she be given her own voice (when does a mother get to speak, where are the case studies of women as mothers in the work?), you none the less remain essentially in the same referential frame. (Parker (1995) explores most fully the issue of maternal ambivalence, addressing Winnicott's work, notably his 1949 paper 'Hate in the counter-transference' (Winnicott, 1979)). As long as the question remains: what would be a truer representation of the mother, the limits of knowledge as knowledge remain untouched? Which is not to dismiss that question but to suggest that things become even more complex when we throw the unconscious back into the frame. Speaking on behalf of unconscious ambivalence is not the same thing as trying to address what the unconscious does to any position from which we might speak. These quotations are from 'The psychoanalyst's use of free association' (1992c):

Regardless of how well analysed we may be, we shall always be a subject who only ever partly knows. Partly knows the other. Partly knows the self. Partly knows life. Most of our life is lived unconsciously, in dialogue with the other's unconscious, within the field of unconscious social processes.   (pp. 116–17)

I do not agree [that it is possible to comprehend our patients]. I think we fail to 'grasp' them, because anyone – including oneself – is substantially beyond knowing. [. . .] the unconscious never ceases its work and the psychic material in which it plies its trade is profoundly beyond our knowing.   (p. 131)

It is, as Bollas states in his Introduction to *Cracking Up*, the founding paradox of analytic work that the analyst aims to 'understand unconscious communication in terms of a theory of the unconscious which theoretically makes such communication impossible' (1995c, p. 6). This could suggest that one of the roles of the mother, in theory, has been to carry the burden of that paradox.

I will now therefore turn things around a little and make my question not what the mother does to the category of knowledge, but, as a way of extending that question, what she is being asked to bear. In what has become one of her most famous essays, 'Stabat Mater', written shortly after the birth of her son, psychoanalyst and writer Julia Kristeva (1986) comments:

> Belief in the mother is rooted in our fascinated fear with the impoverishment of language. If language is powerless to situate me for, or speak me to, the other, then I presume – I yearn to believe – that someone somewhere will make up for that impoverishment. Someone, or rather someone female, before there was speech, before it – before the unconscious – spoke, before language pumelled me, via frontiers, separations, vertigos, into being.   (pp. 175–6)

'Let us call "maternal",' she says near the start of her essay, 'that ambivalent principle that is bound to the species on the one hand, and on the other stems from an identity catastrophe that causes the proper Name to topple over into the unnameable. It is that catastrophe which we imagine as femininity, non-language or the body' (1986, pp. 161–2). I read Kristeva as saying that language fails us, both because of what it cannot speak and because the entry into language is a type of forced passage in itself. To recognize that, or to be in touch with the points where language brushes against its limits, is a type of catastrophe for those subjects (pre-Freudian we might say) who have vested their all in the accomplishment of identities and their poise. This felt catastrophe is simply the fact that there is an unconscious, that we cannot fully know, as Bollas puts it in those quotations, either the other or ourselves. We try to limit the damage, we protect ourselves from the felt danger, by fleshing out our anxiety, giving that zone of anguish a name: femininity, nonlanguage, body. But the name we give it before all others, the one we really hold answerable for it, is the mother.

One could then say that, if mothers know anything – to give them back their subjectivity in the matter for a moment – it is the travesty of that projection. Maternal love, Kristeva writes, is 'a surge of anguish at the very

point where the identity of thought and the living body falls apart'
(Kristeva, 1986, pp. 175–6). Do not idealize the early union of mother and
child, not just because things are more complex than that, but because that
vision of union has so often served in Western thought to veil over the
disunity of being to which motherhood, if anything, owes its most fundamental allegiance. 'I am breaking apart like the world' (I take that line from
Sylvia Plath's extraordinary voice poem, 'Three Women', in which three
women's voices speak across and through each other in a maternity ward).
Once again this goes beyond the question of the complexity, agency of the
mother. It is more, what this figure of the mother forces us to confront
about the limits of our being. What passes through the mother, writes
Kristeva, 'gnaws away at the all-mightiness of the Symbolic' (Kristeva,
1983, p. 185).

Even more perhaps, that vision or fantasy of primary union hides the
extent to which the mother and child, in their negotiations with each other,
however playful and loving, are, amongst other things, up against a radical
confusion of tongues. This is Jean Laplanche, in his book *New Foundations
for Psychoanalysis*, glossing Ferenczi's famous formula (Ferenczi, 1933). He
is discussing what he sees as the incommensurable dialogue between the
mother and her infant: the mother a sexual being, the infant thrown into a
world of words and desires to which it is quite impossible that she or he
could be equal:

[We are dealing with] an encounter between an individual whose
psychosomatic structures are situated predominantly at the level of
need, and signifiers emanating from an adult. Those signifiers pertain
to the satisfaction of those needs, but they also convey the purely
interrogative potential of other messages – and those other messages
are sexual. These enigmatic messages set the child a difficult, or even
impossible, task of mastery and symbolisation and the attempt to
perform it inevitably leaves behind unconscious residues. . . . We are
not, then, dealing with some vague confusion of tongues, as Ferenczi
would have it, but with a highly specific inadequacy of languages.

(Laplanche, 1989, p. 130)

And again:

The primal relationship is therefore established on a twofold register;
we have both a vital, open and reciprocal relationship, which can truly
be said to be interactive, and a relationship which is implicitly sexual,

where there is no interaction because the partners are not equal. . . .
Someone is moving from the straight and narrow; we have here a
'Traviata', someone who has been led astray and seduced.

(Laplanche, 1989, pp. 103–4)

Or, to use terms that will be more familiar – the last but not least of the
eighteen reasons Winnicott offers as to why the mother hates her child: 'He
excites her but frustrates – she mustn't eat him or trade in sex with him'
(Winnicott, 1949, p. 201). If the mother feels hate for her infant, it is
because she loves the infant – the form her love takes at moments is – too
much.

If, as I have been describing so far, I read a progress or move in Bollas's
writing towards the vanishing point of all knowing, I equally read an
increasing and symmetrical stress on what is excessive or unmanageably
baffling about the nature of the world for the child. Though in relation to
sexuality, would it be fair to say that, although there is an erotics of the
idiom and frequent discussions of object choice, there is not much sex in
the good, or bad, old perverse Freudian sense, in this writing? (There are
the essays on the trisexual in *The Shadow of the Object* and on homosexual
cruising in *Being a Character*, but these are, I think, cases apart (Bollas,
1987j, 1992f)). I also remember that when Laplanche, in a talk to the
Institute of Psychoanalysis more than ten years ago, said something similar
to what I have quoted here, his suggestion that the mother's message to the
child might be bafflingly sexual, might indeed be sexual at all, caused
something of an outrage (in the discussion Juliet Mitchell suggested that
what was going on was in itself a 'confusion of tongues').

But it does seem to be the case that in the later writing, notably in the
wonderful (1992e) essay, 'Why Oedipus?', there is a new emphasis on the
madness, not of the mother, but of the options open to the child as he
negotiates his way through a set of essentially unresolvable predicaments –
that madness as Bollas puts it in one of my favourite of his formulas, 'that
ego psychology terms reality' (p. 243). We are dealing, as he puts it in the
later essay, 'Cracking up', with 'a world of the real that is deeply thoughtless' (1995b, p. 243). 'For this is the age, is it not,' he asks in 'Why
Oedipus?', 'when the child comes to understand something about the oddity
of possessing one's own mind?' (1992e, p. 239). The oedipal child's
'moment of truth', he continues, is a discovery 'that in some ways matches
the search that Oedipus inaugurates when he aims to get to the origin of a
curse that dooms his civilisation':

That curse is the bittersweet fact one suffers in having a mind, one that is only ever partly known and therefore forever getting one into trouble, and one that in the extreme can be rather lost (as in the losing of a mind) and one whose discovery by the child is a most arresting moment. (Bollas, 1992e, p. 240)

It is not possible to get justice in relation to the conflicts of the family scene, and the realm where we are meant to seek it, that of the group, is, as Freud himself pointed out, the bearer of its own insanity. 'We are,' Bollas states, 'amidst two quite profound unconscious orders – our own mind and that of the group – which break the symbiotic and Oedipal cohesions' (1992e, p. 244). Crucially, none of this can be laid at the door of the mother. These dilemmas, which will 'check our dreams of safe haven for ever after', no one is accountable for: 'Our own subjectivity,' he exclaims, 'will abuse us all!' (1992e, pp. 240–1).

So why do we lay so much on the mother? What is it, finally, ultimately, that we are asking her to protect us from? In 'What is this thing called self?', one of the essays from the latest collection, Bollas writes: 'The mother who gives birth to us also brings us in touch with death' (1995e, p. 174). (Likewise Kristeva describes motherhood as 'a veiling over of death in death's very place' [1983, p. 177].) In Freud's (1913) essay on 'The theme of the three caskets' (Freud, 1958), silent Cordelia, dumb in the face of her father's demand for love, bearing a love in excess of speech, is also, going back over an old mythological equivalence, the representative of a death to which she finally brings him (cradled in Lear's arms in the last scene, her latent identity as mother surfaces inside out at the end of the play). Again, a line from Plath's poem 'Three Women', this time the second voice: 'the world conceives/Its end and runs towards it, arms held out in love' (Plath, 1971).

I do not think it would be going too far to suggest that this is also a strand which runs through Bollas's writing. In this, as with everything else I have described, he could be seen as bringing to the surface of a whole tradition in relation to the mother what she is being asked to carry. He could be showing us what psychoanalysis – writing of her and returning to her in what so often feels like a punishing scrutiny – no less than any other discourse, repeats. (Why do we expect psychoanalysis to be free of all this?)

In the first essay in *The Shadow of the Object*, in a sense the flagpiece for what's to come, there is an extraordinary line: 'the search for the perfect crime or the perfect woman is not only a quest for an idealised object'

(1987i, p. 18). That sentence, with its brazen equation, brought me short and sent me looking for other signs in the writing of this link between woman and crime. For that early paper, these fantasized figures are seen as making good a deficiency of early experience, which at this stage of the writing can lead only to the mother. But, as I have been arguing, Bollas also has, to my thinking, some far better ideas. Perfection (I reread his sentence) is criminal, women must be perfect, because it is the woman who, by wresting us from a world of certainty, committed the first crime.

Mother as criminal may seem an odd note with which to conclude, but it is in a sense where Bollas's own writing leads. The last collection, *Cracking Up*, ends with two papers – 'Cracking up' (1995b), and 'The structure of evil' (1995d) – which read like alternative versions, back to back, of each other. In the first, evil is described as the compulsive repetition of a death-in-being in which the infant was once the victim of a crime, the 'murder' of the true self (1995d, p. 195). Only this can explain, Bollas convincingly argues, the extraordinary balance struck by those we consider evil between benign and inhuman authority, the way that the serial killer for example lulls his victim into a false dependency which he is then so hideously able to turn inside out and exploit: 'Shocking harm erupting in the midst of a benign texture of the real . . . the grandmother turns into a hungry wolf' (1995d, pp. 191–2). Unknowable, unpredictable – 'we cannot see where he is coming from and . . . whatever we know about him does not help us find him' (1995d, p. 190) – the one we consider evil presents us with a grotesque, inflated, parody of our inability to control our own ends and the ends of the world.

In the next and final essay, 'Cracking up' (1995b), mother once again rushes in, only this time with a difference. This mother is a clown. Death-defying, she goes back in the opposite direction from the serial killer, turns 'disaster into pleasure', taking into herself 'right before the baby's eyes', the baby's own 'internal madness': 'Does she do,' he asks, 'what comics and humorists have been doing all these centuries, taking up into their bodies and souls these disturbing aspects of life?' (p. 242). 'Is [the comic moment] death defying? . . . For a brief moment, then, the funny man defies the forces of life and death. He does deliberately what most of us do by chance' (p. 253).

And if death is in the frame, then so, exceptionally I would say, is sexuality. The instincts, explicitly sidelined in the rest of the work, return when it is a question of really cracking up – control of the world, of bodies, of thought all falling apart: 'The force that the humorist grasps when he crosses the boundary is the constant unconscious movement of instinctuality. . . . The comic moment may be a descent into the underworld, where it dips into the force of instincts and returns with enough energy to split sides' (pp. 252–3).

I like this mother as clown. I think it's the best version we've had so far. Not least of all, because the excessive, unmanageable nature of what she is being asked to carry has become the explicit theme. As if that tension, dialectic, balancing act between knowing the mother and the flight of knowledge, has finally toppled over, as if it had to come back to the mother where she is rediscovered as negotiating boundaries whose nature is to be unnegotiable. (As the *I Ching*, in fact one of the most patriarchal texts ever written, would put it: 'no blame'.) Once we are in a world of instincts and unconscious, there are some things, rather a lot in fact, that not even a mother can do.

I want to end by trying to convey a sense of how maddeningly hard I have found it to write about the work of Christopher Bollas. I decided in the end that it was not just that I was being difficult, but even more because of the type of demand that he places on his reader, a demand connected, I think and in the best sense, to what I have been trying to describe. It is not just the extraordinarily powerful way that Bollas evokes the analytic scene, the extent to which, because he is so often writing about the limits of its own capacities, he mimics in his writing the form of a theory which *should* be ungraspable if it is to remain faithful to its object – the unconscious as an ever-receding form of truth. It is more or as much, since the two are not unrelated, that he issues a very particular challenge to the reader. I would say that Bollas asks his reader to treat him like his ideal version of how a mother would treat her child. He thereby undoes, by passing the position back to the reader and out into the world, the extent to which, if there is an ideal mother anywhere to be found, it is the analyst – or rather this analyst – himself (the strongest desire of this writing seeming to be at moments the desire to be one's own mother). Read me, hold me, but don't crush me, don't get too close. Above all, don't think you know, and I would want to add, don't expect to get it right.

Literary critics who have turned to Freud in the last decade have spent a lot of their time concentrating on footnotes and asides (it started with the case of 'Dora', the argument being that if you wanted to find an answer to everything that went wrong with that case, it was in the footnotes – indeed by Freud's own acknowledgement – that it could be found) (A point made by a number of the essays in Bernheimer and Kahane, 1985). So I end with one aside and one footnote. First the aside, from the Introduction to *The Shadow of the Object*: 'I do not discuss how one might analyse the presence of the actual mother's mothering. I look forward to doing so in another work' (Bollas, 1987c, p. 7). Second, the footnote, from the essay 'Violent innocence' in *Being a Character.*

As reconstructions decrease, and as the patient's character is increasingly understood within the transference, the question of what the mother actually did, or who she actually was, fades into its proper place: into the areas of speculation and hypothesis, profoundly tempered by a forgiveness intrinsic to the more important realization of one's own generated disturbances. I intend to discuss this important question, of the invocation of the name of the mother in psychoanalytic reconstruction, in a future essay   (Bollas, 1992d, p. 178)

In response to which, I would simply want to say (it is the message of this entire paper): I can't wait.

NOTES

1. Melanie Klein was of course the first analyst to concentrate on the mother. For more recent analysis of the mother–child bond, see Benjamin (1988); and for an analysis of the absence–presence of the mother in Freud's work, see Sprengnether (1990).
2. 'Some of these ideas were already present in the earlier work (1987g), but the later paper goes further in its account of this uncanny proximity, with the analyst creating a somatic double' of the patient.

REFERENCES

Benjamin, J. (1988) *The Bonds of Love.* New York: Pantheon.

Bernheimer, C. and Kahane, C. (Eds) (1985) *Dora's Case: Freud–Hysteria–Feminism.* New York: Columbia University Press.

Bollas, C. (1987a) At the other's play: To dream. In C. Bollas, *The Shadow of the Object: Psychoanalysis of the Unthought Known.* London: Free Association Books.

Bollas, C. (1987b) Expressive uses of the countertransference: Notes to the patient from oneself. In C. Bollas, *The Shadow of the Object: Psychoanalysis of the Unthought Known.* London: Free Association Books.

Bollas, C. (1987c) Introduction. In C. Bollas, *The Shadow of the Object: Psychoanalysis of the Unthought Known.* London: Free Association Books.

Bollas, C. (1987d) The liar. In C. Bollas, *The Shadow of the Object:*

Psychoanalysis of the Unthought Known. London: Free Association Books.

Bollas, C. (1987e) Loving hate. In C. Bollas, *The Shadow of the Object: Psychoanalysis of the Unthought Known*. London: Free Association Books.

Bollas, C. (1987f) Normotic illness. In C. Bollas, *The Shadow of the Object: Psychoanalysis of the Unthought Known*. London: Free Association Books.

Bollas, C. (1987g) The psychoanalyst and the hysteric. In C. Bollas, *The Shadow of the Object: Psychoanalysis of the Unthought Known*. London: Free Association Books.

Bollas, C. (1987h) The spirit of the object as the hand of fate. In C. Bollas, *The Shadow of the Object: Psychoanalysis of the Unthought Known*. London: Free Association Books.

Bollas, C. (1987i) The transformational object. In C. Bollas, *The Shadow of the Object: Psychoanalysis of the Unthought Known*. London: Free Association Books.

Bollas, C. (1987j) The trisexual. In C. Bollas, *The Shadow of the Object: Psychoanalysis of the Unthought Known*. London: Free Association Books.

Bollas, C. (1989a) The analyst's multiple function. In C. Bollas, *Forces of Destiny: Psychoanalysis and Human Idiom*. London: Free Association Books.

Bollas, C. (1989b) The ghostlike personality. In C. Bollas, *Forces of Destiny: Psychoanalysis and Human Idiom*. London: Free Association Books.

Bollas, C. (1989c) Historical sets and the conservative process. In C. Bollas, *Forces of Destiny: Psychoanalysis and Human Idiom*. London: Free Association Books.

Bollas, C. (1989d) Off the wall. In C. Bollas, *Forces of Destiny: Psychoanalysis and Human Idiom*. London: Free Association Books.

Bollas, C. (1992a) Aspects of self experiencing. In C. Bollas, *Being a Character: Psychoanalysis and Self Experience*. New York: Hill & Wang.

Bollas, C. (1992b) Being a character. In C. Bollas, *Being a Character: Psychoanalysis and Self Experience*. New York: Hill & Wang.

Bollas, C. (1992c) The psychoanalyst's use of free association. In C. Bollas, *Being a Character: Psychoanalysis and Self Experience*. New York: Hill & Wang.

Bollas, C. (1992d) Violent innocence. In C. Bollas, *Being a Character: Psychoanalysis and Self Experience*. New York: Hill & Wang.

Bollas, C. (1992e) Why Oedipus? In C. Bollas, *Being a Character: Psychoanalysis and Self Experience*. New York: Hill & Wang.

Bollas, C. (1992f) Cruising in the homosexual arena. In C. Bollas, *Being a Character: Psychoanalysis and Self Experience*. New York: Hill & Wang.

Bollas, C. (1995a) Communications of the unconscious. In C. Bollas, *Cracking Up: The Work of Unconscious Experience*. New York: Hill & Wang.

Bollas, C. (1995b) Cracking up. In C. Bollas, *Cracking Up: The Work of Unconscious Experience*. New York: Hill & Wang.

Bollas, C. (1995c) Introduction. In C. Bollas, *Cracking Up: The Work of Unconscious Experience*. New York: Hill & Wang

Bollas, C. (1995d) The structure of evil. In C. Bollas, *Cracking Up: The Work of Unconscious Experience*. New York: Hill & Wang.

Bollas, C. (1995e) What is this thing called self? In C. Bollas, *Cracking Up: The Work of Unconscious Experience*. New York: Hill & Wang.

H. D. (1974 [1956]) *Tribute to Freud*. Boston: David R. Godine, 1974.

Derrida, J. (1988) Telepathy (trans. N. Royle). *Oxford Literary Review*, 10: 3–41.

Ferenczi, S. (1933) Confusion of tongues between adult and child. In S. Ferenczi, *Final Contributions to the Problem and Methods of Psycho-Analysis*. London: Hogarth Press.

Freud, S. (1932) New introductory lectures on psycho-analysis. *Standard Edition*, 22. London: Hogarth Press.

Freud, S. (1957 [1915]) The unconscious. *Standard Edition*, 14: 159–204. London: Hogarth Press.

Freud, S. (1958 [1913]) The theme of the three caskets. *Standard Edition*, 12: 289–301. London: Hogarth Press.

Freud, S. (1959 [1926]) To Romain Rolland. *Standard Edition*, 20: 279. London: Hogarth Press.

Freud, S. (1961 [1925]) Negation. *Standard Edition*, 19: 233–9. London: Hogarth Press.

Kristeva, J. (1986 [1983]), Stabat mater. In *The Kristeva Reader*. (Ed.) T. Moi. Oxford: Blackwell.

Laplanche, J. (1989) *New Foundations for Psychoanalysis* (trans. D. Macey). Oxford: Blackwell.

Parker, R. (1995) *Torn in Two: The Experience of Maternal Ambivalence*. London: Virago.

Plath, S. (1971) Three Women. In S. Plath, *Winter Trees*. London: Faber & Faber.

Sprengnether, M. (1990) *The Spectral Mother: Freud, Feminism, and Psycho-analysis*. Ithaca, NY: Cornell University Press.

Winnicott, D. W. (1979 [1949]) Hate in the counter-transference. In *The Maturational Processes and the Facilitating Environment*. London: Hogarth Press.

8

The Poetics of Analysis: Klein, Bollas and the Theory of the Text

Joanne Feit Diehl

What does Object Relations offer the reader of poetry, and how does a study of poems contribute to psychodynamic insight? If Object Relations is to be useful to the literary critic, it might be understood as a way of reading psychic conflict that enables us to satisfy our epistemophilic quest for origins, a search for the beginning of literary production. Although I do not imagine anything so simple as an unmediated relation between those psychic origins and the production of poetry, what does engage me are the psychodynamic issues that are reenacted in a work of art. The character of that reenactment warrants close attention, for it is within its processes that we witness the distinctive, transformative capacities of the imagination. I shall first discuss the applicability of Object Relations analysis to aesthetic theory and then go on to elaborate my observations through a reading of three works by the contemporary American poet, Elizabeth Bishop. My initial premise is that aesthetic productions can be viewed as embodying traces of the earliest Object Relations, for these relations comprise the grounds of future creativity. As Christopher Bollas asserts, 'the aesthetic experience is not something learned by the adult; it is an existential recollection of an experience where being handled by the maternal aesthetic made thinking seemingly irrelevant to survival'.[1] The relation of such 'existential' recollections to the production of poetry is my major concern in what follows. I suggest that artistic structures can be viewed as reparative gestures made to the feared and always potentially aggressing mother; that literary texts may be viewed as reconstituting the very conditions that inform the initial mother–infant relationship. Such a supposition draws upon an Object Relations approach to human experience, and, particularly, to the transmutations of anxieties associated with a specifically female-identified psyche. This gender-inflected reading attempts to articulate the reciprocal relationship between the maternal idiom of care and the literary idiom through a process of interpretation that attends to the motives and impulses that inform creative activity.

Essential to this critical method is the conceptualization of an informing consciousness, an authorial presence that acknowledges psychic resonances as it remains attentive to the literary word. I introduce this investigation into Bishop's work by way of Melanie Klein's essay, 'Infantile anxiety situations and the creative impulse' in order to articulate the psychic origins that inform it.[2]

Describing the origins of creativity for the visual artist Ruth Kjar, Klein delineates what, to her mind, is the fundamental anxiety situation in female children. Klein describes that situation as follows:

> The little girl has a sadistic desire, originating in the early stages of the Oedipus conflict to rob the mother's body of its contents, namely, the father's penis, faeces, children, and to destroy the mother herself. This desire gives rise to anxiety lest the mother should in her turn rob the little girl herself of the contents of her body (especially of children) and lest her body should be destroyed or mutilated. In my view, this anxiety, which I have found in the analyses of girls and women to be the deepest anxiety of all, represents the little girl's earliest danger situation.... When the little girl who fears the mother's assault upon her body cannot see her mother, it intensifies the anxiety. The presence of the real, loving mother diminishes the dread of the terrifying mother, whose image is introjected into the child's mind.   (Klein, 1987, p. 92)

Fear of her own anger and her mother's imagined retaliation trap the little girl in the snare of anxiety. To free herself from that anxiety, the little girl makes reparation to the mother, as she attempts to compensate the mother for her own potential destructiveness. That reparative gesture can, in artistic women, result in the creation of imaginative or aesthetic productions. Such productions may themselves reenact or recall the initiating traumatic feelings associated with the infantile anxiety situation. Individual works, moreover, may revise that recollection, transmuting powerful feelings into narrative actions as literary texts construct scenarios that echo the lineaments of the infantile trauma.

In terms of the construction of narrative, the relation of the authorial psyche to its imaginative creations may be likened to the relation enacted between a dreamer and her dream. As understood by Christopher Bollas, the dream experience mirrors the dynamics of intrapsychic life. Rather than delineate a comprehensive subjectivity, Bollas asserts, 'in the dream one portion of the self is represented through an illusion that the experiencing subject in the dream is the entire self, while the other portions of the self may be represented through the dream events and other aspects of the dream script'. (Bollas, 47). He goes on to ask the question, 'How is the experiencing subject handled as an object by the dream script?' (Bollas, 47). This is akin to the question I will be addressing to the literary works under discussion: 'How is the poetic subject handled as an object by the narrative structures in which it is embedded?' Answers to both these questions are predicated upon Bollas's assertion that 'the dream experience constitutes an object relation in its own right and can be examined as such in terms of the dreamer-subject's experience of the dream event' (Bollas, 47). In literary terms, the aesthetic scenario constitutes an object relation, one that can be viewed as reenacting the traumatic core of the maternal–infantile paradigm.

Crucial to the acquisition of self-knowledge on the part of the dreamer is the recognition that the dream articulates a space wherein the self as object engages in symbolic relation. As Bollas writes,

> Whatever the dreamer's experience of the dream script, it is relevant to our psychoanalysis of the person's relation to himself as an object **to consider the dream space as a particular kind of unconscious holding environment** in which the dreamer may be the object of a presentation of desire, guilt, and historical notation, from an unconsciously organized and interpretive portion of the self.
>
> (Bollas, 47)

Thus, the poetic persona can be viewed as a a split-off part of the creative self whose experiences occur within an aesthetic holding environment, and who, like the dreaming subject, is affected by the presentation of 'desire, guilt, and historical notation'. To be sure, while the dream is constructed by unconscious forces, the poem is the production of a highly mediated, imaginative consciousness. Yet, I speculate that the underlying psychic structures of poetic texts may nevertheless reflect what Bollas names the maternal 'idiom of care', that 'archaic object relation' whose character informs all future relations between the self and the objects it creates or perceives (Bollas, 27). Furthermore, by engaging in creative activity, the author can be understood as participating in a quest for 'the transformational object' which possesses the 'capacity to resuscitate the memory of early ego transformation' (Bollas, 27). The poetic process functions to create the transformational object, and, in that creation, the poem reenacts the intrapsychic structures that inform the earliest manifestations of object-relating.

This transformational object harks back to 'the object as process', the experience of the mother as a 'region or source of transformation' (Bollas, 28). As Bollas asserts, 'the aesthetic space allows for a creative enactment of the search for this transformational object relation, and we might say that certain cultural objects afford memories of ego experiences that are now profoundly radical moments' (Bollas, 29). He continues, 'in the arts we have a location for such occasional recollections: intense memories of the process of self-transformation' (Bollas, 29). It is crucial to a study of aesthetic objects that we remember Bollas's assertion that 'transformation does not mean gratification'. 'Growth,' he explains, 'is only partially promoted by gratification, and one of the mother's transformative functions must be to frustrate the infant. Likewise, aesthetic moments are not always beautiful or wonderful occasions – many are ugly and terrifying but nonetheless profoundly moving because of the existential memory tapped' (Bollas, 29). If 'existential memory' resides within the aesthetic moment, then one means of locating that memory will be to attend to the dynamic structures which inform that moment. Thus, a theory of reading might be posited which would advocate an analysis of how the persona in a poetic narrative is treated and treats its environment in order to draw us back to a discovery of the existential memory of infantile object-relating. The nature of that existential memory will, if we invoke Klein's description of the infantile anxiety situation, include the recollection of crisis. If we invoke Bollas's description, it will include the frustration that he views as instrumental to the process of psychic maturation. I wish to make it clear that I do not advocate a mode of interpretation limited to the quest for an existential memory contained within the poem.

What I do find potentially useful, however, is the contribution attentiveness to such psychodynamic issues makes to the pluralistic act of reading. As a poet of a discreet and impassioned subjectivity, Bishop provides an evocative proving ground to observe the articulation of a distinctive 'human aesthetic' (Bollas, 3).

Bishop's poem, 'The Prodigal',[3] can be viewed with particular attention to the affectual and experiential situations in which the poetic subject finds himself, situations that, I suggest, reflect an originary experience that characterizes the infant's early encounters. 'The Prodigal' evokes the consciousness of a male persona and creates a narrative fiction that dramatizes feelings of loss, isolation, and abandonment – feelings that bespeak a primary trauma of the nascent ego. To be sure, the Biblical story of the prodigal son forms the ostensible occasion for such feelings, but the frame narrative itself may be considered, if not a screen, then a structure that preserves ego states that respond to trauma. Here is the poem:

> The brown enormous odor he lived by/ was too close, with its breathing and thick hair,/ for him to judge. The floor was rotten, the sty/ was plastered halfway up with glass-smooth dung./ Light-lashed, self-righteous, above moving snouts,/ the pigs' eyes followed him, a cheerful stare – even to the sow that always ate her young –/ till, sickening, he leaned to scratch her head./ But sometimes mornings after drinking bouts/ (he hid the pints behind a two-by-four),/ the sunrise glazed the barnyard mud with red,/ the burning puddles seemed to reassure./ And then he thought he almost might endure/ his exile yet another year or more.

> But evenings the first star came to warn./ The farmer whom he worked for came at dark/ to shut the cows and horses in the barn/ beneath their overhanging clouds of hay,/ with pitchforks faint forked lightnings, catching light,/ safe and companionable as in the Ark./ The pigs stuck out their little feet and snored./ The lantern – like the sun, going away/ – laid on the mud a pacing aureole./ Carrying a bucket along a slimy board,/ he felt the bats' uncertain staggering flight,/ his shuddering insights, beyond his control,/ touching him. But it took him a long time/ finally to make his mind up to go home.

Bishop seizes upon the experiential aspects of the story (Luke 15:11) to emphasize the immediate perceptual responses of the Prodigal. From the poem's opening, the environment impinges upon the Prodigal's perceptions. The atmosphere, 'the brown enormous odor he lived by', is palpable, experienced with an olfactory immediacy which is so pervasive, it can no longer be identified. The Prodigal's surroundings are further enumerated with a specificity that graphically illustrates disgust. Yet the repugnant scene the poem describes has an attractive quality as well, for the text aestheticizes the very conditions which render the Prodigal's situation horrific. The dung is 'glass-smooth', the sunrise glazes the 'barnyard mud with red' and 'the burning puddles' seem 'to reassure'.

The pigs participate in this paradoxical scene: 'Light-lashed, self-right-eous, above moving snouts, the pigs' eyes followed him, a cheerful stare – even to the sow that always ate her young – till, sickening, he leaned to scratch her head'. Sickened presumably by the sow's cannibalistic propensities, the Prodigal does not turn away but, in a sympathetic gesture, 'scratches her head'. This admixture of revulsion and sympathy marks the surreal relation the Prodigal has to his environment. Visual alterations that may be ascribed to his drinking create illusions that offer some comfort. With such reassurance comes the thought that the Prodigal almost 'might endure his exile yet another year or more'. One can only speculate as to the terrors the forsaken homeground must hold if these illusory signs of reassurance can lead the Prodigal to believe that he might prefer enduring his present circumstances to return. The signs of reassurance disappear in the poem's second fourteen lines to be replaced with a new form of exile and the threat and attraction of departure.

Taking care of the animals, the farmer has created a haven for them as 'safe and companionable as is the Ark'. Excluded from that ark, an alternative haven of safety, the Prodigal is again thrust into the position of an outcast; this time, however, into an exile not of his own making or of his own choosing. This experience awakens in him feelings of deprivation as he associates the farmer's receding lantern with the cosmic effect of the 'sun, going away'. At the poem's close, the Prodigal undergoes an intermingling of external and internal worlds: 'Carrying a bucket along a slimy board, he felt the bats' uncertain staggering flight, his shuddering insights, beyond his control, touching him'. These embodied insights violate the Prodigal's autonomy and threaten his ego.

No longer able to employ the psychological mechanism of projection as a means of warding off anxiety, the Prodigal is invaded by his fears. Just as the sow served as a repository for images of infanticide, so the bats become shuddering forms that escape the Prodigal's capacity to neutralize them by means of externalization. Fusing the internal and the external, the Prodigal becomes a paranoid subject, tormented by what lurks within him. Despite the warnings awakened by the sightless bats' touch, it takes the Prodigal 'a long time/finally to make his mind up to go home'. Caught between two exiles, one self-imposed and the other produced by the farmer's neglect, the Prodigal delays his decision to return home, and, in the space of that delay, creates an alternative, alienated homeground that comments upon the inherent aversiveness of his two choices. This view of the paranoid subject assessing his alternatives is a brilliant tour de force. For, not only does Bishop evoke an aura of intimate feeling as she re-creates the psychological reality of the Prodigal, she also gives him a sensibility that strives to compensate for the home he has lost. With astonishing compression, the poem describes a world where objects of disgust assume a compensatory loveliness cast by a subtle change of light, the perceptual effect of an intoxicated subjectivity. Paranoia becomes a mode of survival as the self postpones the decision to return home. What does this portrait of the exile reveal about the authorial imagination that creates it? What might 'The Prodigal' have to tell us about the sources of the creative energies that produce the poem?

Central to these energies is the restitutive capacity of the Prodigal to aestheticize his surroundings, to convert the rotten floor and the dung-filled sty into sites of apparent reassurance. Yet such illusory loveliness does not suffice to stave off the encroaching fears embodied by the bats. The conflict provoked by the Prodigal's 'shuddering insights', presumably the result of observations made regarding his surroundings and his aversion to return home, create a delay, a period of indecisiveness that gestures towards the antipathetic cast of his alternatives. Doubly cast out, the Prodigal perceptually creates a tentative reassurance that dissolves in the presence of external warning signs. If the poem serves as a repository of memory, then what the artist remembers for us here are precisely those fears or primordial presences that evoke our deepest anxieties. Along with these expressions of feeling is a yearning for protection and nurturance, a desire for aesthetic satisfaction in the external world. The primal infantile anxiety situation, here defined as abandonment and loneliness, can, in the context of the poem, be reexperienced in a space that experiments with the powers of an aestheticizing sensibility exercised both by the poetic subject and by the authorial imagination. For, if the Prodigal's perceptual distortions create a world of incipient loveliness, the author of the poem designs a poetic structure adequate to convey traumatic experience. In the creation of that structure, foundational anxieties are contained within an aesthetically determined form. By submitting themselves to the vicissitudes and play of poetic language, these terrifying conflicts can be registered on the reader's psyche without overwhelming it. With the threat of incipient trauma controlled by the reiterated assurances of aesthetic form, the primal infantile anxiety situation can be reenacted in a space that is imaginatively alive, freed from the force of uncontrollable anxiety. Thus, what is transformative about such a poetic production is the extent to which the poem enables us to witness a traumatizing situation handled in such a way that it is released from its capacity to overwhelm without sacrificing its meaning or its affect. As far as the reader is concerned, the ability to reflect is acquired as the immediate traumatic force is contained. With the advent of pleasure, we are held in a good-enough artistic milieu. Of such successful attempts to contain trauma to achieve aesthetic viability, Bollas asserts, the aesthetic moment is a

caesura in time when the subject feels held in symmetry and solitude
by the spirit of the object. 'What would characterize experience as
aesthetic rather than either cognitive or moral,' writes Murray Krie-
ger, 'would be its self sufficiency, its capacity to trap us within itself,
to keep us from moving beyond it to further knowledge or to practical
effort.' While such moments can subsequently be flung into hermeneutical explication, they are fundamentally wordless occasions, notable for the density of the subject's feeling and the fundamentally
non-representational knowledge of being embraced by the aesthetic
object.   (Bollas, 31)

The reader feels held by the poem to the extent that it achieves a balance
between a representation of suffering and a basis for empathic identification.
Whereas Bollas describes such aesthetic moments as 'wordless occasions', I
contend that it is through the presence of language that the transformative
experience occurs – the word is the transformative means that renders
trauma acceptable to the readerly self. In 'The Prodigal', themes of exile,
abandonment and infanticide collude to create a profoundly sad occasion,
but this sadness is itself distinct from trauma because the affect bears a
trace of reflection acquired through a process enacted by language that
renders indivisible the fabric of psychic consciousness and aesthetic form.
It is with the deployment of language, in the rhetoric, not the experience of
trauma, that infantile anxiety situations create a transformative medium.

If the work of art can be understood as an act of restitution, then the
forms that restitution assumes reveal much about the initiatory trauma that
constitutes its occasion. In Bishop's story, 'The Sea & Its Shore', the
protagonist, Edwin Boomer, shares the Prodigal's isolating circumstances,
but here the compelling subject is language and its effects upon the psyche.[4]
It is Boomer's task to rid the shore of its detritus of printed matter. In his
obsessive activities connected with this task, Boomer signifies the literary
individual *in extremis*. So all-consuming becomes Boomer's obsession that
the 'world, the whole world he saw, came before many years to seem
printed, too' (Bishop, *Prose*, 178).[5] His occupation is, finally, destruction –
'But the point was that everything had to be burned at last' (179). Here,
the protagonist's relation to printed texts is that between self and world.
The task, for Boomer, is to ward off becoming engulfed by the world as
text, by the imprint of external life. In terms of Object Relations, one might
view Boomer's occupation as an attempt to maintain requisite space for the
ego. As in the archaic paradigm of the early feeding situation where the self
strives to achieve a balance between getting what it needs and protecting

against being overwhelmed by those supplies, here, in the realm of the Lacanian Symbolic, the world comprised of language, the readerly subject attests to the supreme importance of words and their capacity to inundate him. A middle ground, that of confusion, is one possible resolution to this crisis. Problems of understanding arise as Boomer cannot always adequately decipher the applicability to himself of the subject matter he reads. That failure of understanding can be seen as a means of modulating the power of language. A willed ignorance functions as a successful defence which allows the self to gain the power of regulating what will reach and what will miss Boomer's receptive imagination. Fear of engulfment creates in the psyche the necessity of protecting the self by categorizing everything outside it in relation to its needs; so Boomer organizes the printed matter he collects according to three classifications.

First, and most numerous: everything that seemed to be about himself, his occupation in life, and any instructions or warnings that referred to it.

Second: the stories about other people that caught his fancy, whose careers he followed from day to day in newspapers and fragments of books and letters; and whose further adventures he was always watching out for.

Third: the items he could not understand at all, that bewildered him completely

> but at the same time interested him so much that he saved them to read. These he tried, almost frantically, to fit into first one, then the other, of the two categories. (Bishop, *Prose*, 175)

The danger in this obsession with print is that the world as text will not yield up its meaning.

> The more papers he picked up and the more he read, the less he felt he understood. In a sense he depended on 'their imagination', and was even its slave, but at the same time he thought of it as a kind of disease. (Bishop, *Prose*, 177-8)

The only way that Boomer can resolve this dilemma is to burn the papers. 'Burning paper was his occupation, by which he made his living, but over and above that, he could not allow his pockets to become too full, or his house to become littered' (Bishop, *Prose*, 179-80). What Boomer most craves, that with which alone he remains in constant relation, is what he must destroy. So, in pychodynamic terms, the relationship between Boomer and the world beyond is endangered; relationality can be maintained only through a ritualistic process of destruction. For Boomer, conflagration becomes a means of controlling the incursions of print; symbolically, for the experiential ego, survival is achieved through the protective effects of aggression. The apparent, ironizing simplicity with which this story is recounted contributes to its effect, for we acquire access to the workings of the literary imagination as we simultaneously witness the rites of the embattled ego. Humour plays its role here; among the pieces of paper in the third group 'that fascinated but puzzled', Boomer saves a small, untorn strip of pink paper' which describes the use of 'JOKE SPECS WITH SHIFTING EYES' (Bishop, *Prose*, 172–7). The understanding of the instructions on this piece of paper eludes Boomer as do the psychic functions of his behaviour. The figure of Boomer himself remains ambiguous; mock heroic and grotesque, he nevertheless assumes his place in an extremely picturesque scene, 'in some ways like a Rembrandt, but in many ways not' (Bishop, *Prose*, 180). Here the aestheticizing of Boomer in his surroundings is incomplete – as partial as his own success in interpreting what he reads. Boomer's negotiations in the realm of the Symbolic are fraught with the tensions carried over from the earlier pre-oedipal stage, the issues of supply and demand that are at the core of the infantile feeding situation. This transfer of the issues associated with the demands at the breast to the time following the acquisition of language is characteristic of the way developmental trends can be seen as informing theoretical observations about verbal communications. The psychological dynamics associated with the literate and literary life find their trace in the non-linguistic, pre-oedipal past.

Not every relationship, however, is conveyed through the means of thematizing psychodynamic interactions. Something as amorphous as mood may be read as a marker, a trace of a flaw in a relationship, the moment when parental empathy breaks down. Speculating upon the role mood plays in the clinical setting, Bollas theorizes that 'moods are often the existential registers of the moment of a breakdown between a child and his parents, and they partly indicate the parents' own developmental arrest, in that the parent was unable to deal appropriately with the child's particular maturational needs' (Bollas, 115–16). In literary representation, the evocation of mood, delicate as it is, may be seen as similarly leaving a trace, gesturing towards a moment of crisis that resides in the past. However mood is conveyed, it can be considered a sign of a past object relation that leaves its mark on the present. In Bishop's poem, 'Sestina', mood is, as so often in her work, conveyed by description of place and attentiveness to external process (here especially the weather, which is complicit in its creation).

'September rain falls on the house', forming the background to a scene of inscrutability enacted by a child and her grandmother. As each keeps her tears secret from the other, the tears continue to proliferate until they are everywhere – in the grandmother's teacup, in the child's drawing, between the pages of the almanac. This covert display of sadness with its hidden elements of a common grief points towards the creation of a mood that must be stifled to preserve appearances. If the poem is lent an autobiographical context, we might bring to our reading the suggestion that the grief that is shared resolves around the absent mother, Elizabeth Bishop's own mother, who was institutionalized when Elizabeth was five years old. Weeping from unarticulated causes, the child and the grandmother share a common mood and a reciprocal feeling. If a mood can be interpreted as the registration of a 'moment of breakdown between a child and his parents', then the poem simultaneously represents the outcome of that breakdown as it alludes to its origins. This dual representation is inherent in the communicative power of mood to function as a signification of breakdown, a sign of trauma that operates in a realm of temporal displacement. The mood experienced in the present testifies to an emotional fissure residing in the past. Mood inscribes that fissure in contemporary experience, creating thereby a signifying trace that speaks to origins associated with loss and lack. 'Sestina' reenacts the signifying function of mood, for it marks as it simultaneously displaces grief. By displacing human tears into a world of external objects and representing those objects in a literary form, the author separates from as she aligns herself with the immediacy of grief. The poem, therefore, constitutes a double act of displacement and signification which suggests that interrelational failures can be simultaneously represented and contained. Writing functions to articulate boundaries which allow the authorial ego to express feelings through the act of redirection and containment, much as the child's drawing transmutes tears into buttons.

In their very different ways, 'The Prodigal', 'The Sea & Its Shore' and 'Sestina' all offer possibilities for Object Relations-inflected interpretation. The range of concerns spanned by these texts suggests the broad scope of such a psychoanalytic inquiry. Emphasizing the dynamic processes that inform interactive relationships, this branch of psychoanalysis contributes to literary interpretation by offering insights into the fundamental mother–infant dyad. If the creative enterprise can be understood as a process of restitution, as an ongoing, reparative gesture made to the archaic mother, then the form of this enterprise can also be interpreted in terms of intersubjective phenomena. Ways of being with the Other are transcribed by language into an aesthetic discourse that harbours traces of its psychohistorical origins. Thus, the act of interpretation includes a return to the dynamic sources of literary production. At the heart of these sources is the concept of gift exchange, the transactions enacted by mother and infant at the site of the mother's breast. Whereas, in my earlier work, I invoked this concept to explore the subject of literary influence, what has interested me here are the links between archaic infantile interactions with the mother and the sphere of literary representation. While these two areas may seem far apart, I agree with Klein and Bollas that throughout life the initial, infantile experience is reenacted through all future relationships, including the literary. To view literary production as a form of relationality is itself to insist upon the intersubjective properties of creativity. Such an understanding is predicated upon the theory that the energies that fuel creative production are themselves linked to the psyche's initial experience of nurture. The aggressive drives associated with securing the mother's milk, the oral dynamic enacted in the early feeding situation, the over-whelming feelings experienced by the infant as s/he responds to satiety and frustration all inform the more modulated, intrapsychic processes that underwrite creativity.

In the examples I have drawn from Bishop's work, issues associated with the idiom of care, the infantile anxiety situation, and the dynamics of breast feeding have played a major role. Governing all of these aspects of the mother–infant relation is the question of reciprocity, the impulse on the part of the maturing psyche to make reparation to the mother. Efforts of literary creation can be understood transferentially, as attempts to make reparation in the verbal sphere, for, with its representational capacity, language can articulate as it masks over a reenactment of the processes that govern the psyche's earliest transactions with its source of life. Given such a model for aesthetic activity, poetic representation can be viewed as the creation of an alternative narrative of pre-oedipal history, 'alternative' because in addition to the task of representing historical material, the poem enacts a revisionary gesture that re-constitutes the underlying fantasy of the initial mother–infant relation to construct a verbal holding environment. Thus, a narrative space is created that, through the processes of figuration, converts the maternal idiom into literary style. Verbal acts, therefore, can be viewed as dynamic, psychic events that seek to redress the balance between the maternal source of nurturance and the activities of the infantile self transformed into the poetic ego. This process of restitution involves a continual displacement, as memories identified with the powerful Other are resituated in the external world or find a home within. Thus, creativity is linked to the process of mourning as internalization of the good Object becomes the restitutive aim of the poetic ego.[6] Such psychic purposes inform linguistic choices, as the writerly subject constructs a verbal form whose shape is inflected by her/his intrapsychic needs.

Reading Bishop with such a paradigm in mind is not simply a process of uncovering biographical material; it is, instead, a process that remains open to the dynamic nature of the relations figured within the poem. Metaphor and metonymy play a part in this figural notation as rhetorical choices determine the associative connections which link up primitive materials with their aestheticizing environment. Such associations themselves delineate structures of identification as feelings identified with the primal self and the nursing mother are refashioned to assert the authority of the poetic ego. Containment, displacement and thematization remain the major routes for this literary transformation of affectual life. The proliferation of rhetorical effects within a poem can be seen, in part, as a gesture towards containment, the search for verbal forms that will simultaneously convey the initial trace memory of infantile experience and refashion that memory into a narrative that both echoes and reconstructs the initial psychic situation. Here memory is linked to desire as the poet invents structures of containment that preserve fundamental infantile experience as she devises strategies for repositioning the poetic ego so that it inhabits a position of mastery.

The intense aura of subjectivity conveyed by Bishop's poems (despite their overt acts of rhetorical distancing) derives from this thematic and affectual reenactment of early forms of Object Relating. The 'existential recollections' embedded in her work manifest themselves in narrative structure, interrelational dynamics, and mood. An Object Relations-inflected interpretation offers the conceptual means to reach back through these forms to consider the intimate origins of consciousness and to apprise oneself of the residual conflicts that underlie literary creativity. The aesthetic resolution of such conflicts constitutes the stylistic idiom of the poet, and that idiom can be viewed as the trace of intrasubjective defences transferred into the realm of style. Psychic restitution is made through verbal articulation; the restitutive is transformed into the rhetorical as interrelational structures are transferred into the linguistic medium. Thus, the processes of intrasubjectivity, through the deployment of language, find an aesthetic outlet and reparative resolution. Reading through the lens of Object Relations affords us a means for examining these intrasubjective forces as they emerge in Bishop's work. Applying the theoretical concepts of Klein and Bollas to the process of interpretation enables us to trace with greater precision the intricacies of poetic subjectivity and to approach the underlying origins of Bishop's creative impulse.

NOTES

1. Christopher Bollas, *The Shadow of The Object: Psychoanalysis of the Unthought Known* (New York: Columbia University Press, 1987), pp. 34–5. All other references to this book will appear in parentheses in the text.

2. See Melanie Klein, *The Selected Melanie Klein*, edited by Juliet Mitchell (New York: The Free Press, A Division of Macmillan, Inc., 1987), pp. 84–94.

3. Elizabeth Bishop, *Elizabeth Bishop: The Complete Poems, 1927–1979* (New York: Farrar, Straus, Giroux, 1991).

4. As others have noted, Edwin Boomer shares initials with Elizabeth Bishop.

5. Elizabeth Bishop, *The Collected Prose*, edited by Robert Giroux (New York: Farrar, Straus, Giroux, 1984).

6. For a provocative and groundbreaking discussion of the relationship between the role of mourning and the depressive position, see Melanie Klein's 'Mourning and its relation to manic-depressive states' in *The Selected Melanie Klein*, pp. 146–74.

9

'If My Mouth Could Marry a Hurt Like That!': Reading Auto-Mutilation, Auto-Biography in the Work of Christopher Bollas and Sylvia Plath[1]

Michael Szollosy

In his 1992 book, *Being a Character: Psychoanalysis and Self Experience*, in a chapter straight-forwardly entitled 'Cutting', Christopher Bollas illustrates an intimate portrait of a self-cutter he refers to as 'S'. Languishing under the radically depersonalizing, patriarchal institution of a psychiatric hospital, S cuts herself both in defiance of the authorities that seek to control her and to reassure herself of her own existence. For S, auto-mutilation serves the dual function of auto-biography, a self-articulation, and (re-)ontologization, a confirmation through pain of her own being. Bollas presents the vast majority of this chapter as a first-person narrative, impersonating the voice of this institutionalized analysand. This narrative strategy makes an essential contribution to the ideas that Bollas conveys in this piece: by choosing to represent S's narrative in the first person, he constructs a porous, dialogic narrative that, like the cuts that S makes on her own body, is open to the interchange of objects that facilitate the production of meaning. Both practices, auto-biography and auto-mutilation, seek to inscribe a concrete text, a record of experience, and both seek to create spaces – *potential spaces* – in which subjects can meet and creatively articulate their own idiom.[2]

S reminds us that 'Sylvia Plath cut herself in 1962', referring to her poem, 'Cut':

> What a thrill –
> My thumb instead of an onion.
> The top quite gone
> Except for a sort of hinge
> of skin . . .
>   (Bollas, 1992, p. 139)

Following this lead, I will in this chapter examine 'Cutting' and the work of Sylvia Plath, especially her collection of poems *Ariel* and her novel *The Bell Jar*, in an attempt to demonstrate how auto-mutilation serves as a means to self-articulation. I will demonstrate how S's cutting and Plath's writing, both often only read as expressions of a desire to die, demonstrate a desire to *live* in the world. Of course, Plath's texts are different in that they represent linguistically these recourses to the realization of being.[3] But S and other cutters are also writing, making a record of their struggle to survive, by scarring their own bodies; self-mutilation may thus be regarded as another strategy in the attempt to write one's own story, to be the author of one's own subjective experience. However, rather than using the page and pen, as is the typical strategy employed in conventional forms of auto-biography, here we see inscription taking place on the body – and while I contend that self-experience is always concretely inscribed, S's means are more immediately gratifying, more direct and desperate. I also hope to show how literary and cultural critics may utilize Bollas's ideas in approaching fiction and art in general. Despite a long-running love-affair with psychoanalytic thought, humanities scholars have only recently begun to look outside orthodox and French psychoanalysis for ideas – and I believe that Bollas's strategies and approaches in particular will make important contributions to literary and cultural theory as we work to address, and redress, contemporary issues.

'AXES . . . AND THE ECHOES!'

Before we hear S tell her own story, we are allowed briefly to eavesdrop upon other voices talking about her. At a conference table in a psychiatric hospital on a Monday morning, therapy staff, medical directors and nurses react to news that another patient has cut herself; we hear voices, speaking in turn, offer their opinions:

'Well, clearly S cuts because she is testing limits. It is boundary testing'. . . . 'Obviously S cuts because she poses the question, "Who is to control my body, the body in question?". . . . 'We must ask the analyst, or S, or both, "What is happening in the transference to inspire the analysand to cut her analyst at this moment?" ' / 'Cutting is a relief. The patient cuts to free herself of her persecutory inner contents, which she lets out concretely by bleeding. . . .'

(Bollas, 1992, p. 138)

Each of these voices represents a theory of self-harm that one can easily recognize from the psychoanalytic literature and I would not dismiss, whatever my own focus here, any of these as irrelevant or a mis-recognition of what are often very real motives behind self-harm. However, the potential of self-harm to provide a moment of experience, a sense of being, is strangely overlooked at this conference table. It is as if Bollas is suggesting that these voices of the institution cannot recognize how their discourses and practices might themselves deny or negate the possibility for experience itself.

Another quality about Bollas's representation of these voices that I immediately recognize is the authority which they try to claim for them-selves. 'Well, clearly . . .', 'Obviously . . .', 'We must . . .', the certainty and finality behind decisive statements such as 'Cutting is a relief'. You can imagine each of these voices dripping with pretentious, empty knowledge, illustrating the archetype of the disengaged, unlistening analyst. Perhaps it is a stereotype that makes many psychoanalysts recoil with frustration and embarrassment, but this portrayal is found again and again in literary representations of the analytic scene. S does not see her analyst as capable of communicating with her; he makes no attempt to contain her anxieties. 'If my doctor knew me he would know when I felt like cutting' (Bollas, 1992, p. 141); 'He has no insides for me. No place for me to look inside him. Just phallic externality, that compost heap of exposure, that medicality embodied' (p. 143). Plath, too, often writes of such analysts. 'Lady Lazarus' is addressed to 'Herr Doktor . . . Herr Enemy . . . Herr God, Herr Lucifer'; she sarcastically taunts, 'Do not think I underestimate your great concern' (Plath, 1981, p. 246). Dr Gordon, Esther Greenwood's similarly esteemed psychiatrist in *The Bell Jar*, immediately challenges Esther on their first meeting, 'Suppose you try and tell me what you think is wrong' (Plath, 1963, 137).

I turned the words over suspiciously, like round, sea-polished pebbles that might suddenly put out a claw and change into something else.

What did I *think* was wrong?
That made it sound like nothing was *really* wrong, I only *thought* it
was wrong.   (Plath, 1963, p. 137)

Dr Gordon, who is usually more interested in reminiscing about the pretty
WAC girls who used to be stationed at Esther's college than hearing about
her symptoms, confidently prescribes electroshock therapy during only their
second meeting. For Esther and S, these positivistic, authoritarian voices of
the medical establishment are part of an all-pervasive patriarchal system,
the 'phallic externality . . . the medicality embodied'.

Bollas similarly presents each of these voices at the conference table as
speaking so as to be monolithic in their diagnoses and monologic in their
(grammatical) structure. Each voice here asserts its own theory in such a
way as to close down the possibility for other interpretations and the
possibility that other voices, including that of the analysand herself, might
enter into the debate. They appear as 'spiritual imperialists, greedily moving
through others, militantly affecting people in destructive ways' (Bollas,
1992, p. 63). And as these voices speak with a closed, disengaged, objective
tone, they cannot understand the experience of cutting, or that their
analysands cut out of the need for experience. S's analyst 'reads and reads
these petite cuts with all the earnestness of an anthropologist whose only
fieldwork among the natives will be in the library' (p. 142).

We can thus see the significance of the narrative strategy that Bollas
adopts for this essay. Bollas does not rigorously theorize in a clinical,
dispassionate language the motivations behind self-harm, and even though
he sometimes writes in the voice(s) of clinicians, he resists assuming such a
definitive language himself. In so doing, I think, he realizes the full potential
of the uniquely psychoanalytic narrative, initiated by Freud, that allows the
permeation and mingling of multiple voices, and therefore multiple meanings, into the text. Bollas states at the outset of *Being a Character*, 'Each
essay is an effort to put a very particular kind of self experience into words'
(p. 6). Bollas states that

> [t]he reader will notice that I periodically narrate my own life history
> and my own nature to investigate or to argue a particular topic. I
> believe this is because, at certain moments, I have needed to conjure
> my own self experience in order to write about a topic – to be
> informed from within, so to speak, rather than to think about the
> particular self state by discussing a patient. After all, Freud suggested
> this form for the writing of psychoanalysis in his *Interpretation of*

Dreams, a work which includes his own dreams together with those of his patients in an evolutionary dialectic that supports the construction of his theories. I think this is a unique literary form for the writing of psychoanalysis, enabling the reader to participate in that unconscious movement that contributes to a psychoanalyst's clinical practice and informs his creation of psychoanalytic theory.   (Bollas, 1992, p. 6)

The inclusion of his own voice(s) creates a text that is *dialogic* and *polyphonic* – it represents a multi-voiced and multi-layered conversation in which meaning is not sealed and the sole preserve of one author(ity) but constantly generated through negotiation and re-evaluation. Bollas expresses how he, like Freud, conceives of the psychoanalytic scene and text as an 'evolution-ary dialectic' – for which I substitute the word 'dialogue'[4] – that combines the analyst's dream with the analysand's in the construction of theory.

Notice too that Bollas wishes to include the ever-important, yet often excluded, *reader* in the creative production of meaning in his texts. With the objective, scientific voice that encumbers much writing about psycho-pathology, including some of Freud's own (in spite his own best efforts to the contrary), the reader, like S and Plath, is shut out from entering the text. The discourses of the doctors who treat S lack this dialogic, inviting property. They are monolithic and monologic and seek to exclude the voice of the (usually female) patient. S asks

Where do I find representations in the icons of my civilisation for such a hole, an o-ffence? Greek and Roman men still walk the museums of our world with representational arrogance flaunting this penis, but where are our vaginas?

Perhaps in the ellipses, the gaps in consciousness. The holes in minds that do not represent.   (Bollas, 1992, p. 141)

It is in these ellipses, the gaps in consciousness, language and the body, that the possibility for dialogue exists. S dramatically emphasizes this intimate relationship between cutting, writing and gender by speaking of her 'cuɽts'. In answer to the flaunting penis, the phallic externality of the medical establishment, S finds her cuɽt to be the open spaces, determined both by her gender and her razor, that opens her body and her discourse to the potential for intersubjective meaning.[5]

In contrast to the solid, smooth discourses of her doctors, then, S's narrative is punctuated with such opportunities, refusing to close down the production of meaning. In fact, for Bollas, the 'analysand's discourse always undermines the authority of the analyst'; 'the mere fact of free association deconstructs any tragic hero's destiny. . . . The self that wants to master its narration is continuously slipping up in its intentions' (Bollas, 1995, p. 224). When, for example, S refers to Plath's poem she only quotes the first five lines, ending with ellipsis. S, or Bollas, could have gone on to recite the whole poem, and perhaps then also have gone on to offer an exegesis that would seek to *define* what this poem means and thus assume the role of the spiritual imperialist, negating the potential that the poem or any object has for helping to elaborate an idiom. Such a strategy stifles the creative production of meaning (as I will hopefully not do below); the ellipses leave open the poem and its contribution to the meaning of the essay. Plath's voice is not appropriated but added to the concert of voices playing in the essay.

Narrative strategies such as those Bollas employs here therefore *cut* into these monologic discourses, opening the text to the participation of the analyst, the analysand and the reader. Like Bollas's idea of *cracking up*, S is *cutting up*, using horror instead of humour to undermine the authority of her analyst. However, just as with any venture into a potential space where meaning can be constructed, the threat of liminal uncertainty always looms. Bollas appreciates the risk in such a narrative strategy and realizes that there is always a degree of security in writing as the sole author(ity), in closing down the text to other meanings and thus securing one's own singular version of truth.

> Of course, Freud knew that he left himself open to a particular kind of reading which would disclose his self deceptions, but the revelation of such blindness is a crucial feature of this literary form. Naturally I am well aware that my essays leave me in a similar position, but if we are to *open up the writing* of psychoanalysis to bring it closer to the nature of psychoanalytic practice – and to the to-and-fro of blindness and insight – then it is a literary risk well worth taking.
>
> (Bollas, 1992, pp. 6–7; italics mine)

Bollas's often courageous writing is thus productive, facilitating and inclusive; by opening spaces for the two-way, in-and-out flow of meaning, it circumvents and subverts, like S and Plath, the authoritarian monologism too often plaguing scientific discourses, and it is this dialogic quality that psychoanalysis, like fiction and poetry, can and should encourage. Bollas presents, through S, a polyphony of voices that we might imagine S having been subjected to over the years of analysis. I hear echoes here of

Winnicottians, Kleinians of all stripes, Freudians of all shapes, Lacanians, French feminists and many others who have written from various perspectives on self-harm. So too, though, there are Bollas's voices, the voices of at least one analysand (though I suspect S represents more than one analysand), and, of course, Sylvia Plath's.

When S cuts it can be thus rightly interpreted as a challenge to and an attack upon the author(ity) that dares to speak for her. Questions of authority and control are constantly raised in S's narrative; 'Who owns the razor I use? With whose hand do I make these incisions? Is it my hand? Who cuts me?' (Bollas, 1992, p. 139). On the one hand, when S cuts, she is trying to manipulate her body, to control *when* and *where* she bleeds.

> Sometimes blood comes and I turn into pretend surprise: Oh! Blood. But I can control it. . . . When I get my period, well, a day or two before it actually happens, I change. We all change differently. I feel cross, irritated by small things, and I cut myself off from my friends, as I don't want to be a pain. I get an unpleasant full-body feeling, a container stretched to its limits, about to burst its skin. My breasts, tender. Pain. It *is* pain. Every bloody month.   (Bollas, 1992, p. 141)

It seems that S cuts in order to gain a degree of control in the articulation of her experience, but also so as to achieve a degree of control over her body. This latter motivation of self-harm, although immensely important, significantly contrasts with the experience of self-harm that is the specific focus of this study. Cutting to control one's body involves a psyche-somatic *split* rather than an attempt to achieve a moment of psyche-somatic integration. Trying to control one's own body, perceived to be a foreign entity, at the expense of integration is an attempt by a disembodied *mind-psyche* (Winnicott, 1949) to seize a temporary sense of omnipotence, representing the triumph of 'mind over matter'.

But S also cuts so as to (even temporarily) gain a degree of control over her own subjective experience. She seeks, in pain, a creative, purposeful act of self-authority. To achieve this, she must rupture the control exerted on her by her doctors, and slash through the smooth surface of the doctor's correct discourse, creating a space in which she can enter.

> So I am cutting him up. He tells me so. Well, good. That's what I desire. I want my cut to signify him. 'Oh, Dr Y,' his colleagues inquire, 'how is S doing?' The doctor whose patient cuts. Ha! The doctor defined by cunts, the doctor who does not know so much, who

not know when the blood comes. Let him be a cunt. A little cunt. I
bleed: he bleeds.   (Bollas, 1992, p. 142)

S wants to create spaces for/in/on herself while making him, quite literally,
shut up. 'My cunts shock the analyst. I flash my bleeding wound and force
his lids shut' (p. 141). Cutting for S provides an opportunity to open the
sealed discourses and to create spaces so her own internal world may flow
and spill out into the world, and to control when and where such spaces are
open to such scrutiny and potential attack. Plath also cuts using language.
Her poem 'Words' begins:

> Axes
> After whose stroke the wood rings,
> And the echoes!
> Echoes travelling
> Off from the centre like horses.
>
> The sap
> Wells like tears, like the
> Water striving
> To re-establish its mirror
> Over the rock.
>   (Plath, 1981, p. 270)

Plath's words, like S's cuts, work like axes resonating with multiple voices
that de-centre authority and chop down the phallic monolithic signifier,
letting the 'sap' – internal contents – ooze into the world. Bollas finds that
'unconscious freedom' is achieved through a process analogous to cutting
and pasting discourse; it is 'found in the necessary opposition between the
part of us that finds truth by uniting disparate ideas (i.e., "condensation")
and the part of us that finds the truth by breaking up those unities' (Bollas,
1995, p. 3).

'I DO IT SO IT FEELS LIKE HELL. I DO IT SO IT FEELS REAL'

This reading, I think, challenges the all-too commonly held notions that
both those practising self-harm and Plath's work are governed by preoccupations with death that could only ever be resolved in a successful suicide.[6]

However, as I have stated from the outset, auto-biography and auto-mutilation are strategies often used to achieve a moment of psyche-somatic integration and to experience one's own subjective existence. Bollas also finds the slashing suicide attempt by Tom, a normotic – a subject who has no inner life, no subjective element – to be about much more than literal or psychic death. 'It is my view that Tom's breakdown constitutes a mute refusal to live within normotic culture, even though at the point of his suicide attempt he had not discovered other avenues for the expression of his feelings' (Bollas, 1987, p. 151). Rather than death, then, I argue that Plath's poetry and S's cutting are about *survival* – resisting death and non-being and instead trying to *live*. Susan Bassnett makes a similar point with regard to Plath. 'The most straightforward way to reject the writing-as-prelude-to-dying reading is to go back to the poems and prose and look again at them. *The Bell Jar* is a novel about a suicide attempt that fails; but is also a novel about a woman who learns how to live with herself and how to come to terms with the world, that world of destruction and horror' (Bassnett, 1987, p. 122).

Cutting can be a defence against what Winnicott (1992 [1952]) describes as 'Anxiety associated with insecurity'. It can defend against disintegration and depersonalization, the lack of a relationship of psyche to soma, by re-enforcing somatic boundaries and re-integrating the body and the mind. Winnicott also describes a third anxiety, when 'the feeling that the centre of gravity of consciousness transfers from the kernel to the shell, from the individual to the care, the technique' (1992 [1952] p. 99). Bollas similarly describes a depersonalized analysand as having an 'absence of a sense of self', his inner world a mere 'empty space' (1995, p. 159). Like the desubjectified normotic, his life lacks spontaneity and creativity, and is instead dominated by schedules and mechanized ritual. S also suffers from this sort of depersonalization. Her 'hospital body' is an empty shell. 'My cunts aren't the real thing, are they?' she asks. 'I usually just scratch my surfaces' (Bollas, 1992, p. 141). S recognizes that 'this cunt is only a cul-de-sac, it has no interior to it, no complex folding of skin layering its way to my insides. I present the doctors with a medical model of my cunt, a cut version, with no inside to the body, just a surface representation for diagnostic familiarity' (p. 141). For Schwartz and Bollas, Plath also 'announces in her works an absence at the centre of her being' (Schwartz and Bollas, 1979, p. 180). They point out that Plath illustrates a 'machine-like' adherence to ritual, 'an exaggeration perhaps of her true defensive functioning, but nonetheless a poignant depiction of how she feels she must exert self control' (p. 181). 'Not surprisingly,' however, 'the defense becomes the enemy, the machinelike self receives a brutal and haunting attack from Plath in "The Applicant"' (p. 181). In this poem, Plath becomes the victim of her own depersonalizing, disengaging defence; she describes a suit that is the hard, impenetrable shell allowing nothing to seep in, withering the kernel:

> How about this suit –
>
> Black and stiff, but not a bad fit.
> Will you marry it?
> It is waterproof, shatterproof, proof
> Against fire and bombs through the roof.
> Believe me, they'll bury you in it.
> (Plath, 1965, p. 6)

However, there is ample evidence in Plath's poetry to argue against such a complete abdication of the potential for being. For me, the very *existence* of Plath's text (like those of Charlotte Perkins Gilman, Marie Cardinal, Joanne Greenberg and Ntzoke Shange *et al.*), the very act of writing, demonstrates an attempt to struggle against the anxiety of non-being, as does S's practice of self-harm. In 'Stings', we again see Plath hint that cutting can be a means to grasp this potential being and resist the depersonalizing threats of institutional forces and discourses.

> They thought death was worth it, but I
> Have a self to recover, a queen.
> Is she dead, is she sleeping?
> Where has she been,
> With her lion-red body, her wings of glass?
>
> Now she is flying
> More terrible than she ever was, red
> Scar in the sky, red comet
> Over the engine that killed her –
> The mausoleum, the wax house.
> (Plath, 1981, p. 215)

The queen that Plath believes she can recover is perhaps the kernel, the *true self* that lies protected in the hive, protected by the drones who, like false selves, are sent out into the world to perform mechanistic, uncreative functions.

S recognizes that cutting is a 'thrill' – 'A celebration, this is,' she says, alluding further to Plath's poem, 'Cut.' But as S asks, 'What do I celebrate when I cut?' What does Plath celebrate? A degree of control over one's boundaries and limits, a confirmation of self, a recognition of being alive, a moment of self-experience, a *'jouissance* of the true self, a bliss released through the finding of specific objects that free idiom to its articulation' (Bollas, 1992, p. 17). For S, cutting can be a playful, creative act. She says, 'it gives me pleasure to laugh when he takes my little cunts so seriously. It gets him all twisted up inside. I can see his worry, his *uncertainty*. He is no longer so sure of himself' (p. 142). For Plath, too there is a creative element in her self-harm, even if, like S, the enjoyment seems to be heavily imbued with a sense of irony.

> Dying
> Is an art, like everything else.
> I do it exceptionally well.
>
> I do it so it feels like hell.
> I do it so it feels real.
> (Plath, 'Lady Lazarus', 1965, p. 9)

In Plath's *The Bell Jar*, Esther Greenwood attempts to commit suicide by swimming so far out into the ocean that she believes a return to shore to be impossible. Abandoning her attempt, yet still suffering from a great deal of (self-inflicted) pain and strain, Esther describes:

> As I paddled on, my heartbeat boomed like a dull motor in my ears.
> I am I am I am.
>
> (Plath, 1963, p. 167)

This moment of being is recorded and remembered, again when Esther is facing death. At the funeral of a friend from her institution she relates, 'I took a deep breath and listened to the old brag of my heart. I am I am I am' (Plath, 1963, p. 256). Notice here that the mere act of *breathing*, 'when experienced and enjoyed', as Winnicott would say (1991, p. 69), can serve as a creative act re-affirming the ontological status of the subject.[7]

The play, the uncertainty, the integration of psyche-soma and the realization of being, are all characteristic of Winnicott's *potential space*, a concept of which Bollas makes extensive, yet typically idiomatic, use. Here, in this third or intermediate area, creative articulations of subjectivity can be realized; it is a place that is created through dialogue between the internal and the external worlds and between subjects. This potential space is a shared reality, populated with – it is hoped – an endless variety of objects and subjects; a place that is both me and not-me, where the subject learns that sustained paradox can have positive value. For Bollas, this place is where the meanings of the world and its objects reside, 'where subject meets thing, to confer significance in the very moment that being is transformed by the object' (Bollas, 1992, p. 18). It is also where subjects meet, 'two very complex creatures are at play: idiom-to-idiom' (Bollas, 1992, p. 28).

When this area is misappropriated it leads 'to a pathological condition in which the individual is cluttered up with persecutory elements of which he has no means of ridding himself' (Winnicott, 1971, p. 103; Schwartz and Bollas, 1979, p. 200), and perhaps cutting allows a space through which one may release such objects. S cuts to challenge boundaries, not only the skin-boundary between inner and outer worlds, but also the boundaries that prevent her from entering the space of creative play. When doctor's discourse becomes less authoritarian – 'he is no longer sure of himself' – it creates the potentiality for such a space for S to enter. In their analysis of Plath, Schwartz and Bollas also believe that 'Plath could imagine such a space for herself, as she could imagine tenderness, playfulness, wit' (p. 200).

'IF I COULD BLEED, OR SLEEP!'

Another useful way of looking at self-harm and Plath's poetry is offered by Marike Finlay-de Monchy (1995), who discusses auto-mutilation using André Green's terms of *l'anxiété rouge*, red horror that is related to an attack on the body, and *l'anxiété blanche*, the white horror of non-being. For the hospitalized patient, red horror provides a moment of relief; spilling red blood upon the sanitary white sheets, white nurses, white doctors, and white walls of the hospital or the myriad of other institutions that deny the realization of being, provides a momentary respite from the threat of subjective annihilation. Notice how such imagery appears when S describes another patient's experience of cutting:

L cut herself on the upper left arm, just below the shoulder, in a very special secret place, and the blood flowed all the way down her arm, trickling off her finger into her bowl of cereal, mingling with the milk and cornflakes. She stirred and stirred. What a shock! Who could dare to look at this! It was enough to bring a horrified silence to the breakfast room. A mummy nurse led her away from her bowl of milk, but the men – ha! – they could not move. They can't take this blood, they can't deal with this, our cunt, that moves around our bodies to new secret places.   (Bollas, 1992, p. 140)

Red and white imagery is abundant in Plath's poetry. Like L dropping and swirling blood in a bowl of milk, in many of Plath's poems we see drips or streaks of red punctuating whiteness. In 'Cut', Plath describes her thumb,

> The top quite gone
> Except for a sort of hinge
>
> Of skin
> A flap like a hat,
> Dead white.
> Then that red plush. . . .

In 'Contusion', 'Colour floods to the spot, dull purple/ The rest of the body is all washed out,/ The colour of pearl' (Plath, 1981, p. 235). And for Plath, as for S and the other women on the hospital ward, an explosion of red can shock and defy the patriarchal authority figures; after describing at length in 'Lady Lazarus' how she is merely 'flesh and bone', a suicide-case subjected to the control of 'Herr Doktor . . . Herr Enemy', Plath warns:

> Beware.
>
> Out of the ash
> I rise with my red hair
> And I eat men like air.

However, *l'anxiété rouge* does not always offer a simple, acceptable remedy to *l'anxiété blanche*. As the story of L's above demonstrates, it may also be the case that while proving a degree of relief for the white-gowned patients in the hospital, there are those for whom the white setting of the hospital provides a defence against the threat of meaningful experience. As Winnicott and Bollas recognize, entry into the potential space can be a frightening experience, fraught with the anxiety of uncertainty and the dissolution of boundaries. For some (many?) subjects the very *possibility* of ontological realization and meaning is too much to bear and to be avoided at all cost.

The poems of Plath's that for me most dramatically portray the struggles between red and white horror are 'Tulips' and 'Poppies in July', both from *Ariel*. In 'Tulips', Plath takes solace in the white horror of institutional non-being.

> The tulips are too excitable, it is winter here.
> Look how white everything is, how quiet, how snowed-in
> I am learning peacefulness, lying by myself quietly
> As the light lies on these white walls, this bed, these hands.
> I am nobody; I have nothing to do with explosions.
> I have given my name and my day-clothes up to the nurses
> And my history to the anaesthetist and my body to the surgeons. . . .
>
> They bring me numbness in their bright needles, they bring me sleep.
> Now I have lost myself I am sick of baggage –
>
> (Plath, 1981, p. 160)

White dominates the environment; white lids hide her eyes – 'Stupid pupil, it has to take everything in'. The red tulips, which promise to cut through the white and bring the hint of life to her environment, are unwelcome and perceived as a threat.

> I didn't want flowers. I only wanted
> to lie with my hands turned up and be utterly empty. . . .
>
> The tulips are too red in the first place, they hurt me.
> Even through the gift paper I could hear them breathe
> Lightly, through their white swaddlings, like an awful baby,
> Their redness talks to my wound, it corresponds.
> They are subtle: they seem to float, though they weigh me down.
> Upsetting me with their sudden tongues and their colour,
> A dozen red lead sinkers round my neck. . . .

And I see myself, flat, ridiculous, a cut-paper shadow
Between the eye of the sun and the eyes of the tulips,
And I have no face, I have wanted to efface myself.
The vivid tulips eat my oxygen.

Before they came the air was calm enough,
Coming and going, breath by breath, without any fuss.
Then the tulips filled it up like a loud noise. . . .

The tulips should be behind bars like dangerous animals. . . .

(Plath, 1981, pp. 161–2)

The tulips, like her blood, like the 'awful baby' and the rest of her internal contents, are wrapped up in a thin, white membrane, waiting – or threatening – to erupt to the surface. This metaphor of a thin membrane also appears regularly in Plath's poems; in 'Cut', for example, she describes 'I have taken a pill to kill/ The thin/ Papery feeling' (Plath, 1981, p. 235). 'Tulips' offers many parallels with S's narrative: the 'two-lips', in the word-play parlance of the French feminists, represent women's way of speaking with multiple voices, so that Plath's tulips, like S's cuɴt, draws together slashing, sexuality and the potential for plural, idiomatic meaning. The tulips correspond to her wound and to those 'sudden tongues' that threaten to erupt from a gap and speak. There is also a distinction to be made here, I think, between a mechanical breathing that is performed merely to keep the subject alive – 'Before they came the air was calm enough,/ Coming and going, breath by breath, without any fuss' – and the type of breathing that the tulips are engaged in, eating the oxygen, hungry not just to stay alive but to enjoy the experience of living.

Finally, in 'Poppies in July' we again see the red flowers paradoxically as both a *threat to* and a *release from* the white horror of institutional non-being.

Little poppies, little hell flames,
Do you do no harm?

You flicker. I cannot touch you.
I put my hands among the flames. Nothing burns.

And it exhausts me to watch you
Flickering like that, wrinkly and clear red, like the skin of a mouth.

A mouth just bloodied.
Little bloody skirts!

There are fumes that I cannot touch.
Where are your opiates, you nauseous capsules?

If I could bleed, or sleep! –
If my mouth could marry a hurt like that!

Or your liquors seep to me, in this glass capsule,
Dulling and stilling.

But colourless. Colourless.

                                            (Plath, 1981, p. 203)

There emerges in the narratives of Plath and S a pattern of oscillation between defences, from the comfort and relief of white horror to the celebration and relief of red horror and back. Plath first pleads for the poppies to make her feel – she puts her hands in the flame but 'nothing burns'. It exhausts her to watch the flowers, as in 'Tulips', and she longs for the colourless opiates, the nauseous capsules. But she is torn, caught between conflicting desires: 'If I could bleed, or sleep!'. She cries to opiates, capsules and liquors to dull her senses, yet she also longs to speak through the wound of experience, the poppies 'like the skin of a mouth'. This mouth is the cut. It articulates experience, and shouts in defiance. It has skin and therefore sets a boundary, but it is also an orifice allowing the flow and exchange of elements between worlds. The exclamation, 'If my mouth could marry a hurt like that!' succinctly expresses the desire, shared by Plath and S, to negotiate the spaces constructed in and through writing and self-harm, auto-biography and auto-mutilation and the potential experiences that these enable.

NOTES

1. I am grateful to Professor Robert M. Young, Caroline Tapping, Joseph Scalia and Lucinda Mitchell and especially Dr Sue Vice of the University of Sheffield for their constructive comments.
2. I will not here attempt to reduce Bollas's terms and concepts, such as *idiom*, into concise, and I think shrivelled and lifeless, definitions. As it will become clear in this

chapter, I believe that Bollas himself plays with these terms in his own idiomatic manner – and I think he wishes for his readers to do the same, rather than doctrinally accepting any singular meaning. He reminds us that 'our words often need displacing (as I may be doing with Winnicott's phrase "true self" by substituting "idiom" for it) because the overusage of a term, thought transitionally essential to individual and collective efforts of objectifying the signified, eventually loses its meaningfulness through incantatory solici- tation, devaluing any word's unthought potential' (Bollas, 1992, p. 64).

3. While I do not wish to engage in an analysis of Plath-the-poet, there is evidence to suggest that Plath did, at least once, purposefully cut herself in such a manner, though the usually private nature of self-harm and the speculative mythologizing of 'Plath' make any definitive statement as to the occurrence or frequency of this impossible. In *Letters Home*, Plath's mother writes:

> One unforgettable morning, I noticed some partially healed gashes on her [Sylvia's] legs. Upon my horrified questioning, she replied, 'I just wanted to see if I had the guts!' Then she grasped my hand – hers was burning hot to the touch – and cried passionately, 'Oh, Mother, the world is so rotten! I want to die! Let's die together!'   (p. 124)

4. Although this present chapter is not the appropriate place to elucidate this difference, I use the term 'dialogue' in the a sense derived from Russian literary critic M. M. Bakhtin.

5. Although I return to this image frequently below, I think that much more can be, certainly *needs* to be said with regard to the image of the cut and the explicit connection Bollas makes between self-harm and sexuality. This connection is re-enforced by the data offered in every study that informs my reading of self-harm (from the mid-1960s to the present day) that, by an overwhelming majority, it is women who practise cutting.

6. To an extent, this includes Schwartz and Bollas's claim, in 'The absence at the center: Sylvia Plath and suicide,' that 'Plath created in her poetry a world in which she could no longer find the possibility of survival' (p. 181).

7. In *Playing and Reality*, Winnicott explains that creativity is

> something that can be looked at as a thing in itself, something that of course is necessary if an artist is to produce a work of art, but also something that is present when *anyone* . . . looks in a healthy way at anything or does anything deliberately, such as making a mess with faeces or prolonging the act of crying to enjoy a musical sound. It is as present as much in the moment-by-moment living of a backward child who is enjoying breathing as it is in the inspiration of an architect who suddenly knows what it is that he wishes to construct.
>   (Winnicott, 1991, p. 69)

REFERENCES AND FURTHER READING

Alexander, P. (1991) *Rough Magic: A Biography of Sylvia Plath*. New York: Viking.

Axelrod, S. G. (1990) *Sylvia Plath: The Wound and the Cure of Words.*
    Baltimore, MD: The Johns Hopkins University Press.
Bakhtin, M. M. (1981) *The Dialogic Imagination: Four Essays* (trans C.
    Emerson and M. Holquist). Austin, TX: University of Texas Press.
Bakhtin, M. M. (1986) *Speech Genres and Other Late Essays* (trans. V. W.
    McGee, (Eds) C. Emerson and M. Holquist). Austin, TX: University of
    Texas Press.
Bassnett, S. (1987) *Sylvia Plath.* London: Macmillan.
Berman, J. (1985) *The Talking Cure: Literary Representations of Psychoanal-
    ysis.* New York: New York University Press.
Bollas, C. (1987) *The Shadow of the Object: Psychoanalysis of the Unthought
    Known.* New York: Columbia University Press.
Bollas, C. (1989) *Forces of Destiny: Psychoanalysis and Human Idiom.*
    London: Free Association Books.
Bollas, C. (1992) *Being a Character: Psychoanalysis and Self Experience.* New
    York: Hill and Wang.
Bollas, C. (1995) *Cracking Up: The Work of Unconscious Experience.* London:
    Routledge.
Bollas, C. (1999) *The Mystery of Things.* London: Routledge.
Burnham, R. C. and Giovacchini, P. L. (1969) Symposium on impulsive
    self-mutilation: discussion. *British Journal of Medical Psychology*, 42:
    223–9.
Finlay-de Monchy, M. (1995) The horrified position: an ethics grounded
    in the affective interest in the unitary body as psyche/soma. *Body and
    Society*, 1(2): 25–64.
Kafka, J. S. (1969) The body as transitional object: a psychoanalytic study
    of a self-mutilating patient. *British Journal of Medical Psychology*, 42:
    207–12.
Kroll, J. (1975) *Chapters in a Mythology: The Poetry of Sylvia Plath.* New
    York: Harper.
Pao, P.-N. (1969) The syndrome of delicate self-cutting. *British Journal of
    Medical Psychology*, 42: 195–206.
Plath, S. (1963) *The Bell Jar.* London: Faber.
Plath, S. (1965) *Ariel.* London: Faber.
Plath, S. (1975) *Letters Home: Correspondence, 1950–1963*, A. S. Plath (Ed.).
    New York: Harper and Row.
Plath, S. (1977) *Johnny Panic and the Bible of Dreams.* London: Faber and
    Faber.
Plath, S. (1981) *Collected Poems.* London: Faber and Faber.
Podvoll, E. M. (1969) Self-mutilation within a hospital setting: a study of

identity and social compliance. *British Journal of Medical Psychology*, 42: 213–21.

Schwartz, M. M. (1993) Where is literature? *Transitional Objects and Potential Spaces: Literary Uses of D. W. Winnicott*, Peter Rudnytsky (Ed.). New York: Columbia University Press, 50–62.

Schwartz, M. M. and Bollas, C. (1979) The absence at the center: Sylvia Plath and suicide. In *Sylvia Plath: New Views on the Poetry*, Gary Lane (Ed.). Baltimore, MD: The Johns Hopkins University Press.

Winnicott, D. W. (1991 [1971]) *Playing and Reality*. London: Routledge.

Winnicott, D. W. (1992 [1949]) Mind and its relation to the psyche-soma. In *Through Paediatrics to Psychoanalysis: Collected Papers*. London: Karnac, 243–54.

Winnicott, D. W. (1992 [1952]) Anxiety associated with insecurity. In *Through Paediatrics to Psychoanalysis: Collected Papers*. London: Karnac, 97–100.

10

Painting into a Corner:
Representation as Shelter

Greg Drasler

The relationship between object and process is something I thought I knew about, being a painter; the work of making something in my studio, with intuition and anxiety, is familiar to me. But the making without knowing that Christopher Bollas explores introduced me to the ghost in my machine. Knowing a painting as an object and as a site, I can understand it as an environment, and Bollas's concept of the Transformational Object (TO) transforms objects into the kind of environment that enables a self to be a subject. The TO represents a familiar unconscious place that prescribes agency in the world and reveals the power of self-identification. To me it suggests a threshold. The perception of an object as an environment or place, a familiar state of being with both its own inertia and its own drive, thrills and confronts me as a maker, a viewer, and a subject. The reconstitution of symbol, metaphor, and trope proposed by Bollas's transformation of our understanding of the object urges me beyond a semiotic forest of signs into an allegorical poetic imagination.

My first paintings were based on images of workers, guys with jobs, culled from self-help publications such as the *How-to-Do-It Encyclopedia* and *Popular Mechanics*. The work evolved into allegorical images of the body as an accumulation of tools of the trade. Eventually I found a seemingly endless variety of objects and jobs with which to be self-identified. I was drawn to baggage, in the sense of luggage, the suitcase, as an evocative symbol for freedom of movement and the anxiety of homelessness, a place to put it all. The luxury of travel and the rootlessness of the dispossessed came to cohabit in scenes of baggage-claim areas and piles of luggage waiting to be collected. Next I began to focus on the interior of the suitcase, on images of a suitcase being packed, an allusion to the packing of a metaphor. The difference between the scuffed and scarred exterior and the plushly appointed interior seduced me into the work that has occupied me for the last ten years.

My paintings of the interiors of rooms are meditations on the empty suitcase, the same box being packed and repacked with different objects. What I call the 'Cave Paintings' (1994) are concerned with a sense of shelter and with specific accommodations, rarely with where this place is. Rooms, corners, ceilings, and doors become places into which a subject can expand, places where defences can be let down, where a subject can float into imaginative flight and unguarded repose. Like taking in a deep breath and letting it out, to internalize a place, a privacy, or a pause seems to allow consciousness, seems to allow a subject to exist. The place occupied by a subject, the place of collecting oneself, seems, like the process in an object, to embrace the material and to expand the implication of the imagination imbedded in the symbol.

I would begin these works with an elaborate ceiling, a place of dreaming, the vista when I was lying flat on my back. The appointments of the rooms dripped down from these ceilings: I was drawn to wall paintings of panoramic landscapes, tropes of nature, as if the sense of security in the painted rooms could be burnished by fixing an image of nature on the protective walls. These paintings on the room's walls gave way to patterned wallpapers, which inscribed the space with a wide range of often conflicting iconography yet maintained a pattern of inward containment. My preoccupation with regular patterns allowed me to concentrate on an elemental place of privacy and protection, the corner of a room. A tension simultaneously claustrophobic and agoraphobic is encoded in these patterned corners.

In painting one corner, I removed the iconography in the wallpaper and replaced it with geometric stripes, finding a richly coloured airless corner, but I could not get the painting to gel with the elements I had prescribed for it. It wasn't working as a place; I couldn't get into it. In a last-ditch effort to resolve it, I hung a toy truck from a rope in the centre of the image. It worked, I didn't know why or how. This was not a new device for me, but it felt different: it seemed to operate the way graffiti can on an advertisement, breaking the spell of the sell into its basic elements and making it readable.

A psychologist friend of mine asked me how my work was going. I must have assumed an odd expression; I tried to explain what had happened with the truck, and my confusion and pleasure with the new painting. My friend asked me if I had read Christopher Bollas. I hadn't, but if he had thought of this writer in relation to what I had just told him, I needed to immediately. *The Shadow of the Object: Psychoanalysis of the Unthought Known* became my companion for the next several days. I gorged myself on the first chapter, 'The transformational object' (TO). The implications of the concept made my head swim, giving me a way to reread my own work from a different place. I could now examine the intuition that had driven my work as an internal progression and process. I had a deeper and more accepting confidence and curiosity in the voice and choice of my intuition. Continuing to nibble at the text, I discovered new resonances with every rereading.

My work is finding the place to put myself in producing a subject. A place of work, a studio, houses the process of making an object, and the traffic of inside to outside and outside to inside informs the structure of my studio. This is how I had thought about a subject/object relationship (internal/external) before considering the intersubjective states suggested in Bollas's practice.

'Symptom' strikes me as a club of a word in referring to my studio. In trying to 'enjoy my symptom,' as Slavoj Zizek recommends, I must admit that my symptom is my studio. It's a place where I can do my work, where I can think about being. I am reminded of a remark by Philip Guston:

> When you go into the studio to paint, everybody is in the studio, your friends, art writers, they're all in the studio and you're just there painting. And one by one they leave until you're really alone, and then that's, that's what painting is. They leave you where you've prepared yourself to be. To paint. There is nobody there. Then, ideally, *you* leave.[1]

It is hard for me to find a grammar that would allow me to contain and expand these implications for myself. My habit is deliberately to lose myself in order to approach the familiar from a different angle. To think of images through semiotics seems clinical to me, an atomized attempt at diagrammatic relationships. I am drawn instead to allegory, with its assemblies of signs, symbols, metaphors, displacements, dramas, cycles and authority problems. Opposites attract, however, and a polar relationship has re-emerged that embodies my particular concern: I imagine myself comfortably between two extremes, agoraphobia and claustrophobia, the cardinal navigation points of my work. Being either thrown into the world or boxed up, feeling either exposed or homebound, frames my dilemma. The picture plane is the threshold on which teeter my various acts of action and delay. Whether to reveal or to obscure this place between, to illuminate it or shade it, these questions contain and hold me within the work. They define a place for me to be.

Being present and not there conjures a different attitude than that of embracing a malady with gusto. Bollas animates the unacknowledged labour of sheltering oneself in gestures like these. He reveals the necessity of building a familiar world with simultaneous transparency and opacity. How Bollas opens objects into being a place also objectifies fugitive expressions such as attitude and posture into things and thus possessions. When examining self-representation and identity this TO becomes the material and spatial 'thing' between two subjects. The light touch and circular route with which Bollas has outlined this site of interpretation engages me with its compassion and intellect. Bollas has put space in its place. Becoming familiar with the unthought known must happen somewhere.

It's a small world unless you have to clean it.   Barbara Kruger

Inventing a space, a world, is a vast undertaking, suggesting a desire for a long view, a mute identity, control. Inventing a room is different: I am seeking less a total makeover than a place for the night. After the work comes the occupation or inhabitation of the constructed place, for occupied space becomes a place. The transformation of the space of a world into a place allows the kind of subjective interplay between artist and viewer that is familiar to me. The place becomes an object of privacy that communicates subject-to-subject.

Bollas's concept of the TO bolstered my confidence in my repeated painting of interiors. I intend to produce a subject, but the unconscious production of an environment as a means of communication is not apparent to me in the moment of painting. I invent rooms and interiors that give privacy and ease to a subject, rooms that offer accommodation, rooms that are occupied. Bollas's writing helped me to see how these images express the dilemma of the self inside and the self outside, doing so through the familiar, the 'unthought known'. It also helped me to recognize the interior as a place to contain consciousness, and the self as an object that is imaginatively portable.

PAINTING INTO A CORNER

In trying to understand my painted places more elementally, I chose to eliminate the domesticating appointments of everyday comfort and the orientation provided by the whole room. Instead I began to paint myself into a corner. The corner gave me a protective structure and just enough room to breathe. Inventing disruptively designed wallpaper patterns for these protective corners, I inscribed them with inconsistencies. These were places I could imaginatively enter, in which I felt uncannily alone, yet that felt occupied. They emphasized privacy and even intimacy. In simplifying the architectural protection to a corner, I aimed to present an elemental space sealed within an image. The painted corner supplies the minimal perception of space necessary for the effect of crossing a threshold into the image. I have painted that place like the sheet music of a song, articulating it with the evocative touch and materiality of paint, as evidence of occupation and voice. Reduced form and inscribed pattern operate as texts, providing a surface for an occupant to read. The familiar is prompted by the depicted place, which one can imaginatively enter and occupy.

The symbolism of this subdued encoded form allows me to represent presence in absence. Image begins to give way to ambient texture, an accumulation of passages. It comes to feel like a record of random thoughts and notations. Lost in simplicity, an awareness surfaces of tendencies, distractions, and incorporations. Like a car alarm in the middle of the night, an anxious disruption is lulled and smoothed by a desire to dream. If I have been able to approach the unthought known, it is in these paintings.

THE FAMILIAR

The familiar that Bollas is speaking of, as I understand him, does not represent but is present. It is not easily recognized by the maker/subject. I believe that it is the familiarity of the unthought known that generates the dispersion of responses that accompanies a work of art. I view my paintings as sites in which interpretation and response are located. In this sense they are places in which subjects can interact, and they interact through the familiar. The idea of the unthought known adds a startling principle to the familiar and reveals a mute but fundamental underpinning of the subject in the artwork. I see my uses of the familiar as unreserved, and containing a dimension of alternative meaning with an opening for other significance. I find shelter in the symbolic and alternative references of painting, a place for less obvious personal thoughts.

Unconscious production, a response to existential states, can be fraught with emotion. What happens in a work of art is the production of a subject, or of a place for a subject. Through Bollas I understand my moods, the emotional environment that I wrap around myself, as a place that I try to objectify. The representation of a mood (attitude, criticality, disturbance) through a symbolically significant sign (a metaphor, a gesture, an object) or position (critical, imaginative, or supportive) needs shelter within a familiar location. Hiding in plain sight, accommodation serves both the viewer and myself. My painting suits the viewer's unconscious need to understand, to get to the bottom of something. It conforms by allowing an unconscious fit to appear as a place, housed beneath or around explicit references. Logic and knowledge can become lost in these places. Covering as much as they reveal, my paintings contain places a subject can occupy and in which I can breathe.

The use of something familiar to unlock the place within a work forms a threshold. It is an introduction, an association that breaks the ice between the viewer and me, and between me and myself. In this sense Bollas's *Shadow of the Object* changed my understanding of my own work. Beyond the recognition of everyday readability, the mechanism of insight opens a place of shelter. The same tendency that makes a mark into a gesture, or an image into a symbol, affirms the intuitive attraction between viewer and maker through the object's conjuring of a subject. The insinuation of a sense of the familiar in representation is aimed not at comfort but at depth. Disruptions cannot occur without a framing sense of order, nor can a discordant image identifiably be woven into anything but accord. My uses of domestic environments lend my paintings the sense of familiar surroundings to be disrupted and known.

The place in the work, which is informed by both a reductive sensibility of essences and an additive scheme of baroque accumulation, offers the artist privacy amid public display. A corner is reductive in relation to an interior environment, and contains a privacy for me. It is simultaneously casual and omnipotent. The embrace of restraint as an aesthetic introduces a barrier between the object and the person. Conversely, an overdetermination of meaning, through symbol, sign, and gesture, offers another kind of cover through its demand for interpretation and understanding. These strategies combine with tendencies of subversion, acting, and collecting, opening a chasm between the production and the produced. I begin to see these two intentions of expression as more related than I was able to imagine before my introduction to Christopher Bollas.

THE OBJECT

The subject, the individual, emerges out of a defensive posture into a sheltering place. (Four walls around me to hold me tight, roof over my head, in a lover's arms, perhaps even in the heat of battle, or in the moment of the dance.) The concept of the TO releases me from this interior. In linguistic terms the TO is more preposition than noun or verb, driving conditional applications to substantiate the idea of action or being within the object. Is this object a passage or vessel, a yardstick, or a fragrance? A will to categorize this shape-shifter object puts me through the paces. I am reminded of the golem and the rabbi, who conjured up unformed matter to lend him a hand. I like building places that do not require disclaimers, but I am reconciling myself to the idea that they *are* disclaimers.

Does the TO inspire its own interior co-ordinates? Does it contain a room of its own? The object seems to be a place. I construct subjectivities expressing my shifting needs for survival. Will I occupy this painting or will it occupy me? The shadow and its associations with Plato's cave supply a conditional limit that at this point I find consoling. That limit seems to accommodate claustrophobia and agoraphobia, the squeeze and the tease, accumulation and essence, as material prescriptions for another character.

The investigation of a specific site is a matter of extracting concepts out of existing sense-data through direct perceptions. . . . One does not impose, but rather expose the site . . . the unknown areas of sites can best be explored by artists.   Robert Smithson[2]

REPRESENTATION AS SHELTER

Once that threshold has been crossed, the appointment of the place, its particular breathability, the height of the upholstery and the polish on the floor, facilitate particular qualities of occupation and habitation. The place has been outfitted. A tight space or a high and wide one will lead eventually to the prescribed and inscribed agency that the space allows an occupant. Sunlight cast on the wall becomes an object of the day. The corner, a joining line between the walls, describes integral strength, privacy and isolation in the crease of a room. To speak of rooms and interior rather than space in a general sense gives specific determined character to a potential occupant.

In the same way that I have been able to use Bollas's writings as texts for understanding my painting, I like to use painting as a place to understand the construction of self-accommodation. I hope I have described the effort of looking for a little cover within a public practice that leaves the maker room to move and breathe. Between what I paint and what I represent exists a gap that I define as an interior space. The 'space between' is rarely public, and the appointments and accommodations contained there are various. That is where I mean to represent myself. In contrast to Buckminster Fuller's dictum 'I seem to be a verb', I seem to be a preposition. Hiding in plain sight, agoraphobia, expressions of the void, and the making of aesthetic equivalents are common not only in my painting but in contemporary cultural production. Coded meanings and hermetic practices aim at the desubstantiation of the objective world in order to conduct a transcendent life above, below, outside, or inside the process. This happens by making an object transformational.

I use representation to contain a place that provides a subject with shelter and occupation. The navigational aspects of perspective provide entry to a picture allowing a sensory body access to a space. The unthought fit of the maker's measurements on the made gives dimension to that place between representation and presence.

In the leap from the internally familiar to the externally discursive, the desire we express, as psychological beings, acknowledges and transforms the pain and struggle documented in the case studies with which Bollas gives dimension to his insights. With gratitude and respect for these accumulated efforts, I hope to have shared some of the revelations these insights have inspired in my practice of painting. It is a constant for me to try to translate whatever I am reading into its implications on and for my studio practice. Bollas's writings are the first I have read that acknowledge the dynamic potential of interior space as a place with a life of its own, often separate from my obvious intentions. His sensitivity to the subtle articulation of the power of the interior life has allowed him to express these concepts in such a clear and fluid way as to need minimal translation.

NOTES

1. Philip Guston, speaking in Michael Blackwood's film *Philip Guston: A Life Lived*, 1980.
2. Robert Smithson, quoted in Lucy R. Lippard, *The Lure of the Local: Senses of Place in a Multicentered Society* (New York: W. W. Norton & Co.), p. 183.

11

Cracking Up the Audience

Kate Browne

The writing of Christopher Bollas has become a great influence on my theatrical work and has helped me galvanize many of the concepts I've been exploring, including my approach to aesthetic form and my relationship with the audience. I frequently suggest to my actors that they take a look at Bollas. An image from a rehearsal that still makes me laugh is of an actor, dressed as a polar bear, sitting quietly in the corner, reading *Cracking Up*.

> In the sense that the dream experience is a highly sophisticated form of theatre that challenges all our critical capacities, the ego which fashions the dream setting reflects an organized and avowing unconscious whose discourse, as Lacan has argued, is structured like a language: the speech of a visual theatric that both represents and veils thought. The syntactical forms of this Other are the dream, the joke, the fantasy, the symptom, the intrusive gap in the subject's discourse, and the meta-discourse of all object relating.
>
> (*Shadow of the Object*, p. 67)

I have always felt constrained by narrative, plot-driven theatre: it tends to spoil language and put audiences to sleep. The linear form doesn't really ask that much of the audience, doesn't challenge them or upset them. Instead, by engaging only the rational, conscious level of their brains, it permits them to be distant watchers of a theatre that plays servant to the freeze-dried psychological arcs of stock characters.

Today's culture is drenched in narrative. It's all too easy to see our lives reflected in clichéd magazine personality profiles, memoirs, plays, sitcoms, people reciting their life stories on TV tell-alls. It's all too easy to understand our lives through these shorthand narratives, neat little parcels of experience, their characters tidy snapshots of the people we are supposed to identify with or not, us and the others, the employee or the boss, the poor or the rich, the abuser or the abused. These narratives, in a very unsurprising way, educate us in what we already know.

A friend once said, Freud ruined the theatre of the twentieth century by placing the onus on the psychological state of the character. I think she's right (though perhaps it's not all Freud's fault) that the lead character's psychological story has become the paramount thing. 'Unfortunately, Freud was less than interested in the specific formal intelligence or aesthetic of any person's ego, so little that even though creating a dream is an aesthetic action, Freud preferred to see it solely as one of necessity' (*Cracking Up*, p. 41). From the playwright to the director to the actor, the focus is now intensely inward – on building the character – not outward – on experimenting with the aesthetic form of the play and unnerving the audience. Because this process only confirms what we already know about personal morality and uses an aesthetic form constrained by stringent structure, people rarely become alarmed in today's narrative theatre.

The narrative play tends to keep us from our anxieties, from what is buried in us, from what we think we do not know, or have hidden within ourselves. The belief that this is good and that anxiety is bad, something for playwrights, actors and directors to avoid or sidestep, is the crux of the matter. Rather than using anxiety as a catalyst in opening our mind to creativity, the neatly organized, accessible and friendly play comforts and pampers us.

It's always been my contention that theatre should be different. It should stir things up. It should lure people in, then sideswipe them. It should get inside their heads and their unconscious, bop them in a way that short circuits their thought process, causing cognitive mishaps and a multitude of mental spinoffs. Bollas has given me a blueprint to the workings of the unconscious and what it responds to, how to put it in a state or mood. His work has educated me in the uses of anxiety and nothingness in contemporary theatre. I have always wanted my work to wield the psychological power of trauma, as well as exhibit the nothingness, the empty spaces, that are present in our lives. These are the times when we are no longer able to choose or verbalize words, and must rely on the millions of particles of images entering the brain.

That nothingness is always there, whether it momentarily mutes speech, swallows up memory, refuses to yield an idea struggling to come into thought, or receives all the faint and discarded images and words that pass by in the back of my mind on an endless conveyor belt, from the unconscious passing briefly through consciousness to oblivion. (*Cracking Up*, p. 59)

It is in this endless passing unconscious, the audience's mental processes, where I attempt to get them to turn off their well-trod routes and travel an unknown road. My plays are visceral pieces that create a mnemonic theatre of hallucinogenic clarity, where audiences unexpectedly find themselves experiencing their own creative process,

> ... that occasion when a person is shaken by an experience into absolute certainty that he has been cradled by, and dwelled with, the spirit of the object, a rendezvous of mute recognition that defies representation.   (*Shadow of the Object*, p. 30)

After a performance one night of my play *The Lost Tensions*, in Boston, a woman in the audience told me, 'I was moved in a way that I could not fully comprehend.'

My work's relationship to the audience is an 'unconscious communication', which endeavours to make them part of the lived experience on stage, without asking them to come on stage or talk back to the actors. One way to do this is to move from something that is known or soothing – the actors sitting down to eat a meal, or meeting the gaze of the audience with a welcoming smile – to a state that overloads the audience's mental capacities with the unexpected, in an attempt to cause disorientation and anxiety. This is an uncomfortable state to be in, but one that is very creative. If I can put the audience in this state, if they allow themselves to be put in this state, then I have tapped into a wild and unclaimed territory that has yet to be digested by rational thought.

> Because a latent thought is an unconscious idea, it differs from the way the conscious mind, with its discretionary powers of judgment, rationally bifurcates lived experience. It is laden with psychic materials that consciousness knows to be crucial to its own development: the stuff of somatic registrations, bodily recollections or dispositions, instinctual excitations, sensed memories of previously lived experience, elicited laws of being and relating that have been part of the individual's history, object–relational evocations in which specific unconscious relations to persons in one's past life are brought partly into being again, and so on.   (*Cracking Up*, pp. 48–9)

Sufficiently jarring the audience's thought process puts different gears into motion than those required to drive the token interpretive skills required by most narrative theatre. These different brain gears dig deep through conscious thought down to a level where creative impulse and images are generated. It is kind of like a huge seismographic reverberation in the audience, a giant fulfilling fuck moment, a churning up of a lush abundance of lost images and sensations, and the point to the theatre I make.

HOW I DEVELOP MY THEATRE PIECES

Text and images (deep memory)

Our collective agreement that the world is shared by us all is matched by another poetic license, that the terms we use to describe the world are adequate to represent it. The mathematician who writes 'let $X=1$' acknowledges the arbitrary nature of the symbolic. Language functions through illusion.   (*Shadow of the Object*, p. 30)

I grew up near the Village of Uno in central Pennsylvania. The Village of One. U-N-O, Uno, pronounced 'you know', like 'you know something'. My first word joke 'that acknowledges the arbitrary nature of the symbolic' (*Shadow of the Object*, p. 30). As a child I remember my father standing on the porch in the summertime, perhaps thinking about mowing the lawn, reciting Gertrude Stein. I sat on the lawn staring at the green grass while I heard 'a rose is a rose is a rose', the words and images smashing together in the hot sun.

As a child, listening to my father recite Stein, I thought I would be a poet. I was never much for narrative. I had always had difficulty reading and although I read a lot I often accidentally missed words or skipped whole lines on the page. One sentence would become part of the next without my realizing I had skipped commas, periods, whole phrases. So I didn't learn narrative in a traditional way or even read traditional narrative in a traditional way. In a sense, without knowing it, I was breaking form.

When I was in my thirties, a doctor realized that although I had 20/20 vision, my eyes each saw at different levels. They always had. My horizon never met. For me the horizon was a line in constant flux, jagged and jumping up and down. When I read the newspaper, I looked at each word individually by covering up the others with my hand. My language had become fractured. In a way this was a gift. I was in a way experiencing the conscious world in the form that I wish to express it.

> . . . inevitably we must turn to the aesthetics of form – the particular
> way something is conveyed – as an important feature of unconscious
> communication.   (*Cracking Up*, p. 41)

I work within visual and spoken rhythms and patterns, word play, visual
and word jokes, a kind of high jinx of the mind. The plays I create are full
of surprises and they hang in what I think of as the territory of the stage.
In the beginning of a new piece, the territory of the stage is the rectangle in
which I draw the images that go with the text. Later this becomes the
three-dimensional performance space where the play takes place. It is a
territory that is wide open, very American, a place where anything can
happen.

I begin my plays by writing text and dialogue and drawing images of
how the stage should look. The words and images develop along side one
another, equally, neither carrying more weight than the other. A little later
in rehearsals, spontaneous gestures and movement are added. The movement bounces off and reverberates with the language. The piece is then
musically scored, and rehearsals begin again. At the same time, the props,
set and lighting design are also being developed.

A sense of everyday existence is juxtaposed with abstract reality so that
these elements read to the audience as both oddly familiar and a fractured
abstraction. Take props, as an example. In *The Cassandra Project*, a blue
bird that sits on a rudimentary tree of three grey planks crudely nailed
together is paraded slowly around the stage like a saint. Later, a man shoots
a small chair with a pistol, picks the chair up, and hugs it to his body as his
face very slowly contorts into a mute cry. Later still, 24 pink rubber ears fly
out of a red hole in a green mound, then a man walks on stage and carefully
numbers each ear like a table at a banquet, with a plastic numbered card on
a metal stand. These are all symbols without explicit meaning, which allows
the audience to enter into the dreamscape of the stage and make it their
own. A dreamscape or nightmare where the audience can experience a
series of creative surges or 'psychic intensities' that tap into their deep
memory, as well as their own creative thought processes.

> Indeed, the more profound a psychic intensity, the less permanent its
> registration in consciousness, for the ideas deriving immediately from
> it soon give birth to a plenitude of further and divergent thoughts
> which disseminate in countless ways.   (*Cracking Up*, p. 53)

Working with actors (deep memory)

For the actors in my theatre pieces, a movement must be specific, clear and readable to the audience, familiar, but also peculiar and strange. Actors should be open to their unconscious, and its changing associations, in order to impart or transfer it to other actors during the long rehearsal process. This means that they must not think about character and plot, but instead be aware of the endless snippets of thoughts, images, textures going through their unconscious, while they concentrate on their bodies repeating the movement and gestures they are learning for the play.

Bollas's description of the analytical couple – the psychoanalyst and the patient – best explains this bond I am speaking of when I talk about sparks of creativity transferred by the actors in rehearsal.

> Even though each will have only a fractional conscious understanding of the other at any one time, both are nonetheless deeply involved with each other, and although unconscious communication is by definition out of sight and outside of consciousness, any well-functioning analytical couple would say that paradoxically what they cannot bring into consciousness about their collaboration – that which is always unconscious – is the deepest matrix of their work together.
>
> (*Cracking Up*, pp. 46–7)

If the unconscious is in play during the rehearsals and performances, there is a greater possibility of it awakening in the audience. A spark that runs through the group also runs through the audience as a kind of chain of unconscious transference.

I ask actors to see where they are in the territory of the stage, to look especially at the minute details where their hands are, where their fingers are, and is this finger moving quickly or incredibly slowly or has it stopped for a second on the last word in the sentence, or for a count of 20 seconds in silence? It is these details that the mind absorbs and that the body remembers, and their repetition on stage becomes a ritual act that has no attachment to a culture beyond the play's own internal world.

I want actors not to think like characters, but to perform precise movements without having to think about them, because once they're in the groove interesting things happen. A good analogy comes from sports. As athletes like to remind each other, 'thinking is stinking'. Take basketball: you practise your jump shot over and over, getting the body to remember just how the hands should hold the ball, the legs should position and jump, the shoulders square to the basket, so that come game time, you don't have to think about these things. If, during the game, you think a lot about who you are – your own personal narrative or character as a basketball player, you will surely miss your best game shot. If, however, you let yourself run on automatic, letting the body remember, not letting the brain get in the way, then you will play the game in a very magical and surprising way.

In workshops we run through and run through and run through movement until something makes sense in what we are creating and then that tiny bit is added to the piece. To be repeated throughout like a musical composition, to be done slowly and speeded up. Then we continue, we run through and run through and run through until bang there it is again a gesture to be used by a single actor or by the group. It is about waiting and patience, looking and listening for a pattern to be developed and broken.

For some actors this is an extremely painful process. 'Why? Why? Why am I doing this? Why? Why? Why do I walk from here to there?' Some actors even get panicky about this patient, silent process. The pieces are very individual because the actors who make them up put themselves into them, not a character or life story, just bits and pieces of what they do every day internally. I am asking the actors to make a piece out of threads, weaving and weaving the unconscious dialogue that we are having as a group in the workshop and later with the audience.

Props, set and lights

When I say that my work is very open I mean that, although the plays run like clockwork from moment to moment, the aesthetic form leaves openings for the audience to enter the play. Props are symbols that lead the way into these openings. They are signposts or guides that say to the audience, 'Here, over here. Come down this path with me.' The actors treat the props as if they hold considerable power. The props make sudden and unexplained entrances on stage, through an open hatch in the ceiling, for instance, or holes in the walls of the set. They are a fluid set of symbols unattached to any culture beyond the internal world of the work.

Take, for example, the 24 pink rubber ears mentioned earlier. The ears are not identified as belonging to anyone, no comment is made on how they became separated from their original owners, or why they are suddenly catapulted out of a red hole in a green mound and litter the stage, or why an actor carefully numbers them like banquet tables, or why two actors then dance wildly among them. But the ears morph from unknown object to labelled object to ground covering pushing the audience at every evolution, not to interpret or identify the reason the ears are in the play but to turn to some strange and bizarre place in their own minds.

Individual props mean one thing to one person, another thing to someone else.

> the idiomatic significance of any signifier to the individual: 'my' signifiers will be different from someone else's. As we meet up with objects – literally a tree, or the word 'tree' – the signifier divides into separate ideas, which in turn divide into still other ideas.
>
> (*Cracking Up*, p. 62)

People's conversations after a performance about their disparate visions of what they saw become a chain of events where each vision from each person leads to a new vision. 'Each idea is a kernel of some truth. As we speak the idea, it gives birth to other thoughts, each of which is itself a new kernel of yet another truth' (*Cracking Up*, p. 62)

Like the words, the props hang in the set, the territory of the stage. It is important to bring up the meaning of territory again, because the set and lights represent it to the audience. It's a territory rather than landscape because landscape denotes tamed and manicured space, a well-planned garden, and territory is an environment that is wild and unexplainable. Like the actors' movements, it is familiar yet unsettling. The familiar living room that is not quite right, dislocated and disturbing, causes a reverberation and schism in the brain.

The set and lights are a visual territory of the mind. This returns to the concept that these are created dreamscapes with many juxtapositions and fluid paths. The theatre I create is, like life, full of visual surprises. These surprises are like dreams, but on stage they are outside the head. When we see a surprise happen in the territory of the stage, the unexplainable moment, it carries a great deal of weight: 'such experiences crystallize time into a space where subject and object appear to achieve an intimate rendezvous' (*Shadow of the Object*, p. 31).

MY APPROACH TO AUDIENCES

While such moments can subsequently be flung into hermeneutical explication, they are fundamentally wordless occasions, notable for the

density of the subject's feeling and the fundamentally non-representational knowledge of being embraced by the aesthetic object.

(Shadow of the Object, p. 31)

Earlier I talked about my work's unconscious communication with the
audience, and my endeavours to include the audience in the dreamscape on
stage. Following is an example of how I attempted to do that in a scene in
Needles that begins with the sound of crickets.

The sound of crickets holds nostalgic power. It is a potent noise, much
used in theatre, from Tennessee Williams, where it evokes sultry Southern
summer nights, to Sam Shepard, whose too loud California crickets in *True
West* are commented on by the character Austin as in fact being too loud.
All this was my starting point. What I wanted to do was use cricket-sounds
to begin the expected mood, then turn that mood on its head by juxtaposing
it with elements that would overload the audience's rational thought
process, surprise and move them unexpectedly.

In the scene in *Needles*, the actors have just finished a meal in a set that
has taken on an oddly familiar and homey atmosphere. The audience begins
to hear the sound of crickets. They are lulled by the sounds that evoke a
restful summer evening. Then an actress wearing a low-cut, fluffy bird-like
dress begins to lower light bulbs through holes in the ceiling of the set. She
lowers them slowly, one by one, in no particular order. They begin to blink
like fireflies as the crickets get louder, and the sounds and lights wrap
everyone in a comforting blanket of nostalgia.

Then everything begins to change. The light bulbs are no longer in the
background but become a visual obstruction, blinking brightly in the actors'
faces. The sound changes from crickets to electrical crackling. The light
bulbs begin to blink slow and fast with no obvious pattern the audience can
comprehend. To add to this disorientation, as actors bump into the bulbs,
the bulbs swing slightly and create moving shadows, which transform the
set's homey feel into an unbalanced, dream-like environment. The audience's thought process begins to unravel. The blinking stops, silence.

The actors step away from the light bulbs and towards the audience.
The actors meet the gaze of the audience and smile a comforting smile,
once again soothing the audience. The actors move closer to the audience.
In the silence, there are intermittent sounds of electrical crackling. The
actors' gaze begins to oscillate between smiling and menacing. Closer still
to the audience, one actor speaks softly to them, a nonsense verbal imagery,
'Many people think that it is an impossibility that shoes fall from the sky.'
(Silence. Smile.) 'Metaphysically impossible.' (Silence. Smile. Then he

speaks with hate.) 'Quiet. Isn't it?' Shortly thereafter, he makes some proclamations, 'The world is round.' The others join in menacing the audience, 'Yippee. Yippee.' He proclaims, 'It's not square.' 'Yippee. Yippee.' Then he commands loudly, 'Bring me my fork!' He is handed a rat.

The audience has now received an onslaught of words and images, their brains are discombobulated and working overtime. The interpretation of what's been experienced, in a very American and democratic way, is up for grabs. There is a fair amount of anxiety in the air, then perched high above the actors, the actress in the fluffy bird-like dress holds up a poster bearing the word *vanilla* in large graphic letters. As if it were a word they had never seen, or a language they did not speak, the actors try to sound out the sounds and syllables of *vaaa-nnnn-illl-aaa*.

At this moment, performance after performance, audience members began silently mouthing the word *vanilla* along with the actors. The expressions on the audience members' faces were completely blank as if they were participating in a mute, religious ritual. It seemed to me that a gap had been bridged and everyone was now participating in the dream. I think this is what happens with *vanilla* and the nervous, unyielding overload that oscillates between menacing and comforting the audience. It causes a cosmic pool of anxiety alongside moments of nothingness. The audience is participating in a way that they do not fully comprehend or even know.

We are not in continuous unbroken discourse with our self, but, rather, constantly breaking the textures of inner experience with the movement of nothingness, with abrupt questions, diversions, turning points, ruptures, and elisions, and these are part of the pattern of the inevitably tattered fabric of being.   (*Cracking Up*, p. 59)

Or, as Wilhelm says at the end of *Needles*,

Pleasures.
Beside Nothingness.
The glimmer glamour world.

REFERENCES

Bollas, C. (1987) *The Shadow of the Object*. London: Free Association Books.
Bollas, C. (1995) *Cracking Up*. New York: Hill & Wang.

Plays written and directed by Kate Browne

The Big Window, Theatre Workshop, Edinburgh Festival Fringe 1994;
    Women's Project and Productions (directed by Joan Vail Thorne), New
    York 1995.
The Cassandra Project, Bogota, Colombia; Ontological Theater, New York
    1996.
The Host Tensions, Rose Art Museum, Boston 1998.
Needles, New York Performance Works, New York 1999.
Reworking Cassandra, Gateway Theatre, Edinburgh Festival Fringe 2001.

PART III

A Conversation with Christopher Bollas

Christopher Bollas

interviewed by Anthony Molino

The following interview, which took place in London on 9–10 January 1995, explores themes taken up by Bollas mostly in *Being a Character*, his most recent book at the time.

Anthony Molino: *In his book* The Postmodern Condition, *Jean-François Lyotard, citing the work of Wittgenstein, writes: 'The social subject itself seems to dissolve in this dissemination of language games. The social bond is linguistic, but is not woven with a single thread. It is a fabric formed by the intersection of at least two (and in reality an indeterminate number of) language games, obeying different rules. . . . [T]he principle of unitotality – or synthesis under the authority of a metadiscourse of knowledge – is inapplicable.' In a similar vein, much of your work on the self also goes against the grain of any unitotality. And yet in an earlier book,* Forces of Destiny: Psychoanalysis and Human Idiom, *you put forth what you call a theory for the true self. Is there a contradiction here? As clinician and theorist, how does Christopher Bollas understand the self?*

Christopher Bollas: In *Cracking Up*, there's a chapter on this thing called *self*. Winnicott's concept of the 'true self' and what we mean by the self are not the same. The true self was just his way of designating the presence of spontaneity: the true self as gesture. The false self, the only other 'self' he wrote about in relation to the true self, indicates its presence through compliance: it describes a reactive attitude. My belief is that we have a sense of self that exists within an illusion of integration: an illusion essential to our way of life. Even those who see themselves as radical deconstructivists cannot, and do not, live a life without that illusion.

AM: *Michel Foucault has also written about postmodernism and, more or less directly, about psychoanalysis, in the contexts of his 'histories' and 'archaeologies'. In line with his thinking, where he argues for 'the insurrection of subjugated knowledges', of what he calls* anti-sciences, *where and how do you* *situate your writing? Can psychoanalysis be something other than what Foucault calls a* totalitarian theory?

CB: Already Freud's *Interpretation of Dreams*, in his writing of his self-analysis, and the reporting of his dreams to interpretation – in what was so remarkable an event, and so very fertile an occasion – doesn't support a totalitarian structure. If, like Freud, psychoanalysts write openly, if they provide enough detail, if there's enough saturation with the unconscious, then any reader will re-read and re-write a text in such a way as to undermine any thematic totality. It is those psychoanalytical writings, written with a greater degree of unconsciousness, that are, to my way of thinking, the more interesting. I include in this area the writings of Jacques Lacan, for example, where something primitive, something mythological and elusive persists, that leads one to imagine them, and open them up in so many directions. Harold Searles's writings are unconsciously rich. Each psychoanalyst must, no matter whether he or she does it consciously, re-invent psychoanalysis for themselves. It's those analysts who show the re-invention that sustain a level of creativity that's essential to the development of thinking. One can see this in certain contemporary analysts, like Andre Green, Adam Phillips, Michael Eigen, Harold Boris, James Grotstein, Joyce McDougall. All these people are recasting psychoanalysis, and re-creating it.

AM: *Along these lines, is there an element of a 'project' in your work?*

CB: I can answer that question only toward the end of my life, when I look back. I don't wish to develop a 'Christopher Bollas theory'; nor do I wish to re-use or echo terms which first served simply to establish a point I was intent on making in a single, earlier essay.

AM: *Speaking of archaeology, Freud had already used it as a metaphor for psychoanalysis. In your book,* Forces of Destiny: Psychoanalysis and Human Idiom, *you seem to be inviting something new when you write: 'Perhaps we need a new point of view in clinical psychoanalysis, close to a form of person anthropology.' In a postmodern world, where the self, for one, is described as fragmented, decentred, discontinuous, multiple . . . take your pick! – what would a 'person anthropology' entail?*

CB: It would be an analysis of any individual as a privately evolved but structured culture. It would mean that those signifiers that were currently important to an individual could be deconstructed; or, to think, when analysing someone for the first time, that we're to enter a foreign country. It's like going into a different culture with a different language. Psychoanalysis then becomes in part a process for the translation of a person's different and changing perspectives, a way of deciphering all the many rules of foreign lives, of private cultures . . .

AM: *In* Forces of Destiny *you take issue with D. W. Winnicott's notion of the true self, where he links it with the id (in juxtaposition to the false self and its connection to the ego). Yet you rarely speak of a false self; it seems, rather, that there exist only degrees of realized potential of true self, owing to the interplay of trauma and what you later, in* Being a Character, *call 'genera'. Is this so? And if it is, why resort to adjectives like 'true' and 'core'?*

CB: I resort to them because I come from a particular intellectual and analytical tradition, and have felt it important to indicate those origins. As for Winnicott, I think my critique of the link you mentioned was an incomplete critique. I think I understand why Winnicott linked the true self up with the id, as he was trying to get to something viscerally powerful and primitive. He did not want it linked to the ego because of that. On the other hand, I believe the organizational density of the true self, what I call *idiom*, is too intelligent a phenomenon to be, as it were, ascribed to the id. As a seething cauldron of primitive urges, the id did not, at least in the Freudian structural theory, have the kind of thick intelligence to it that I think exists for the true self, or indeed for idiom. Conversely, when Freud theorized the unconscious ego, he got to something which had that kind of dense intelligence to it: something that really has to do with the aesthetic organization of the self, or with the self as an aesthetic organization. Ultimately I think it is understandable why Winnicott linked his idea of the self with the id; but too much of his concept of the true self would still have to find a place in Freud's theory of the primary repressed unconscious, or later, of the unconscious ego. So, it was a failed effort, I think, to link it up to the structural theory.

AM: *Your reflections on the self, on idiom, have taken you to explore the realm of 'character', a word which appears prominently in the title of your last book. It's not a concept usually invoked by psychoanalysts . . .*

CB: I think that 'character' is an aesthetic. If our way of being refers to our very precise means of forming our world, both internal and intersubjective, then each of us is a kind of artist with his or her own creative sensibility. We know that the distinctiveness of that creation is the particular form we have brought to it. We will share many contents with other beings; we share many phenomena in common, but we render them differently, and it's the rendering of a life that is so unique to us.

It is a pleasure to express and articulate the self: there's an erotic dimension to that kind of representation. Indeed I think Freud's theory of the instinct with its source, its aim and its object is an arc . . . a pure arc . . . without any actual 'other' present in a way. But it's almost a pure arc of the pleasure of representation, because the erotics of the instinct drive is not simply in its final gratification through an object: it's the entire process . . . In order for there to be the reduction of excitation, for there to be pleasure, representation is needed.

My own view is that in the formation of character we similarly have that arc: except I would say that, instead of there being a pure line from source through aim and object, there are many lines that fragment and break, in something like a vast symphonic movement which is, in and of itself, a pleasure. It is not the end point, not what we find at the end, not the objects that reduce the excitation, that constitute the pleasure. The pleasure is in the entire movement: which none the less remains something far too complicated and condensed, too thick, to be reduced to a single meaning, or even to two or three meanings, or two or three interpretations.

AM: *What about Winnicott's distinction between the optimal progression of an ordinary human life and what he views as the superior development of the creative artist or artistic personality?*

CB: I think by 'ordinary' he means a return to the unformed existence of an unconscious. Certainly I think psychoanalysis, if it proceeds via the medium of free association, engages the analysand in a process of expression that leads consciousness to realize how extraordinary unconscious life is; in that respect, we must live dangerously, because we do take risks by allowing our unconscious life its freedom. It takes risk to speak what one thinks freely. Therefore, an analysand who is operating within the milieu of free association is living dangerously. And I believe there is a great deal to be gained from that kind of risk: not only is the free-associating analysand creating his analysis, he's creating his life. This is true to the extent that one is not operating through a process of carefully constructed narrative, which then leads the analyst to an equally carefully constructed interpretative narrative, i.e., interpretation of the transference, and so on and so forth.

It leads to something more dense and unconscious . . . more frightening, in a way, for both the analyst and analysand, in a sort of pleasurable way. . . . One does not often know consciously what to make of this, even though one has quite an acute sense that these movements are essential, intriguing, mysterious, developing . . .

AM: *There was an enormously small word in your last answer of some consequence. You said: 'If a psychoanalysis proceeds via free association . . .'. That seems to imply that an analysis could proceed differently.*

CB: There is a fundamental divergence between analysts or schools who see the analysand's free expression of thought and feeling as a priority, and those who don't. There are, in a certain sense, two paths. Along the first, this fundamental expression would have to take priority over the psychoanalyst's interpretation: without this freedom of mood, of thought, of feeling, without this density, the analysand is not going to issue a licence to the unconscious; he or she is not going to find a voice in the context of an analytical situation. For the analyst, this means remaining quiet when he or she can see certain things operating within the transference. The analyst's silence, then, is in the interest of that movement, of that evolution in the analysand which gives rise to meaningful, if limited, self-reflections, to self-generated insights. To insights, mind you, which proceed not only from the psychoanalyst, but from within the patient: insights which over time establish an intriguing relation between the analysand's production of his or her own existence, between the creation of a life through free association and the unconscious movement that informs those insights.

That's one theorization, one path psychoanalysis has taken. On the other path, which is very different but very popular at the present time, is the patient who speaks about his or her life to an analyst, who then translates that speech into a metaphor of the patient's relation to the analyst; or of a part of the patient's self in a here-and-now relation to a part of the analyst. This is something which is not difficult for well-trained psychoanalysts to do, and in my view is also very interesting and meritorious in some ways; but it offers psychoanalysts the opportunity to resolve the ambiguities of a session's unconsciousness through a kind of reliable interpretation of events as they see them taking place. This, I believe, forecloses free association in the analysand, although one could argue that the process is split off within the patient, experienced somewhere but not uttered. Still, the difference between that analysand and the one who's freely speaking is enormous. Well, this difference poses a problem. I have no idea what will happen but, perhaps as time goes on, there will be two substantially distinct traditions in psychoanalysis, and people choosing to have an analysis can have one or the other, and will then know more or less what country they're entering.

AM: *It would seem that each of those paths carries with it, perhaps unconsciously, a very different sense of what a psychoanalytic cure would entail.*

CB: The highly interpretative analyst is very embracing, and promotes a cure by object relationship, by narrative restructuring. Of course, in the best of times, the interpreting analyst is in fact illuminating important pathological structures, important transferential anxieties: and therefore there is enough truth to his exercise for it to be meaningful for an individual. A lot is gained in this kind of an analysis; if it were a complete waste of time people wouldn't stay with it. They might be drawn to it but wouldn't stay with it for such a long time. But unfortunately, there is as much lost as there is gained in this kind of an analytical procedure. What's lost is something truer to life, because in a life we don't have accompanying us, day-to-day, an interpretative companion. We do not have an analyst alongside us interpreting the interactive meaning of every one of our gestures. And so I don't see how, in the end, that kind of an analysis fits in with a human life. However interactive we are, we're living in a fundamentally solitary space where we will always be generating meanings unconsciously, and only partially understanding ourselves. It is, therefore, the first path of analysis I identified that I believe takes into consideration the full nature of a human life: in that it aims to increase unconscious creativity and to situate unconsciousness, or the interpreting part of the self, in a meaningful but modest relation to creativity; whereas the other form of an analysis operates under a very particular illusion that a partnership, between a purely interpretative self and a purely unconscious self, will exist throughout a human life.

AM: *Again on the true self, you write: 'A genetically biased set of dispositions, the true self exists before object relating. It is only a potential, however, because it depends on maternal care for its evolution.' This could read like an essentialist argument, one that some orthodox Jungians might favour. Was that your intention?*

CB: No, though I don't disagree it's an essentialist position. I am arguing that we begin life with an essential core, with a nucleus of logic . . . with logical nuclei ... or, let us say, with 'positions' waiting to come into existence, that we somehow have to account for. How can each infant be so different from any other infant? *Forces of Destiny* had on the cover sets of human fingerprints. So what is the psychic correlate of the human finger-print? I think there is something psychically as irreducibly different about each newborn as the irreducible difference of a fingerprint. And because I don't know where this intuition comes from, I rest back in the area of genetic predisposition. Of course there is a foetal existence, the incredible evolution before birth when the foetus is influenced by the world and engaged in relation to the inside of the mother's body, and to objects beyond the inside of the body. Already then the 'something' that we are is in the beginning of a process of fragmentation, of a creative fragmentation that depends on both its own creativity, as well as on the mother's and the father's medium of care: on whether objects are provided for the infant and child to use and through which to disseminate themselves.

AM: *In what you call a person's 'idiom moves', objects in the environment function both as receptors for our projective identifications and structuring agents of the mind. What is the relationship, or perhaps the difference, between these idiomatic expressions of the self and the symbolic elaboration that is the task of genera?*

CB: I think at any one moment in time, whenever we approach an object, we can say we're either going to use it for its projective potential or for its evocative integrity to structure us differently. There is a different, funda-mental orientational attitude in the subject's use of an object. In the process of our own inner unconscious evolutions, we will be using objects either to contain parts of ourself or parts of the other, or in order to break us up via the structuring dimensions that are inherent to the object's integrity. In other words, more to fragment us than to contain the break. In that way, I suppose, where the elaboration of the self is concerned, the movement of genera depends upon whether at any moment in time we're deploying the objects in our environment, or whether we ourselves are seeking to be redeployed: whether we're putting ourselves somewhere through the deployment of objects, or whether we ourselves are seeking to be thrown into a new organization.

Any child, then, who is privileged to evolve by virtue of maternal and paternal care will have as an unconscious principle the formation of genera and the evolution according to those formations. . . . Psychic genera cannot emerge within the subject unless there has been substantial support for the evolution of the subject's idiom, which is a sort of fundamental paradigm for the genera of the self.

AM: *In your writing the subjective realm of human experience is paramount, from the womb to the grave. I'm reminded of Victor Turner's etymology of the word* experience, *where he derives it from the Indo-European base* per-, *meaning 'to attempt, venture or risk', which also yields the word 'peril'. In an essay of Turner's on the anthropology of experience, he identifies the Germanic cognates of* per *in the German words 'fare', 'fear', and 'ferry'; while the Greek* perao *relates experience to 'passing through', with all the attendant implications of rites of passage. In your elaboration of the strivings of the self and the workings of genera, you seem very much attuned to this tragic quality of much of our existence, as the etymology of the word* experience *indicates.*

CB: I like this deconstruction. In a way, the Sophoclean tragic vision is of violent action that breaks things up, followed then by reflection, seeing and sizing up what's occurred. This Sophoclean vision, cast in Oedipal terms, is of devastation, and involves the realization of the unwitting dimensions of the devastation. Put in terms of Oedipus, we could argue that the entire process is true of the nature of life itself: that consciousness is blind to unconscious development, and that unconscious development is radically destructive.

You could say: 'But what is it destroying?' Perhaps it destroys all mothers and all fathers; perhaps the evolution of any self destroys what was formed for us earlier by the mother, or by the father. Perhaps any evolution is going to break the desires of the other. It is then that we create our destiny, and live it. There are objects of desire and objects of hate, objects of intimacy and corpses of the expelled; and then, when we look back, in a Sophoclean way, one could say: 'My God, what have I done? Only now I understand it all.' And we see that progression as a tragic one, or as the ordinary way in which life is lived, as something unavoidable. Thus, in the notion of existing, or of experience, are the concepts of a ruthless breaking, of an opening up, of a dissemination, of a perilous venture. And, in addition, of something which borders on a kind of reflective faith: a kind of belief, upon reflection, that what's taken place was unavoidable and essential.

AM: *Thinking back at your discussion of the erotics of self-representation and the aesthetics of the self, are these pleasures simply breaks or interludes in the* *context of this greater tragedy? How do the tragedy and pleasure play off each other?*

CB: I think representation is a pleasure; therefore, the representation of Oedipus, the Sophoclean presentation itself, is a pleasure. Whatever the contents of the tale, whatever the story, its telling is always a pleasure. This is why I think, in the end, that Freud's theory of the dream as a wish fulfilment is true: not because the contents of the dream fulfil a precise wish of the dreamer, but because the representation of the dream, its creation, the very act of dreaming, is the fulfilment of the wish. The wish is to represent. So what we do or say is always a pleasure in that sense. Yet the fact that something is pleasing to the subject does not mean that it's good; it doesn't mean that it's going to be morally admirable. The pleasure could be awful, it could be terrible: but it would be, nonetheless, in the service of desire.

AM: *Postmodernism contends that 'the centre does not hold', that the function of narrative – as one way of identifying or cohering around a centre – has essentially been lost. Psychoanalysis seems to oscillate between the free-associative dimension you've emphasized and what you're now identifying as the pleasure of the narrative. Still, I've found that a sense of history is missing more and more in the tellings of patients. There seem to be fewer and fewer stories to tell; and the stories people do tell are often altogether devoid of pleasure. This quality, in my experience, almost takes on a pathological dimension. Is this something that you see as a generalized contemporary malady, or is it something that the very nature of psychoanalysis exacerbates?*

CB: That's a very interesting question. I've not really heard it put like that before. I agree, there is less pleasure in the historical rendering of the self, or the rendering of the self in history than certainly there was in the past. I'm limited here by my American life, because I lived in the USA until I was 30, during the rise of Erik Erikson's work, when the taking of the history and the giving of the history were very important.

Certainly I've understood the phenomenon in terms of the European migrations to America: once one has left one's place of origin for a new country, what one subsequently does becomes in effect a personal account of heroic evolution. The birth of the hero comes with crossing the seas, as Otto Rank said. But the crossing of the ocean, the rebirth on the new continent, and the subsequent evolution of the self, all give rise to a very neat narrative progression, with its emphasis on accomplishment, and so on. A myth, I think, Americans find very palatable. In the world of psychoanalysis and psychotherapy, American clinicians were very very keen to hear the history of the patient, even if the person had been born and raised in the USA. Something of the myth of the hero was an important part of American consciousness. Today in the USA, that is less the case than it was twenty years ago or so, and I think it no doubt has something to do with the failure to imagine a country capable of giving a new birth to the self, a capacity held to be true in earlier decades. That imaginative possibility has broken down, and therefore a certain relation to the history of the self is now more problematic.

AM: *Only occasionally, in your work, is there a mention of Freud's idea of the death instinct, whereas its correlative of the life instinct is given ample press, as evidenced by the emphases on idiom and genera. How do you envision Freud's grand instinctual dualism? And would you grant it a kind of biological status, or does it serve primarily as a metaphor for the inescapable tensions we all confront?*

CB: I think of it as a principle. The death instinct, like the life instinct, articulates or explains certain fundamental attitudes in relation to life itself. That is, if one is going to make use of life, and of all that goes into a life, as an object, we can speak of the life instincts operating; if a person withdraws from life as an object and shuts the self down, then I believe we can talk about a death instinct. Freud's theory of the death instinct, which fundamentally has to do with the decathexis of the object and a retreat into a narcissistic position, is a theory which makes eminent clinical sense to me. One can see it with certain patients who refuse and have retreated from object usage.

However, to give Freud's portayal of these superordinate moving categories an allegorical power, such that we are driven by life instincts or death instincts, is not something I'm comfortable with. Different from Freud's, Melanie Klein's theory of the death instinct seems more configured around the infant's projection of persecutory factors. Though I find this interesting, I also do not agree with the extent of her allegorization of these two forces in the subject's attitude toward life itself. It's gone too far, and doesn't make sense to me.

AM: *You write in* Forces of Destiny *of 'a virtually legal imperative to pursue desire, . . . of the ruthless pleasure of the human subject to find joy in the choice and use of the object. Indeed, there is an urge to use objects through which to*

articulate – and hence be – the true self, and I term this the destiny drive.'
What do you see, then, as the relationship between Freud's pleasure principle
and 'the destiny drive'?

CB: I think they are very similar. I think the pleasure principle generates the destiny drive. All that I'm adding to Freud's pleasure principle is an aesthetic dimension, an aesthetic aim. The pleasure of intelligence that forms the link between an urge, the aim of the urge, its object and the gratification of the precise pleasure of the self. That structure, that aesthetic dimension, is a crucial part of the selection and use of an object, which I see as part of the subject's destiny drive.

AM: *I imagine it is the case with everyone who practises psychoanalysis that one's own analysis has had profound effects on one's life and obviously on one's thinking. Would you be able to say anything about that?*

CB: Well I had three analysts, the first when I was a student at the University of California. He was a Mexican who, to the best of my knowledge, originally had a Kleinian training and then, after coming to North America, was training classically. My second analyst, during my training period in England, was Pakistani, from the Independent Group, who was analysed by Winnicott. And my third – one should never say final analysis! – my third analysis was with an Italian. So all three people were from different cultures, with entirely different ways of viewing life, although each one was operating, in his best moments, in a way that conveyed a sense of the universality of psychoanalytical methodology. So I was always, in some ways, in the same place. I was always somehow within the same method, though there were three different drivers, three different people who operated and interpreted.

Obviously one is profoundly affected by one's analyst, but the last person who really knows in what way he or she has been affected is the analysand, precisely because of the nature of the transference and, arguably, because of the need for true unconscious participation to be unconscious. So, I have only glimmers of the ways in which each of these analysts has influenced my way of practising. And although I was influenced by the best of their work, there are certain ways in which they got me wrong, or said things that were poorly constructed, or took certain positions that I learned from, because I knew they were mistakes. I think I learned from their mistakes as well as from their more creative, technical dimensions.

AM: *Is it safe to assume that all three of these people had a language other than English as their mother tongue? I find that rather peculiar.*

CB: They all had a language other than English as their mother tongue. I haven't thought about this until your question, but I think each of them also had built into him what I would call a generative hesitation. That is, I was not immediately sensible to any of them, but there was built into their speech, into their form of address, a form of translation which slowed down the process. I think this was enormously helpful to me, because the last thing I needed was quick response, or premature interpretation or precocious comprehension. And indeed I suppose I was eventually drawn to the Independent Group because of the high priority placed on analytical quiet, on the essentials of reverie and the permission not to speak, which was part of that group's technique. My first analyst too, though originally Kleinian, certainly gave me very considerable amounts of time to find myself internally before I spoke, and then to lose my self through speech in ways which were intriguing.

AM: *Did it ever happen that because of this intrinsic and fundamental language bridge you had to cross, your own sense of being comprehended was compromised? Was this generative hesitation of theirs paralleled by any hesitation of yours?*

CB: Oddly enough, no. I think this may have something to do with the fact that my father is French. His first language was French, his second language was Spanish, and English was his third, no, his fourth language. He knew French, Spanish, Italian and then English. But the three analysts that I was fortunate to have were all intelligent, gifted people who tolerated not knowing, and who gave themselves plenty of time. When they did speak, they all tended to do so with lucidity, putting their thoughts into language in ways I found creative.

Perhaps one of the interesting facets of translating, not consciously but unconsciously, from a mother tongue or a father tongue to a third or fourth language, is that what one says is always going to be rather idiomatic in its expression, always rather inventive, in its arriving in the moment. I quite liked the odd ways, sometimes, in which my analysts put their thoughts. I liked the invention that took place in language. It had a certain sincerity to it, a certain truth, a lack of guile, a kind of refreshing affection.

Any effort of thought into speech, any real effort, is very intense; it's hard work; and when my analysts made their interpretations, what often impressed me was the intensity and concentration, the sheer effort of putting something into language that had not before been put into language until that moment. And the fact that they were not of the same tongue as was I meant that we couldn't have commonly assumed clichés. There wasn't what I'd call the 'lazy' element of language. I think I benefited from that; in fact, I know I did.

AM: *I'm thinking of your writings, of your acknowledged de-emphasis of interpretation, and your parallel emphasis on nonverbal forms of knowledge, on intuition. To what extent may these attitudes of yours have derived from the experience of your own analyses?*

CB: If I were to go back through my books, there's one correction I would like to make, regarding the unnecessary rivalry between verbal and nonverbal, between the uninterpretative and the interpretative. I would want to go back and, in the interest of accuracy, give a higher priority to the function of interpretation than I originally gave in my writings. I think there is a link between language, between speaking and internal inspiration. Whatever one's intuition is, one does not ultimately know what one thinks until one speaks, and therefore interpretation creates perspectives that are intimately linked with the unconscious work taking place inside. I think, regrettably, that I underplayed that aspect of analysis.

AM: *Has this shift been reflected in your own clinical practice? Do you find that you interpret more now than you suggest in your writings?*

CB: No, I think I always have interpreted more than I was able to bring about in my writing. Actually, it's not that I've interpreted more, but that interpretation was more important to me and to my analysands than I managed to communicate in my written work. Writing in the 1970s about clinical work, I underemphasized interpretation because unfortunately, in Great Britain at the time, it was the view of the Kleinian group in particular that only through interpretation could one gain access to the patient. So I was inside a political and polemical world at that time, and unfortunately went too far to the other extreme.

AM: *I gather from the biographical hints in your own work that you came to psychoanalysis from literature. Could you chart that itinerary?*

CB: I came to psychoanalysis when I was an undergraduate at Berkeley, at a point in my life when I was very distressed. I needed help, and so I went to the Student Health Service, and by chance was assigned to see a psychoanalyst. I had been studying history, and had come to read psycho-analysis because I was working on seventeenth-century New England village life, and was very interested in the Puritan mind. But my introduction to psychoanalysis was really through my own psychotherapy. As an undergrad-uate, then, I studied with Fred Crews; he invited me to his graduate seminar on literature and psychoanalysis, where I became more interested in the intellectual dimensions of psychoanalysis.

After graduation I worked at the East Bay Activity Center in Oakland, with autistic and schizophrenic children. Working with them I found the mystery of their illnesses so compelling and intellectually challenging that I knew I wanted to continue with that sort of work. I didn't know at the time how I could do it, because I didn't want to study psychology, and I didn't want to study medicine. As I was very keen on literature and wanted to go to the University of Buffalo, I went there to study literature and psycho-analysis. It was through the Department of Psychiatry that I was able to continue with clinical work; they created a little niche for me, and eventually we helped form together a university programme in psychotherapy for people in the humanities. When I had to choose, ultimately, between being a professor of literature and clinical life, there wasn't any difficulty for me. I knew I wanted to train to be an analyst. I wanted to train in Great Britain, where I was accepted for training and went in 1973.

AM: *Sometimes, when I read your work, the words* use of the object *echo with a ring of self-serving ruthlessness, where arguably the self being served is only served at the expense of other human beings, of other selves. Is it your position that your writings are intrinsically divested of ideological, moral or ethical implications? I can't help but wonder if the language itself is somehow a by-product of the 'ruthlessness' of the 1980s, and of the social and economic policies of that period. . . .*

CB: One of the difficulties in writing about 'ruthlessness' was the fact that in the 1980s, the term had a very particular moral significance – and correctly so. It was paradoxical that, at a time when the concept of the id – of that which grasps and takes for ruthless, amoral reasons – had departed psychoanalytical writings and been replaced by too sanitized a language, I was, in a way, reintroducing the idea just as a certain type of greed was operating in a ruthless way in the culture at large. This is something I was aware of, and was not all that pleasing to me. But none the less, I spent a lot of time on those essays, going over and over them to try to make clear what I was writing about. In effect, whether we like it or not, if we cannot be ruthless in the primary, instinctual sense, in the sense of the infant's need to feed, if we cannot follow that early urge . . . I don't believe that the true self, or object usage, will arrive. Indeed much of psychic conflict has to do with different forms of antipathy towards urges and drives and so on. But where ruthlessness is concerned, I address it on purely psychological, and not moral, terms.

AM: *A focus of* Being a Character, *already prefigured in* Forces of Destiny, *is your concern with the creative personality; with the fashioning of a life as a work of art. You point out how so much of this effort has to do with the maternal provision of an illusion of creativity in infancy, from which the child secures a sense of somehow engendering the object world. But you also stress repeatedly, albeit in passing, the function of what Peter Blos calls the 'pre-oedipal father'. What about the infant's generation of and introduction to the object world, via the ministrations and presences of both parents?*

CB: We are now having to try to define what we imagine to be the infant's experience of the father. My own imaginings incorporate many of the well-known psychoanalytical views of the place of the father: the father as the embodiment of reality beyond the couple; the father, in the Kleinian sense, as the embodiment of the phallic entry into the mother's body; the father as intergenerational presence, and so on. But to these ideas I would add the 'textural' difference of the father from the mother, or the 'feel' of the father: the father who embodies a different odour, a different smell, who has a different way of holding, of carrying the child; who has a different way of breathing, of walking, a different tone of voice. Qualities which, for our purposes of discussion, I would say embody the masculine. The father is the embodiment of the masculine, much as the mother is the embodiment of the feminine. And I think, at both a biological, sensual level and at a higher level of imaginative distinction, that the mother and the father are enormously different; and that the infant, therefore, is, as it were, carried by two different persons. Arguably, the presence of agreeable difference – of difference not in the violent sense, not in the sense of having either gender eradicated – is an essential part of the child's development of creative opposition.

AM: *Blos talks about the early father's role as being essential developmentally in breaking the somewhat symbiotic bond to the mother and instituting that sense of difference. Would you say something similar?*

CB: Lacan takes that position as well, I think, in his concept of the Name of the Father, invoked to separate the infant from the mother. Yes, this I think is a widely held European view. I think in European psychoanalysis there is a consensus that the father has an important function in separating the infant from the mother. One could call this a kind of early Oedipal formation based upon the father's desire, as it is imagined by the child. In it, the child, so to speak, imagines the father's entry in order to properly create the separation from the mother later in the Oedipal period.

AM: *Before addressing the question of the contemporary fate of our cultural superego, I wonder how you see the origins of the personal superego? Given what you just said, if you take Freud's classic Oedipal conflict on one end, and Klein's much earlier developmental configuration of the superego on the other, how do you see the father's role in the formation of the superego?*

CB: I believe Klein and Freud are talking about two different mental structures; though they both use the term 'superego', they're not talking about the same mental structure. On the one hand, Freud's idea makes enormous sense: that in identification with the father, the child takes in and psychically transforms the actual other into an imaginary companion, as part of a tripartite structure between the instinctual urges and the ego–self's presence. It makes sense if we look at it as the first moment, or moments, in the rise of judicious self-awareness, in which the child is actually weighing up, *in consciousness*, the play of the different elements of the self that get mediated by the ego: of instincts and paternal prohibitions, of paternal views and so on. This theory of the superego, then, has much to do with the arrival of consciousness, of a sort of self-reflectiveness or awareness. But above all else it addresses the child's mediation between the different forces of the mind, the different elements that go into a self.

On the other hand, the Kleinian superego refers to persecutory anxieties the infant projects into the object, which is then imagined to be harmed by those very projections. It has a principle of retaliatory law, an intention to harm the infant. So there is an initial anxiety, perhaps an initial drive, increasing greed and envy in this area, which intensifies the attack on the object and then leads to this kind of projective circle I've just defined. Now, I do believe this is a factor in all infant life, but that it's more decidedly present in infants where there's been a breakdown in· the infant–mother relationship. To such a child the persecutory anxieties become more predominant. I do not think this is linked to the father, as such; this is not part of superego formation. This is part of the formation of consciousness, but is not the moment in which self-awareness arrives in the infant. What Freud envisioned, and how he saw the superego played out within the context of the family, is a very different imagining, of a very particular way, that the child has of conceptualizing himself.

AM: *Quoting you: 'I think that one of the tasks of an analysis is to enable the analysand to come into contact with his destiny, which means the progressive articulation of his true self through many objects.' Very simply, how does psychoanalysis accomplish this?*

CB: By supporting the patient's right to free association. Through free associating the patient unconsciously selects objects of desire and articulates, through these objects, evolving self experiences. Now, some patients have a very real difficulty free associating; for some initially it's impossible, and therefore the analytical task through interpretation and other means is to try to free this person up so that he or she can actually speak more freely, in order to develop a form of unconscious creativity. Once that occurs, once the analysand is freely associating, then he or she is quite naturally picking objects up. We're talking here, of course, of mental objects: of objects that come into mind through which nascent self-states are released into articulation.

AM: *Is it free associating, ultimately, that you see as being the curative or reparative factor even in dealing with the scars that result from the early breakdowns or failures in environmental provision?*

CB: I certainly think that the capacity to freely associate is the most important curative dimension of the psychoanalytical treatment. It is the medium, in my view, through which analysands can articulate themselves, reflect on what they mean by what they say, and ultimately develop a good enough intrapsychic relation between the unconscious part of the self – which is ultimately beyond knowing – and consciousness which wishes to know something and to make something out of unconscious processes. This I think happens through the process of free association, which is a kind of intermediary between purely unconscious phenomena and lucidity. In short, free association is the presence of the true self in a session.

AM: *In this light, what about the dialectic of transference and countertransference? As forms of knowledge encapsulated outside of words, in the realm of the*

psyche-soma, how can their dynamics 'provide' for destinies to unfold? Could you
relate some clinical examples?

CB: As I said a moment ago, it's through free association that the destiny
drive has its purest form or path. But patients also use their analysts, or
they use part of the analyst's personality, quite unconsciously, I believe, in
a way that this usage remains unconscious even for the analyst himself.
Through the use of an analyst, the patient can elaborate, or give rise to and
articulate, different parts of the self.

This, I think, is where there are very profound differences among
patients who do not make a lot of sense when looked at according to
psychoanalytical psychodiagnostics. For example, one can be working with
a narcissistic analysand or a borderline analysand. The two can have similar
pathologies. With the borderline there can be a movement between claustrophobic anxieties and agoraphobic anxieties, a back-and-forth oscillation;
with a narcissistic patient there can be a kind of autistic, enclosed dimension
to his or her object relating. One can see these shifts in both, but with one
of these individuals there may be a much greater use of the analyst. For
example, one borderline patient might be relatively nonverbal, relatively
dead; another might be more verbal, describing different experiences with
very different shades of affect that in turn elicit different feelings, different
associations, or different responses from and inside the analyst. In the latter
situation the psychoanalyst is being used much more complexly; the
patient's degree of object use is much richer. Both patients are the same
psychodiagnostically, but when it comes to the use of an object, the object
is being used very differently.

This kind of transference, which Winnicott only implied in his concept
of the use of an object, is not something to be found in the psychoanalytical
literature. There one customarily finds references to fairly clear coercions,
or fairly clear projective identifications, which have a particular sort of
effect upon a clinician: inevitably, the outcome of the pathology. The logical
extension of Winnicott's thinking, where the use of an object is concerned,
is to look not so much at the pathology of the analysand, but at what
outside the area of the illness are the capacities of the personality in relation
to the other. That is, how can this personality use the other? This makes all
the difference in the world so far as the ability to make use of life as an
object is concerned.

Thus, we can take a borderline personality like Sylvia Plath, who had a
tragic life and committed suicide . . . and yet, at the same time, she wrote
some of the world's greatest poetry, with a capacity to relate to her cultural

objects that was quite profound. Another borderline personality, not a poet, who was restricted in many areas, might not make use of any objects and would have an even less enriched life. Sylvia Plath was mentally ill, as indeed are all borderline personalities, but unlike some, she also made use of life: which perhaps is one of the reasons why we look to her as such a tragic figure. If her life had been an irremediable write-off, if she had been a total loss to herself and all others, then individuals reading her works and reading about her would not feel such a loss. But it's because she enriched herself and others through her use of the object world that to see her kill herself, we feel an even greater loss. Because this was not a dead soul. There are some patients, unfortunately but true enough, whose lives are so bleak, who are so profoundly without creativity, so unnourished by any part of their life experience, that one can feel in the countertransference that one is not being used as an object, one is not being utilized unconsciously. With such patients, there's very little life present; whereas in other persons, with similar structural difficulties and with similar pathologies, there is a more complex and enriched use of the self.

AM: *You mentioned a type of patient who presents him- or herself as dead, and often stays that way for very long, excruciating stretches of time. Technically, where free association is not within the patient's repertoire, do you just wait out that person, or that self state?*

CB: I don't have, as I expect you'll appreciate, categorical, technical moves. Inevitably, my response would rely entirely upon who that particular patient is, where that particular patient was in the analysis, what understanding if any I had of what the aim was of that deadness. There are certain situations in which I will be quiet and say very little, if anything, in an hour, or in the course of days. But there are other occasions in which I will be talking to the patient, telling him or her what I think this means, what is happening. In the best of times, psychoanalysts hopefully find themselves approaching a problem with a particular patient differently than they would any other patient. Our own technical interventions, I think, are thus part of the unconscious work occurring usually, spontaneously and freely within us.

AM: *In your concluding chapter to* Being a Character, *you talk surprisingly about the 'necessity' of a false self; how there is something intrinsic to psychic life that seems to require it. You almost seem to suggest that to fully develop the true self, or to elaborate one's idiom, could lead one to the limits of madness. Could you address this idea?*

CB: The false self allows each person to construct a ready-made means of negotiating with the conventional object world, while preserving the complicated movements of the true self in the unconscious. Winnicott said there was a necessary false self in relation to the object world.

AM: *Is there an echo here of the conservative nature of the life instinct?*

CB: Perhaps there is ... and certainly there is an echo, really and simply, of going back to Freud's theory of unconscious functioning. In remaining true to Freud's theory of the unconscious, we operate as highly complex creatures. The simple operation of condensation or displacement in unconscious life is so thick, so obviously beyond consciousness, that were we to be continuously reminded of our complexity, we would be confronted with a form of madness. We forget, we simply forget about that complexity. In a way we forget about ourselves; and in forgetting about ourselves, we allow the self or selves to get on with their own perambulations, evolutions, interests, curiosities, and so on ... And we benefit from that kind of forgetting.

AM: *Much like Lacan, you too seem involved in a 'return to Freud' that continually mines his findings to rethink his concepts. There is a vitality, in your writing, that in a way returns the unconscious to ontological status. How does Christopher Bollas understand, or imagine, the unconscious?*

CB: When I was re-reading *The Interpretation of Dreams* some years ago, I was struck by the fact that in Chapters 4, 5, and 6, we have the clearest, most lucid charting of the way the unconscious works in psychoanalysis. I was immediately struck by how all of Freud's subsequent theorizings on the unconscious, particularly in Chapter 7 of *The Interpretation of Dreams*, in his metapsychological papers, and then with the structural model, were all much less adequate, much less clear. In those chapters of *The Interpretation of Dreams*, together with his books *Jokes and Their Relation to the Unconscious* and *The Psychopathology of Everyday Life*, Freud indicates how the unconscious works. He shows through examples condensations and displacements, substitutions, assimilations; he illustrates the dense texture that is the unconscious process of an existence.

I was taken by how the dream, as a nighttime representational event, as the mid-point in a total process originating within competing daytime psychic intensities, worked to discharge the excitements and the energies of those very intensities – but without discharging their meaning! I was taken by how, the next day, the breaking up of the dream text occurred, through the process of free association, which in turn breaks open this condensation, and leads to a kind of intense outward movement. That whole arc, that whole evolution, is a remarkable example of how we live unconsciously. It's a process I've verified in my own life, as well as in my work with patients, charting the flows and ruptures of my own psychic intensities.

I came then to believe that Freud's theory of the dream's evolution, of this nighttime event which carries with it the history and experiences of the preceding day, the history of the infant or child, and which brings all this into a text that's broken up through free association. . . . I came to believe this entire process takes place on a much smaller scale, one might say on a less unconsciously creative scale, during our every day. This realization led me to imagine self-experience in ways which, through re-reading Freud, I feel are closer to the way we truly are: that is, at any one moment, under the influence of our entire history. But then something new occurs. We meet up with an object which evokes an intensity within us: not because the object has some inherently meritorious dimension, but because it has to do with our own self. Something I see walking along a street generates an intense moment for me that it wouldn't for you, or for anyone else.

This reaction, then, obviously has to do with one's subjectivity. But without the object there, without the integrity of that object, the reaction is not going to happen. Freud, for example, sees a botanical monogram in a bookstore, an object with quite a powerful evocative capacity to it. At that moment of perception a kind of nucleus is made, and a gravity befalls Freud. We could say this is a type of genera, newly formed. Then, for Freud as for us all, upon the moment's being experienced, upon the completion and fruition of that intensity, certain things will come into consciousness and begin to break up that moment, through the trains of thought that had compacted into its evocative quality. We are then off in a thousand different directions, until the next such psychic intensity. Now, I realize this is too schematic, too simplistic. Intensities are occurring inside us all the time. We can remember an intensity from the day before or a few hours before . . . we don't have to be experiencing an actual object for all this to be taking place. But if we can begin to see this phenomenon as a kind of universe of stars . . . as limitless, gravity-laden intensities that somehow endure and convey themselves, then I think we have a rather accurate metaphor of what we are and how we think: a metaphor that makes room for both our conscious and unconscious minds.

AM: *Where a pathology or a neurosis is present, would you agree that the number of objects that might evoke these intensities in the course of a human life is somewhat limited? And is there invariably a limit to the number of objects that even a healthy personality can be 'intensed' by, so to speak?*

CB: That's a good question; I only wish I knew the answer. Individuals who are ill, who are foreclosed for different reasons, will have a narrower range of objects. They will therefore have fewer generative, evocative experiences of the object. It doesn't mean, however, they're going to have fewer psychic intensities: they could have more psychic intensities than another individual. But they will have fewer generative experiences of the object world. No doubt, in order to protect ourselves against the intrinsic complexity of our capability, we choose to limit the field of the evocative, because otherwise it could be too intense an existence. Certain friends of mine, for example, who are poets, tend to maximize their perceptions of the object world and thus invite quite powerful evocative moments. They live a life of continuous surprise, whereas I myself am too cautious and conservative a person to want to live that stimulated an existence.

AM: *Your emphasis on the object's evocative qualities reminded me, indirectly, of Lacan's idea of the signifying chain. What has been his influence on your work? Unlike Wilfred Bion and Winnicott, whose provisions come across as maternal, indeed as transformational objects or transitional spaces, in the course of your oeuvre, when it comes to Lacan I sense a more 'ghostly' presence. Why is that?*

CB: It's not simply Lacan. I think it's the French, and French psychoanalysis, which I feel very close to. I've read in translation some of André Green's works, as well as Pontalis and Smirnoff, but I have a less consciously foregrounded use of French thinking than I do of British thinking. About Lacan, I did not like his work to begin with. I was unsure whether this was a person who was to be 'believed'. There were grave questions in my mind about whether he was writing in good faith or bad faith, but I benefited from close friends who had studied his work or knew him personally, most importantly Stuart Schneiderman. So I have read Lacan and find him increasingly relevant, but in ways I'm afraid I just don't know.

AM: *When I originally asked the question about Lacan, in my notes I had next to the word 'ghostly', in parentheses, the word 'fatherly', followed by a question mark. When I conceived the question, I didn't know your father was French . . .*

CB: That was immediately how I understood your question, you see! I think that I'm very influenced by my father and his way of thinking, by his whole frame of mind. He thinks, and has lived his life (he's still alive), as a French person does. His world is so much a part of me, so unconsciously absorbed, that it makes the French and their thinking very familiar. I feel in some way as if these are the people from whom one learns. But I don't speak or read French adequately, and that makes for a complex relation to French intellectual tradition. On the one hand, I would like to know more than I do, but I'm restricted by my own inadequacies, as far as the language is concerned.

AM: *Your idea of 'futures' harkens back to the earlier reference of the postmodern 'selves'. The plural is one you yourself often use, as the idea of the self's multiplicity has recently been making a lot of noise: Stephen Mitchell and Jane Flax have both written extensively on it, theorizing multiplicities that James Glass, on the other hand, sees as an unwarranted, and indeed pernicious exaltation of the stakes that inform multiple personality disorders and schizophrenia. What do you mean when you write of 'selves'? How do they manifest in the course of a given treatment? And where do you stand in the current debate?*

CB: It depends upon how the term's being used, on what we're addressing or attempting to articulate. We are 'selves' because in the course of time, of a human lifetime, this self that we are has many representations of itself, along with many representations of the object. In one day alone we go through many different self states, which by itself implies a plurality to our experience of our own being. And it's not an occasional plurality: it's a structure. We're fated to be multiple; to have, in a sense, a multitude of self and object representations. At the same time, I believe that all of us have – if we're fortunate enough – a feeling of unity: a feeling of there being one 'self', even if we were to argue against that possibility. In the spirit of your polarization of the argument, I think that both positions are correct. One without the other is either too simplistic or too dangerous: we are both multiple and one at the same time.

So we do have a sense of a self. In an essay from my book *Cracking Up*, I argue that we have within us a sense of a nucleus that gives rise to our particular aesthetic in being. We have a sense of our own self-authorship, of something that is irreducible and that determines us. It is my point, in that essay, that though we may never know what that 'something' is – in theology some might say it's 'God' – that sense is a kind of organization that somehow determines us, that drives or predisposes us. But I can't say I have a great interest in this particular debate, even though I am sympathetic with those who regard this celebration of multiplicity as too 'over-the-top'; I agree that it is, that it's too celebrated as a kind of accomplishment. We seem to go into fashions where there are these polarizations of one side of a binary process, and I think we are now over-privileging the multiple.

AM: *You quote Madame de Stael: 'The greatest things that man has done, he owes to the painful sense of incompleteness of his destiny.' Is there an echo here, of a Lacanian dialectic of desire and 'lack'? Or does 'the incompleteness we all must endure' refer to something else?*

CB: I think it refers to being a psychoanalyst at work with a patient. To the fact that, as a psychoanalyst, one launches the most intense process of self discovery that we have yet fashioned in Western culture, and that this process can be generated and cultivated by two people working together. And yet, at the end of the day, it raises more questions than it answers. I have to live all the time with my own sense of incompleteness as a psychoanalyst, and my analysand's sense of the incompletion of their own analytical lives ... I'm now 51, and probably more aware than before of what will inevitably be the incompleteness of a life. One can only know, only see, so much. It's not as if there's not a lot more to be seen or known, even within oneself. . . . But we're too unconsciously productive to ever be able to fully grasp ourselves. . . . In that sense we can't get hold of ourselves.

AM: *Last night I had the occasion to hear an interview with Allen Ginsberg. After starting off by revisiting states or stages of Ginsberg's life that might have been reflected by the poet's changing appearance over the years, the interviewer ended up by asking: 'Who is the real Allen Ginsberg?' To which Ginsberg replied: 'Well, they all are, and none of them are.' He went on to relate his experience as a practitioner of Buddhist meditation, and spoke primarily in terms of a Zen orientation. When Christopher Bollas writes about the true self, is there at any level a correspondence with the self that Zen purports to influence?*

CB: If so, it is not intentional. But it certainly has come to my attention, predominantly from people who are Zen Buddhists, that some of what I say resonates with some of their own beliefs. When writing, as in *Being a Character*, about the unconscious as a form of fragmentation, of a psychically intense experience, as a process of deep or thick experience that radiates out and dissolves the intensity, or through which the intensity is dissolved, Zen practitioners have told me that what I'm trying to convey is close to the notion of that which is gained through the dissolution of the ego: a view which, when I first read about Zen Buddhism in the 1960s, I always thought was nonsense, because I understood it in terms of ego psychology at the time. Nowadays, I understand a little bit more about the idea; that is, that a form of consciousness must dissolve in order for a type of freedom to occur within the subject. In that limited area, then, I reckon there is some overlap between what I'm saying and what Zen Buddhists have maintained and believed for a very, very long time. But, as I'm not versed in Buddhist thought, I'm not in a position to comment on confluences in any depth.

AM: *Complementary to your notion of destiny is that of 'futures', what you call 'imaginary objects that are visions of potential use'. 'Fated futures', you write, 'carry the weight of despair' – where you acknowledge the stifling effects of oppressive sociocultural contexts alongside customary environmental and parental trauma. Could you reflect for a moment – perhaps much as you have in chapters from* Being a Character *on 'The fascist state of mind' and 'Generational consciousness' – on the 'futures' that inhabit our present socio-cultural, or 'postmodern', contexts? What do you see them carrying, into the twenty-first century?*

CB: For a black child living in Detroit, in a large family without a father present, and with a mother overwhelmed, perhaps on dope, seeing twenty-year-old blacks being killed, and few surviving into their thirties . . . One would say there's very little in that child's future. There's very little in what he or she can imagine about a future that will facilitate the radical imagining of a self: this is essential, in my view, for any person's envisioning or appropriation of a future, and for its use as an object. Among middle class people, each generation violently destroys the previous generation's ideals and objects; it is through this process of destruction, then, that each generation constitutes its own objects, through which to envision its own future. And it is in this respect that a generation gets hold of its future and uses it as an object.

Much of the literature today, on the so-called lost generation, is a literature written by people in mid-life or older, in which there's a kind of anticipatory grief over what today's youth will not get. I'm suspicious of that kind of writing. I think it reflects more of the generational crisis of the baby-boomers themselves, a generation of great ideals that is now facing its demise and having a very hard time dealing with the losses that are part of that evolution. What's happening, I think, is that this group is projecting its own despair, over its own mortality, into the next generation; so that the adolescents of today, and those in their early twenties, are unconsciously meant not to have as good a future. I don't believe this will be true. I think that young people today, from what I can see, are generating their own idioms: musically, in fashion, in literature . . . and I see no indications that they are bereft of a capacity to envision their futures. They don't imagine themselves in their futures in the ways we imagined ourselves.

When Sputnik went up in 1957, all Americans thought that they were immediately part of a march into the future, called upon to save their nation twenty years hence. And there was an enormous fuss made over our generation, as the one that could save the generations then in power. This made for an over-investment in the politics of future, and in the future of a self imagined through politics. Today, of course, there is enormous despair in the United States and in other countries amongst people of our generation over the so-called failure of politics.

If my generation is critical of contemporary youth, over how they've lost their ideals, have no political aims, or don't seem particularly interested in 'doing' anything, I'd say that criticism is an unfair and inaccurate portrayal of contemporary youth who generally seem to have a more modest idea of what is realizable and can be accomplished in a life. They're not all marching off to Harvard or Yale or looking to get MBAs . . . and I think it's altogether for the better. They're less likely to be materially as well off as our generations were, or so we're told, and so their imaginings of their future seems more modest. But by 'modest' I don't mean less creative: it may well be a more creative generation than ours was.

AM: *In this context, you end your chapter on the destiny drive with a lovely meditation on the richness of the term 'personal effects', and with a mention of the analyst's related work in discerning the analysand's culture. We're back, it seems, in the realm of an anthropology of the person: among objects, structures, and relationships that echo for me Gaston Bachelard's idea of a 'poetics of space'. Would you comment on this?*

CB: I'm pleased you bring Bachelard into this conversation. He is someone whom I read in the late 1960s and was very important in my development. I loved *The Poetics of Space*, *The Poetics of Reverie* and his other books. I think he's had an effect upon my imagining of psychoanalysis, and on the way I think of people. Roland Barthes was also very important to my way of thinking. Some of his early books were very crucial to the way I imagined my patients, if I think of the ways in which he deconstructs cultural objects to reveal mythopoetic thoughts; I found intriguing, for example, his idea of the way a culture thinks through its commodities. And I believe it's not too difficult to move from his analysis of such phenomena to any patient's discussion of an object in a psychoanalysis. These objects are saturated with private meanings and idiomatic significations.

AM: *In your own work you've hinted at some of the 'personal effects', at some of the personal and cultural objects that fill 'your house', so to speak. What are some of those around which your experience has crystallized?*

CB: It's hard for me to know, because I think those individuals whose works influenced me – whether in literature, film, music, or painting – are usually not persons whom I formally turn into objects of prolonged study as such. Ironically, I probably spent more time with certain writers and thinkers whom I believe I should come to terms with, whom I should address or make use of, than those who really and truly affect me. Of these I am less aware. So I have, for example, felt I *should* work with the thoughts and theories of Wilfred Bion. Working with Bion's writings has been important to my own way of thinking, but he's not a pleasure to read. I don't find him such an agreeable spirit, if I can put it like that. His language is, to me, colourless and without poetry, without vitality. But at the same time, he is a profound thinker, and I made a decision that I had to come to terms with him.

Of those people who have really and truly influenced me, most are from outside of psychoanalysis. Some, like Gustav Mahler, or Kant, I cannot even say in what way . . . Mahler has influenced for me a vision of the self, or a vision of life; for several years I listened to his music, read the scores, listening and reading at the same time. . . . But I couldn't possibly say how that has affected me. More recently, I saw De Kooning's exhibit in New York three times; the first time was so overwhelming I had to leave halfway through. Then I returned the next day and saw the exhibit through, and then returned again two days after that. I suppose I spent about seven or eight hours at this exhibition; and I know for sure I have not been so moved by an object in a long time.

I think De Kooning's way of painting captures something about the nature of the unconscious; there's something about his expression of textures, of thought and ambition and endeavour, and about the way he erases. . . . The way he scrapes off certain lines, certain figurations that are

then painted over . . . but the erased lines are still there somewhere. . . .
Something about his vision, his vision and re-vision, really spoke to me.
What he taught me, in a way similar to Freud's theory of deferred action,
is that the unconscious is not just an envisioning, but a re-visioning; and
therefore, while one is writing one's self, one also edits and cuts and pastes
and reviews, again and again and again. I think this was a very profound
'discovery' on De Kooning's part. One has to put it that way. It's in Freud,
but De Kooning actually, literally, illustrated the discovery. So in all I've
been very affected by this, and seeing that exhibit has changed my whole
way of thinking about life. But will I cite De Kooning in my next book?
It's unlikely. . . . It would seem odd, out of place . . . perhaps even a bit
precious . . . And I wouldn't know where to place him.

AM: *There were two other influences I thought you would have mentioned.
What about Melville and Henry Moore?*

CB: There are writers who have been lifelong companions, and Melville is
one of them. Like all American school children, I read his works when I
was very young. I grew up by the sea. As an eleven-year-old I was once
swimming off the coast, about one hundred metres off shore, when a very
small California grey whale – which didn't seem small to me at the time! –
passed right by me. I recall thinking that a reef that had usually been in its
place had unrooted itself and was moving toward me. . . . So I therefore
had a very particular love of whales from that moment on, because I
thought my life had been spared. In an analytical vein, when I was later
doing my dissertation on Melville, I was unaware of the link to my own
boyhood experiences. But Melville's fiction I always found very intriguing.
One has in the very early novels, in *Omoo*, or *Typee*, a sort of adventure
story, a young person's novelistic moment, novels of travel. In his subsequent novels his writings deepen, as more and more repressed phenomena
from his own life start to emerge. And then you get to the profound
engagements in works like *Moby Dick* and *Pierre*. The parts of the self have
by then shaken him deeply, and writing becomes a means of survival. And
to his great credit, mind you, he negotiates and resolves a crisis in such a
way that he no longer has to write.

   As long as you're asking about whom I've read and has influenced me,
I've always read Camus. And there was a period of time when I was very
influenced by the plays of Ionesco and Durrenmatt. I loved Ionesco
particularly; I loved the surrealistic imagination in his plays. In the early
1970s, in London, I taught Modern European Philosophy to a group of

very gifted American undergraduates; I taught Hegel and Heidegger, works like *The Phenomenology of Spirit*, and *Being and Time*. Reading Heidegger was a very important moment in my life, and changed my way of thinking in my twenties. I had been influenced by Heinz Lichtenstein, a psychoanalyst in Buffalo, whose essays were later collected in a book called *The Dilemma of Human Identity*. Lichtenstein had studied with Heidegger, and really had Heidegger in him. And as his own psychoanalytical vision had been informed by Heidegger, when I taught *Being and Time* it was, in a way, Heidegger taught through Lichtenstein.

Henry Moore? I would be hard-pressed to say in what way sculptors like Moore, Gabo or Barbara Hepworth have influenced my vision of life. I actually met Naum Gabo, and learned a lot from his writings about sculpture. I knew Bernard Leach, who was one of Great Britain's great potters. He was a deep and profound man, and any visit with him was a very special occasion.

AM: *Let's follow on this train of thought. Freudians aren't wont to speak of myths generally, outside of Oedipus. Yet in Melville you've mentioned one of the greatest modern myth-makers. How has, or what sense of, myth has informed your thinking?*

CB: I think anyone who grows up by the sea forms a type of myth about the meanings of his or her childhood, that invariably incorporates the order between two entirely different worlds: the terrestrial world and the sea. Being on the boundary of two very different worlds, to be a participant in both, in different ways, to grow up in that place, naturally lends itself to constructing myths out of it. My schoolmates from Laguna Beach have all, I think, constructed quite powerful myths that involve a kind of story or legend of the self alongside the sea, and of how one carries the sea within. I still am very close to my school friends. We see each other every year . . . I'm now referring to people I was with in elementary school and in high school. I know each of them has that part of their life formed into a myth that is always with them, in one way or another.

AM: *You are, after all, an expatriate. Is there something about the sea, for you, that inspires both daring and nostalgia?*

CB: I think that anyone going out to sea as a child, or who is part of a culture that goes to sea, lives in an intimate relationship to that which gives life and takes life. I used to assist as a lifeguard during days when there would be a very powerful surf, with very big waves. And of course I would be part of rescuing people who were close to death, close to drowning. . . . In that kind of situation you also see people who have drowned. So as a child and an adolescent I saw people who were killed by the sea.

AM: *Perhaps one of your most fertile and arguably long-lasting contributions to theory is the idea of the transformational object. How did you come to elaborate the idea, and to what extent was it informed by your clinical work and observation?*

CB: I first wrote about it in my notebooks in 1973, and it was a reflection of my own experience of being in analysis for the first time: of what it feels like to speak oneself and then to be understood in a very particular way, and for that understanding to change one's perspective. It was the generative dimension of that ordinary aspect of a psychoanalysis which got me to thinking, among other things, what kind of object accomplishes that? Or, in the sense of an object relationship, who is that? Later, when I first began doing analysis in 1974, as I was very aware that my analysands would be experiencing me as a process of transformation, as well as of the difficulty of an adequate transformation, I then developed a different view of technique, and of the crucial nature of wording a person to themselves.

AM: *Following up on this, we talked earlier about the dream, especially where your own 'return to Freud' is concerned. You've gone beyond, however, a broad textual re-evaluation of* The Interpretation of Dreams *and of the theory of the unconscious Freud propounds there. The dreamwork, and the dream space, have become in your work not only metaphors but models for both psychic life and the very dialectic of psychoanalytic practice. What about dreams, dream space, and the dream that we are?*

CB: A session is a potential space. As the patient talks, the psychoanalyst associates. Both participants are engaged in a process of free association along the lines of the dream work as defined by Freud. In this respect, both persons are dreaming each other through the workings of substitution, assimilation, condensation, displacement, etc. They may actually form something like a text, as in the analyst's making of an interpretation. Whether or not it is an inspired interpretation, or an inspired comment, whether it comes out of the dreaming between the two of them or not, always remains to be seen. Very often interpretations are matters of routine; whether transference interpretations or not, they may often recur in the analyst's mind. One could say then that interpretation may not come out of the dreaming: the dreaming continues but it doesn't give rise to the comment.

But sometimes what an analyst says to a patient is actually and distinctly different. It's new, it's inspired, and both patient and analyst know it to be so. And I think both know it to come out of the interplay between them. But perhaps precisely because it's inspired and condensed and overdetermined, this kind of interpretation usually has a short shelf-life. The patient makes use of it quickly, unconsciously, and it's then broken up, disseminated, and like a dream it unravels.

I think the dream is the heart of psychic life, and if our patients didn't dream and remember their dreams, if there weren't the possibility of dreams being told, I don't think there would be a thing called psychoanalysis. We simply wouldn't have it. And I agree with Winnicott that the dream really and truly is the pure unconscious, which makes its presence very important to the kind of work we do.

AM: *Would it be correct to say that you view the dream as a locus that replicates, on a daily or nightly basis, the containing function of the mother's unconscious for the infant? You also speak of it as a place where the self is 'loosened', deconstructed, as it were, allowing for what you call 'a plenitude of selves'* . . .

CB: J.-B. Pontalis makes this point. And I agree, that the dream space inherits the place in which the mother functions in relation to the infant. So to dream, to bring oneself together in that kind of place, is based on a kind of memory of being brought together by maternal holding and maternal reverie. The process of dreaming is therefore, intrinsically, a recurring, regressive, refinding of an early type of object relation that was profoundly transformative.

AM: *Clinically speaking, if a patient routinely reported nightmares or disturbing dreams, would you see this as an indication of faults or failures in that person's earliest environments?*

CB: I think invariably so. It's very interesting that most schizophrenic people find their dreams terrifying. Many schizophrenics report no dreams at all, and have managed to eliminate dream life, or at least any contact with their dream life. We can speculate, then, in an individual for whom dreaming is nightmare, that there has been a breakdown in early maternal holding. This is not to say the mother fails the infant, because many things can go wrong from the infant's side of the equation that make it impossible for any mother to effectively hold the child. But something has gone wrong, and therefore there is not an experience of good-enough reverie in the mother.

AM: *What about the place of dreams in clinical practice, in the actual course of a psychoanalysis? Does their unfolding point invariably to the healing effects of treatment, in a somewhat sequential way, or do they function differently, differentially?*

CB: I think one can determine psychic change from dreams. That is, one can tell when a patient has changed in and through the dream, or when the dream registers the change. Take, for example, a patient who never dreamt about her children, and for whom her children were of no psychic significance whatsoever because of a profound pathology of a narcissistic type. When she first included one of her children in a dream, this indicated psychic change; and it was evidence of a change in relation to all of her children. She had created room within herself not simply for the child, but for someone whom she could nurture, whereas in most of her dreams she'd been searching for the nurturing other and unable to hold on to a capacity for nurture. So dreams do register important psychic change. Personally, however, I have never had the luxury to read through the notes of an analysis and systematically study the history of its dreams, in order to be able to comment on whether or not that important private literature is indicative of a very precise kind of evolution and development.

AM: *There's a word you use in* Being a Character, *in the essay by the same title, that I wasn't familiar with. 'We are inhabited by the* revenants *of the dream work of life . . .' I'm left with echoes of remnants and reverie, of covenants . . .*

CB: What I meant by *revenants* are the phantasmatic, the phantasmagoric residues of our dream works, and so of our life as well. It's a word that carries the outcome of our own private unconscious creations.

AM: *When we first contemplated this process several years ago, the lone condition you stipulated was that we record the conversations here in London, in your space, because you needed to provide for what you called 'reverie'. What is reverie for you?*

CB: There are always levels of thought, levels of engagement, levels of response to a question, levels of thinking about something. I can think off the top of my head . . . I can provide a certain level of response to what you might be discussing, or to what a patient might be saying to me. But for reverie to take place, I have to be able to drift inside myself . . . in a more associative way . . . in a less quickly reactive manner. I also have to be relaxed within myself for this to take place, and speaking to you here as opposed to speaking to you just after travelling on an airplane allows me to get to a different level of thinking. It's always a frustration for me when I travel to other countries, as I am never able to get to a level of thought that I value very much. I think it's one of the reasons that I love doing psychoanalysis, because it's a real privilege and pleasure to be working with people within a methodology that frequently allows for this experience of reverie.

AM: *In an earlier conversation, Marie Coleman Nelson and I explored the possible impacts, on both the unconscious and on psychic development, of the techno-culture in which much of Western consumer culture exists: a culture, for example, where ancestral notions of time and space have practically collapsed, and the fertile confusion of tongues that was Babel is being superseded worldwide by an electronic culture of prefabricated images. What do you see as being in store for our species, as language becomes more and more homogenized, less creative, and as our visual capacity becomes increasingly prominent?*

CB: The younger people I see in treatment are indicating a frustration with homogenized imagery and cultural symbols. For example, rap music which is violent, sexist, almost anti-melodic, is exceedingly popular amongst middle-class children all over the world. I take this to be a good sign, a good indication that a revolution of sorts is taking place in consciousness.

These kids do not want to be part of an anodyne world, laundered of the visceral dimensions of an existence. I'm not pessimistic about the cultural future of our civilization. I actually think our generation – I'm speaking now of people in their forties and fifties – has been less creative than it could have been, and it's ironic because it's an unusually self-preoccupied generation: in the sense of the history of generational consciousness, we've been more aware of ourselves as a generation than other previous gener-ations, but not more creative and, if anything, somewhat less creative. If one looks at music, or to fine art, literature or philosophy . . . if one looks around for very creative people who are in their forties or fifties, there simply aren't many. This wasn't the case with earlier generations. I believe we have been in a kind of cultural wasteland of our own creation, something our own generation has created with a certain abandon. I don't understand it myself, but it's there to be seen. And I don't think it's going to last very long. I don't see this period of the Miramax world, let's say, of the homogenized, cinematic productions that have had a culturally devastating effect on European film industries, as proving to be the end of Western culture, or of the generation of meaning in Western culture. We've seen bits and pieces of this, but I think there are also signs of ferment and creative destruction amongst younger people.

AM: *As you've occasionally tackled questions pertaining to the relationship between psychoanalysis and culture, I was wondering how you view the rabid rise of fierce and violent nationalisms and religious fundamentalisms around the world. Today's news alone highlights the ongoing Bosnia tragedy, Chechnyan uprisings, fundamentalist crusades in Algeria and Palestine, and even here in Western Europe the increasing intolerance of immigrants – a topic Julia Kristeva took up in* Strangers to Ourselves. *Is this something psychoanalysis should also be concerning itself with?*

CB: I think psychoanalysis should enter public discourse. I think it has a great deal to offer to a public understanding of destructive processes, and it's a great shame that it has been as little utilized as it has. I was at a recent reunion of the Free Speech Movement in Berkeley, where seminars and discussions on the 1960s were taking place. One of the noticeable absences, in terms of critical perspective, was the psychoanalytical view of culture and social movements, and of the link or relation between violent destruction and economic deprivation. This is less so in Europe, where people make use of psychoanalysts. I am part of a Labour Party think-tank, in which there are two other psychoanalysts, and ten or twelve social theorists and media thinkers. I think it's important that these circles want to have psychoanalysts present, and want us to be part of the cultural deconstruction of contemporary culture.

But getting to the heart of your question, I think that the world has always been a terrible place in many respects. And it's an unfortunate but essential part of every human life that, unless one is immediately and directly affected by extreme political privations, there's some distance we can put between ourselves and the world. One can go through childhood, adolescence and youth without being too aware of this. But by middle-life, one becomes more and more aware of the world at-large, of the processes occurring in and around the world, by which one is not immediately and directly affected, and this recognition brings to mind just how disturbed world affairs are. Yet how is the situation in our world now worse than it was in the nineteenth century or the eighteenth century? Certainly the capacity for destruction is greater, the ability of groups to destroy their societies has been increased by technological developments, and mass communication makes it possible for a man like Saddam Hussein to dominate a large country because he can control it through the media and communication networks. In the nineteenth century, arguably, it would have been harder for someone like him to do this. So, in that respect some things are worse; but I don't think that the world is decidedly more venomous, more malicious than it's always been. It's always been awful.

AM: *You've suggested that you don't think the world is any more of a horrible place than it's always been. Yet throughout the West there's a growing concern with what is arguably a significant increase in crimes committed by juveniles. Aggression seems more and more unbridled among the young, and in our societies generally: to the point that a sense of evil, which you have written about, seems to have become more pervasive, more concrete, less of a metaphysical concern . . .*

CB: I don't think the young are more violent than they were. What they have now that they didn't have before is access to lethal weapons. Access to guns has made the American adolescent in some cities a more dangerous person than he was before. Street violence, street aggression is fairly high in Great Britain, which goes contrary to the notion of this being a gentle country. It's not. But English [*sic*] persons tend not to be armed, and guns are quite rare.

AM: *Amid the general consensus that violence is on the increase, I've often wondered if a sense of group solidarity, of communal values or ideals, is disappearing. With this in mind, I was wondering if psychoanalysis ought to confront the question of whether our dominant models of the superego (Freud, Klein) need rethinking. Are they too proving inadequate in an age when sexuality, arguably – and I'm not sure you agree – is not the unspeakable, culturally repressed force that Freud first unearthed?*

CB: I believe that sexuality is still *the* unspeakable repressed force, and I would take the politically correct movement in the United States, and the fate of certain persons who are right now incarcerated because of that oppression, as evidence of my contention. In the United States there is an epidemic of belief in sexual molestation. Persons accused of molestations are in jail, and we now know many of them are innocent; still, they remain in jail. In religiously fundamentalist families, or in their secular equivalents, one finds situations where there is not a high degree of sexual molestation but a great degree of oppression, where sexuality and aggression are concerned. When children from these families reach adolescence, one of the ways they can imagine sexuality and aggression is through fantasies of violence and of sexual perversion. So, taking adolescent girls, for example, one way they can imagine and talk openly in their family about their sexuality is by putting it in someone else and demonizing it. Then it gets attacked but represented at the same time. So, towards the end of the twentieth century in the United States, there is, from my point of view, a resurgence of the hysterical personality, of hysterical complaints and a mood of hysteria. I would say, then, that sexuality, for its oppression to lead to these rather bizarre forms, is still very much a sufficiently dangerous phenomenon. But I think your question had to do with a breakdown in values in the US, as this connects with something gone wrong in the formation of the superego . . .

AM: *Thinking back at that marvellous essay of yours 'Why Oedipus?', one thing I've noted is that you do seem, in your own reflections on the super-ego within the context of the Oedipus myth, to attribute a shifting but significant power to the group, as embodied in Sophocles's play by the chorus. If this is the case, where can we nowadays locate the voice, the principle, the authority, if you will, of the paternal function? In our own social context, where, in what group, can we locate that function?*

CB: I think it's crucial here that we keep in mind Winnicott's concept of the superego, which Adam Phillips writes up brilliantly in his book *Winnicott*. Winnicott argues, in essence, that the child's sense of what is right emerges out of its experience of being with the mother and the father; he argues, in essence, that the child has an intrinsic sense of right and wrong. This sense is not something internalized, so to speak, by virtue of a reluctant moral appropriation that results from a pure identification with the father; nor, indeed, is it a begrudging accomplishment of Klein's depressive position: i.e., the achievements of a somewhat expedient requirement to maintain the loved object at the same time that it's discovered to be a hated object. Personally, like Winnicott, I think that the child has his or her own intrinsic sense of right and wrong. This doesn't mean that knowing what's right leads the child to behave correctly: one can, in fact, often see a child acting mischievously, looking carefully at the parents, not because he wants to find out if what he's doing is right or wrong, but in anticipation of a certain censorious response from the parent – precisely because he knows that what he's doing is wrong! In a child's participation in culture, he comprehends pretty quickly what is good behaviour and what is bad behaviour. This development is a part of human nature, in a very similar way that the experience of anxiety, or the experience of guilt, or the experience of despair are all natural.

The Oedipal period, then, in which the threesome assumes significance, inaugurates the child's negotiating new difficulties with the mother and father. This is the period when a boy will go through his castration complex, or the girl goes through hers, and each negotiates their appearance of mutilation, and all else that goes into this incredible period of a life. My point in 'Why Oedipus?' is that there is a stage beyond this, a stage that's always existed but only becomes increasingly apparent with a latency or school-aged child. When the child goes to school, and when taking part in the group feels all right, the child is in essence carrying part of the family structure, of the Oedipal structure, inside the self. He or she may in fact be imagining the loving mother and the loving father. And yet their own families are, to their surprise, not powerful or strong enough to sustain the family laws, habits, and idiomatic features away from home; children find that these laws don't always print out on to culture at large, where they meet a different world. They not only find that the world is different, but that each of their peers at school has different families, and that together they're all part of what is in effect a very large group. It's this participation in the group which radically challenges family structures.

And that actual group, moreover, is coincidental with the arrival of an internal group of objects, where the child's self and object representations of the mother and father, of the self and others, is impressively multiple. And because of this multiplicity of structures, this development dissolves the primacy of the dyadic and triadic structures. It does not erase them, however; so that we can and do return in our lives to dyadic and the triadic structures: to the former, for example, by having a relationship, and to the triadic through the creation of a family of one's own. These are, I think, essential transformative retreats from the fact of a human life: from the fact of the actual group, and from the internal group of objects which had earlier dissolved the more simplifying structures. But I think in part we're talking about these issues out of the spirit of your comments regarding the world at large. Is it not a more dangerous place? Is it not a less culturally generative space? From my point of view, it is simply a realization about what is always beyond our families and our private lives. Out there is a

world of a large collection of peoples, of countries, of forces which is
beyond our thinking, beyond our organization.

AM: *In a different vein, you've spoken often of the 'integrity' of an object.
What do you mean by an object's 'integrity' – a word that itself connotes a
certain moral value or quality. What determines an object's integrity?*

CB: I simply mean the structure that any one object possesses. Mozart's
40th Symphony, as an object, is different from his 25th Symphony . . . and
it certainly differs from a Bruckner symphony. So that each time one hears
that symphony, each time one approaches that object, it has a recognizable
integrity to its structure that can't be changed. It can be interpreted
differently by different conductors, but there's a reliable, integral feature to
it. When we choose an object, we very often pick something that will
process us, and the integrity of the object is an important part of the gain
to be derived from that object's selection. Psychoanalysis has tended to
focus too much on the projective uses of an object, on what we can put into
it; it thus has tended to regard objects as sorts of neutral or empty spaces
to receive our contents.

For example, in psychoanalysis we speak of the mother and the father as
if there were no intrinsic distinctions between mothers and fathers, when of
course we know there are enormous distinctions. But we can't make room
for those distinctions when it comes to theories of projective and introjective
identification. Allow me to correct myself a bit: we can with introjective
identification, but we can't so much with projective identification. And we
don't need to really: those theories are important and exist in their own
right outside of their particular frame of reference. But at the same time,
when we make use of objects, when we select a book to read, or a novelist
to explore, we're going to be processed by the integrity offered us by that
object: namely, by its structure, which differs from that of other objects.
That's what I'm really focusing on.

AM: *But in a culture where bombarding images mediate, and often condition
and define the experience of objects, can we still speak of their integrity? I'm
thinking, at a very basic level, of how Madison Avenue manipulates our desire,
and through its selling of sex, for instance, can distort, thwart, or even pervert
our expectations – indeed, our experience – of the opposite sex . . .*

CB: Our experience and use of objects is always vulnerable to an interpretive appropriation of those objects by powerful movements or authorities

outside our realm. So I don't think, for example, that Madison Avenue's interpretation of our sexual objects is more oppressive than the interpretation given to objects by a seventeenth-century minister in New England, who dominated the village and indicated to all and sundry how they were to interpret their environment, or their sexual objects, and how they were to understand their desires. However, there's already a difference between life in an early seventeenth-century New England village and life toward the end of that century in a New England village. The difference is not that the people were any less sexual or less sexually specific in the early seventeenth century, and therefore more liberated in terms of sexual desire in the late seventeenth century. The difference of course was in the mentality. Toward the end of the seventeenth century there was a greater degree of toleration of human preferences, and a less effective oppression created by the church. That's where matters were different.

So in contemporary terms, I don't think the oppressiveness we live in will end people's subjectivities. The politically correct movement, combined with the ability of the media to generate a kind of homogenized vision of life, will not stop people from reading, from writing music, from painting. Their forces are not going to stop civilization. But there is a mentality in these forces which makes the quality of our life different, and thus restricts us. This we must oppose . . . Hence the spirit of your questions. In that sense, I agree: there is something to be opposed. But if you're asking me is this the end of culture, my answer then is no. We have been here before, and we will be here again. Hopefully, though, it doesn't have to happen in the lifetime of every generation. But if we could go back through the preceding generations, we might hear how each generation had a similar experience of the world. Again, it has to do, I think, with the sense of decline that takes over each dominant generation, and its surrender of power to the new generation. It's about the sense of failure, the sense of despair, that arrives over what wasn't accomplished.

AM: *Looking back at your concept of the evocative object, you make a distinction between what you call a 'mnemic' object and a 'structural' one. Can you clarify the distinction?*

CB: The structural object is close to what I later call the 'integral object', which I've written about in *Cracking Up*. The mnemic object is an object that is significant because it has received prior projective identifications on the part of the individual. In *Being a Character*, for example, I pointed to a swing that has particular significance for me. However, a swing is also a

structure, it does something. . . . This comes close to the concept of what
the integrity of the object is, and of how it will have its own particular
effect upon my self. So we can use objects both mnemically and structurally.
Another example: Schubert's 'Unfinished Symphony' was the first symphony I fell in love with as a child, one I'd also purchased through the
Columbia Record Club. In that way it's mnemically powerful for me: it
brings back memories of my life at that time. At the same time, it has an
independent structure to it; it has its own integrity independent of my
projections. And I can also appreciate it as a piece of musical composition
in its own right, and thus see the difference between it and Schubert's
other symphonies. Thus we will sometimes choose objects for their structural capability that may have no mnemic significance for us whatsoever. If
I choose, for example, to go sailing or boating, I pick an object that is part
of a process that engages me, but is not mnemically significant for me.

AM: *In your opening chapter of* Being a Character, *you make a peculiar
reference to what you call your 'postmodernist cousins'. Who are they, and why
do you call them 'cousins'?*

CB: I'm very aware that my own particular development as a psychoanalytical theorist has gone along postmodernist lines in some respects, and I
think many of your questions and comments are quite correct in placing me
within a certain intellectual tradition. I'm also aware of being influenced by
some of the works of Jacques Derrida, for example. And having done my
training in literature at the University of Buffalo in the 1960s, where there
were many soon-to-become postmodernist thinkers, one couldn't help but
be influenced by postmodernist thought. There are, however, some ways in
which my thinking is not postmodernist. You pointed out, for example,
what you regarded as a certain kind of essentialism in my thinking, with
which I would agree. So I see my own positions as a theorist containing
substantial contradictions. And although I can understand why I'm seen as
a postmodernist writer in some ways, I would also say that I'm an
essentialist in others: hence I could not say of Derrida, or of someone such
as he, that he is a brother. But I can see that he is a cousin! There are
familial connections, although not always direct ones.

AM: *Reading your work as an oeuvre that has paid such focused attention to
the subject–object relationship, a flash came to me of the title of a book that was
very important in my formation, Martin Buber's* I and Thou. *Is there a space
where human objects – be they evocative, or objects of desire – or even the*

'ordinary' object world, say, of Zen experience – can engage us as subjects, and collapse the dualism of subject and object?

CB: No, I don't think so. I don't think we can be engaged by the human other in such a way that they cease to be an object for us. In our psyche we will always be unconsciously or consciously objectifying them. But the 'other', the human other, in particular, does have a profound subjective effect upon us: in the sense that our subjectivity is restructured by their processional effect. I tried to get to that side of the equation of object relations by conceptualizing the other as a process, as a transformational object. And I do have a project to try to delineate and differentiate, among the internal objects we hold in us, those that are fundamentally a result of our own work, and those that might be more fundamentally the work of the other upon our self. But I haven't yet reached that point in my writing.

AM: *When you say that objectification of the human other is inevitable, do you mean something more than it can't help but be the recipient of our projections and transferences?*

CB: I simply mean that we form the other as a mental object. For however actual, however substantial, however intimately and profoundly sensitive the other is, and for however much they embody the 'otherness' of the other, we always destroy that sense through our formation of a mental object: as when we change the other according to our own desire, or our own subjectivity. And it is in that act that we always reconstitute the other inside our self.

AM: *And yet you do talk and write about the encounter of unconscious subjectivities in the process of analysis. About how, at the level of the unconscious, we can be subjects to one another . . .*

CB: I understand more precisely your focus now. Both persons affect one another, subject-to-subject, at that unconscious level of interaffectiveness or interrelating. There really will be direct processional effects . . . one upon the other . . . unconscious to unconscious, according to the laws of unconscious condensation, displacement, substitution and so on. However, each person will at the same time be objectifying that experience: that is, bringing it up into mind both unconsciously and consciously, so that those objectifications of the subjective dimension will always be retranslated and re-formed by the subject. Then as time passes . . . we're not talking about a

long period of time, it could be even a matter of minutes . . . there are
subsequent re-editings and changes of that initial engagement. That's why
I like De Kooning's theory of the unconscious, because I think the initial
moment does get erased and changed and then changed again, until the
revision itself is changed and edited.

AM: *There's a marvellous phrase in* Being a Character *that I'd like you to talk
about. In the essay that gives its title to the book, you write, apropos the ego-
psychological ideal of adaptation to reality: 'It seems to me equally valid that
as we grow we become more complex, more mysterious to ourselves and less
adapted to reality.' A sentence like that could drive legions of therapists crazy!*

CB: Another way of looking at it would be to say that reality is increasingly
less available for adaptation. Apropos of your earlier questions of the
disturbing changes in the world, my response in part is that it's not just
that the world is changing, but that we're changing too. This is usually the
sort of perspective of a person in mid-life, or later; but it's one in which
you realize that the world is so complex a place, how could one possibly
adapt to it? So, what is reality? Assuming one could even find it, how would
one adapt to it? I know what ego psychology meant. I know that it was
talking about the broad structures of a life: marriage, children, professional
life, the ability to manage the problems that come with each phase in a life
cycle, and so on. Certainly the concept of adaptation is a useful one, but it's
also exceedingly restrictive and, as a view of what takes place in the course
of a human life, I think unfortunately and substantially wrong. That is, as
we get into mid-life in particular, we enter a phase of the life cycle in which
we become increasingly aware of how complex life is; of how in some ways
it can't be adequately thought. Life is too complicated to be thought out.
And it's not just life as a phenomenon: life, whatever it is, is beyond our
thinking. Political affairs are in some ways too complex for a single thinker
to think out . . . or to be content with his or her thinkings. Each of our own
lives is so complicated. There are so many strands of interest, of conver-
gence and interpretations, that at any one moment in time we ourselves are,
as conscious individuals, beyond our own individual efforts of thought.

   This, I believe, is humbling. I believe it leads us towards more modest
senses of what we can accomplish in life. Another way of looking at this
attitude would be to see it as part of an effort to promote a vision of the
end of an analysis. What is the frame of mind of an individual towards the
end of his or her analysis? I don't think psychoanalysis has offered visions
of the self after a psychoanalysis is concluded. It's left us with metaphors

like 'integration', 'adaptation', 'depressive position', and so on, which are accurate so far as they go, but in and of themselves are rather meagre in comparison to the complexity of a life, and how one looks upon and relates to that complexity.

AM: *What are your hopes for psychoanalysis? Are we a dinosaur close to extinction? Or is there room for us not only to survive but to thrive in contemporary society?*

CB: Psychoanalysis just has to survive 'the psychoanalytic movement'. If it survives psychoanalysts and their schools, then it will grow and develop. But this remains to be seen.

REFERENCES

Bachelard, G. (1969) *The Poetics of Space* (trans. M. Jolas). Boston: Beacon Press.

Bachelard, G. (1971) *The Poetics of Reverie* (trans. D. Russell). Boston: Beacon Press.

Buber, M. (1970) *I and Thou* (trans. W. Kaufmann). New York: Scribner.

Freud, S. (1953–73 [1900]) The interpretation of dreams. *Standard Edition*, 4–5. London: Hogarth.

Freud, S. (1901) The psychopathology of everyday life. *Standard Edition*, 6. London: Hogarth Press.

Freud, S. (1905) Jokes and their relation to the unconscious. *Standard Edition*, 8. London: Hogarth Press.

Hegel, G. W. F. (1977) *The Phenomenology of Spirit* (trans. A. V. Miller). Oxford: Oxford University Press.

Heidegger, M. (1962) *Being and Time* (trans. J. Macquarrie and E. Robinson). New York: Harper.

Kristeva, J. (1991) *Strangers to Ourselves* (trans L. Roudiez). New York: Columbia University Press.

Lichtenstein, H. (1983) *The Dilemma of Human Identity*. New York: J. Aronson.

Lyotard, J. F. (1984) *The Postmodern Condition*. Minneapolis: University of Minnesota Press.

Melville, H. (1981) (1959) *Typee, a Real Romance of the South Sea*. New York: Harper.

Melville, H. (1969) *Omoo, a Narrative of Adventures in the South Seas*. New York: Hendricks House.

Melville, H. (1971) *Pierre, or, The Ambiguities*. Evanston: Northwestern University Press.

Melville, H. (1981) *Moby Dick, or, The Whale*. Berkeley: University of California Press.

Phillips, A. (1988) *Winnicott*. Cambridge, MA: Harvard University Press.

Selected Bibliography

Books by Christopher Bollas

Bollas, C. (2000) *Free Association*. London: Icon Books.

—— (2000) *Hysteria*. London and New York: Routledge.

—— (1999) *The Mystery of Things*. London and New York: Routledge.

—— (1995) *Cracking Up: The Work of Unconscious Experience*. New York, Hill and Wang; London: Routledge.

—— (1995) *Being a Character: Psychoanalysis and Self Experience*. New York, Hill and Wang; London: Routledge.

—— (1989) *Forces of Destiny: Psychoanalysis and Human Idiom*. London: Free Association Books; Northvale, NJ: Jason Aronson, Inc.

—— (1987) *The Shadow of the Object: Psychoanalysis of the Unthought Known*. London: Free Association Books; New York: Columbia University Press.

Bollas, C. and Sundelson, D. (1995) *The New Informants: The Betrayal of Confidentiality in Psychoanalysis and Psychotherapy*. Northvale, NJ: Jason Aronson Inc.; London: Karnac Books.

Index

Printed in Great Britain
by Amazon

77047837R00142